HIGH RIVER AND THE *TIMES*
An Alberta Community and Its Weekly Newspaper, 1905–1966

THE UNIVERSITY OF ALBERTA PRESS

An Alberta Community and Its Weekly Newspaper, 1905–1966

ALBERTA REFLECTIONS

HIGH RIVER
AND THE *TIMES*

PAUL VOISEY

FOREWORD BY THE RT. HON. JOE CLARK, PC CC

Published by

The University of Alberta Press
Ring House 2
Edmonton, Alberta, Canada T6G 2E1

Copyright © Paul Voisey 2004

ISBN 0-88864-411-6 (softcover)
ISBN 0-88864-416-7 (hardcover)

NATIONAL LIBRARY OF CANADA
CATALOGUING IN PUBLICATION

Voisey, Paul Leonard
    High River and the Times : an Alberta
community and its weekly newspaper,
1905–1966 / Paul Voisey.

Includes bibliographical references and index.
ISBN 0-88864-416-7 (bound).—
ISBN 0-88864-411-6 (pbk.).

    1. High River times (1905)—History.
2. High River (Alta.)—History. I. Title.

PN4919.H533T5 2003   071'.1234
C2003-906544-8

Title page photograph: High River. Glenbow Archives
NA-5339-30.

Printed and bound in Canada by AGMV
Marquis Printing Inc., Monmagy, Quebec.
First edition, first printing, 2004
All rights reserved.

No part of this publication may be produced,
stored in a retrieval system, or transmitted in
any forms or by any means, electronic,
mechanical, photocopying, recording, or
otherwise, without the prior written consent
of the copyright owner or a licence from The
Canadian Copyright Licensing Agency (Access
Copyright). For an Access Copyright license,
visit www.accesscopyright.ca or call toll free:
1-800-893-5777.

The University of Alberta Press is committed
to protecting our natural environment. As part
of our efforts, this book is printed on Enviro
Paper: it contains 100% post-consumer recy-
cled fibres and is acid- and chlorine-free.

The University of Alberta Press gratefully
acknowledges the support received for its
publishing program from The Canada Council
for the Arts. The University of Alberta Press
also gratefully acknowledges the financial
support of the Government of Canada through
the Book Publishing Industry Development
Program (BPIDP) and from the Alberta
Foundation for the Arts for its publishing
activities.

 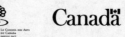

CONTENTS

Foreword by The Rt. Hon. Joe Clark PC CC — **VII**

Preface — **XIII**

Acknowledgements — **XV**

Introduction: The Purpose of a Rural Weekly Newspaper — **XVII**

I TO 1918

1 | High River Before the Times — **3**

2 | The Press Comes to Boomtown — **25**

3 | Boosting the Emerging Metropolis — **43**

4 | Boosterism and the Newspaper Business — **59**

II 1918 TO 1940

5 | The Community in Troubled Times — **81**

6 | The *Times* in Troubled Times — **95**

7 | Rural and Small Town Virtue — **119**

III 1940 TO 1966

8 | The Return of Prosperity — **143**

9 | Fearing for the Future — **163**

10 | The Old, Wild West — **179**

11 | A Parade of Individuals — **201**

IV AFTER 1966

12 | Postscript: High River and the *Times* After 1966 — **215**

Notes — **221**

A Note on Sources — **253**

Selected Bibliography — **255**

Index — **263**

FOREWORD

I AM HONOURED TO OFFER this brief introduction to Paul Voisey's *High River and the Times*. The book grew out of a discussion about the need to record more of the history of the communities that compose this province and country, and to recognize the unusual role in those communities of the local newspaper.

My grandfather started the *High River Times* in 1905, the year the province was formed. My father sold it in 1966, when it became clear that neither my brother Peter, nor I, had the talent or the temperament to carry it on. The *Times* had been a successful paper, High River was a substantial town, and the idea arose that the two together would provide an interesting perspective on Alberta and Canada. In this venture, mine was the easy role of catalyst. It is to Professor Voisey's discipline and scholarship that we owe this book.

The very idea of a community is that it exists before and continues after; the individuals whose lives were shaped by it, shaped it in turn. We are part of our communities in more than the present tense, and in more than the things we actually see and do. Indeed, we are part of them long after they, for all intents and purposes, have disappeared.

In his memoir *Wolf Willow*, reflecting on his childhood in East End Saskatchewan, Wallace Stegner wrote: "I may not know who I am, but I know where I am from." That was not offered as a universal truth. It was about the prairie specifically, and about identities that were just taking shape, yet might prove as transitory as a storm or a dream.

Universal or not, Stegner tells my story. I was raised in a particular time and place—a time that is gone, a place that has changed, lessons that shaped me. Most of the important things I learned of the world, I learned in the community where, as the masthead of our newspaper used to say, "the prairie meets the foothills."

Few of those actual lessons were published in the *High River Times*. It recorded events, not conclusions. But those events describe how a rooted community grew, in a place where none had been before, and how its life was lived, in the detail of day to day. It is, inevitably, a story of individuals— who scored the winning goal, who started the saddle shop, who grew the best gladioli. But, more compellingly, it is a story of community, of people living together, growing together, grieving when one fails or dies.

You will never get me to admit that High River was a typical town, or the *Times* a typical paper. Yet the strength of this story is that it could have been told of the *Brooks Bulletin*, or the *Lacombe Globe*, or the *Stettler Independent*, or the *Wainwright Star Chronicle*, in my mother's home town, or a dozen other Alberta papers, where the town and the editor set high standards.

I commend *High River and the Times*, although I am too close to judge it objectively. This was my father, my grandfather, "our" paper. Paul Voisey, with the distance and the discipline and the empathy of a good historian sees—and records—things I would rather overlook. I don't boast about the inherent "boosterism" of the paper and the town, nor the occasional prejudices of my grandfather. But, certainly, I don't dispute them. They are an indispensable part of a record that Professor Voisey presents fully, cogently, and sympathetically. He tells a story of a time, not just a town, of a profession, not just a paper.

My grandfather published the first *High River Times* on December 13, 1905. For everyone but the Indians, High River was a new place. Almost none of the people who lived there had been born there. Not many of them had known one another before they rolled into town from different points on a large compass. They had no history together, so they began to build one, and the *Times* became its most consistent instrument and record.

Everyone lived the large history of that intervening century—the wars, the weather, the Depression, the growth. The High River story was about how that universal history was lived locally—who went to war, who came back, who did not; whose family visited last weekend, how they looked, where they'd been, what were the plans of the children, and the grandchildren, and the great-grandchildren, who had sprung from this place where there had been no sense of history.

We had our share of outsize personalities and events. The early cattle trade began in these foothills. The "Big Four" ranchers bankrolled the first Calgary Stampede. W.O. Mitchell drew his characters and inspiration from his unsuspecting neighbours, and they were honoured by it. Odette de Foras grew up here, and sang in the concert halls of Europe and New York, and then came home to "her little gray home in the west." The Duke and Duchess of Windsor swanned into town, and got out as quickly as they could. Billy Henry, the gentleman cowboy who lived for a century, and herded cattle to the Klondike for Pat Burns, told the journalist Bruce Hutchison that the people here "dreamed big. They were big dreamers."

And some did. And they are our story line. But the story itself was told more steadily, in children taught, and businesses started, and marriage vows exchanged, and lives lived day by day, but not alone. What started as a place to cross the river, became a community. And each Thursday, when the *Times* was published, the community caught up with itself.

Every job has its formal roles, and some also carry informal expectations. For my father and grandfather, the "job" was to report what happened (or, at least, a good part of what happened), to sell enough ads and printing to keep bread on several tables, and to take their turn as president or chief volunteer of this or that.

They also performed two less formal services. One was to try to understand the community, and reflect what was best about it. Often that consisted of finding the silver lining—what Professor Voisey calls "boosterism." More importantly, they plucked perspective, even pride, from events that might seem ordinary:

Hughena McCorquodale—"Mrs. McCorquodale" to me; a force of nature who was our "editor" for decades—once wrote an editorial about our old Town Hall, which summonsed the ghosts of every meeting, every concert, every local crisis, that had ever happened there.

My father, a photographer, devoted most of one front-page to a photograph of the town's music teacher, Jack Pickersgill, beaming like an angel as he sat at his Christmas piano surrounded by an eclectic choir of the children to whose lives he had brought music.

If the *New York Times* preserves the headline that declared the end of world war, the *High River Times* preserves the celebration of the old Town Hall, and the joy on the face of the music man.

The other informal role was beyond the town. It was as part of the fraternity—they were mostly men—of local editors, who owned and ran and inspired their independent papers in rural towns across the country. No one knew it, but they were an endangered species even then, and virtually none remain, in this corporate age when everything is owned at long distance.

My child's view of those editors is that they were like the kings who came to Bethlehem—fantastic creatures, with stories of faraway places, like Bridgetown, Nova Scotia and Barrie, Ontario and Abbotsford, BC. I grew up with maps of my country, and plenty of history books. But the texture of Canada I learned first from these effervescent friends of my father and my grandfather, who would swing through our town en route to or from a national meeting of editors, and then go back to their own deep and different roots. I was somehow part of that. They were local. We were local. We were all part of something larger.

Looking back later at those editors and publishers—the Canadian Weekly Newspapers Association, as they then were—I realize how central to their nature it was to be simultaneously local and larger. They were of their place, but they were neither confined to it, nor under the illusion that their place was all there was. I think they were the first "national" entity I encountered. They would have understood the idea of a "community of communities."

In 1803, while worlds were shaking elsewhere, the Blackfoot and the Stoney were virtually alone, where the prairie met the foothills, and the river that would be named the Highwood flowed.

A century later, my grandfather, and his second-hand printing press, were sojourning in Okotoks, publishing the *Okotoks Review*, waiting for the break that would bring them to the more promising metropolis of High River.

I am told that, when he first took possession of the *Okotoks Review*, all the hand-set type—by which the paper was printed—had been thrown in a corner by the frustrated editor who had run the *Review* before him. The term of art was: he had "pyed" the type. My grandfather spent literally weeks, sorting out that type, cleaning each piece with kerosene, so he could print words, one slow letter at a time. Today, his great grand-daughter communicates, by instant Internet, with her community of friends around the globe.

I visited briefly, years ago, the building in Okotoks where I believe that type had been pyed. My daughter has not been there and the building is gone. And, in fact, we have no tangible record that the paper was really in that building, or that the type was piled in the corner. It is lore, not history.

As was most of what I knew about my family's paper, my town's history, until Paul Voisey wrote this book, about one town, one newspaper, that records a larger story. If *High River and the Times* does not tell who we are, it certainly helps us know where we come from.

THE RT. HON. JOE CLARK, PC CC

PREFACE

IN 1997 THE RIGHT HONOURABLE JOE CLARK, then temporarily retired from politics, consulted with scholars at Carleton University and the University of Alberta about launching a major research initiative. Under a banner entitled the Canadian Community Project, he envisioned a series of publications related to the history and politics of his era in public life. He hoped that one project might feature his hometown of High River, Alberta. Since the Clark family had owned and operated the local newspaper from its founding in 1905 until 1966, I suggested that a study of the weekly press and its relationship with the community over that period would provide a focused approach to local history. This book is the product of that idea.

The project seemed worthy for two reasons. While historians rely heavily on local newspapers to write about rural and small town life, they rarely study the weekly itself. The neglect seems curious since journalism and its history comprises a huge field of inquiry, yet virtually all of it centres on the metropolitan press. The project also promised to provide a starting point for other studies, including a projected biography of Joe Clark. A study of the *High River Times* would furnish deep background on the Clark family and on the environment that shaped the future Prime Minister in his youth. A preliminary investigation of sources quickly established the feasibility of such a study. Complete runs of the *High River Times*, Clark family papers, and many scattered sources related to High River and district all invited scrutiny.

In pursuing its themes, the study does not employ any overarching theoretical framework. It borrows useful ideas from a variety of disciplines, but does not wade into the murky conceptual swamp of communications theory. Launched by the turgid philosophies of Canadian scholars Harold Innis and Marshall McLuhan, the field has invited many abstract approaches, including postmodernism. But neither its suppositions nor its language appear here, and those looking for the "deconstruction" of text or "discourse analysis" will be disappointed. The aim has been to combine narrative and interpretation in traditional fashion and to present it in a manner that any educated person can read and understand. The topics and themes that dominate the book are the same ones that concerned the newspaper itself.

ACKNOWLEDGEMENTS

MANY PEOPLE ASSISTED IN THIS PROJECT. A helpful archivist is always a blessing, and Doug Cass at the Glenbow Archives in Calgary and Dianne Vallée and Bill Holmes at the Museum of the Highwood in High River provided valuable assistance. The Historical Services Group at the Canadian Heritage office in Calgary kindly allowed me access to its collection of material on the Bar U Ranch historic site. Peter Clark generously permitted me to rummage through a dozen cardboard boxes of Clark family papers and photos. Kimberly Speers conducted many interviews on behalf of the Canadian Community Project to collect information for a future biography of Joe Clark. She agreed to ask her subjects questions relevant to this project and graciously shared her tapes and transcripts. Martin Auger conducted some research in Ottawa. Sean Gouglas prepared the maps. My friend and colleague, David Mills, read the manuscript and offered valuable suggestions. Peter Clark checked it for errors. Other helpful suggestions came from Mary Mahoney-Robson of the University of Alberta Press, and from its anonymous manuscript readers. Thanks also to the book designer, Alan Brownoff, and to the copyeditor, Peter Midgley, for their fine work.

Research always costs money, and the University of Alberta helped in several ways. The Faculty of Arts initially provided seed money to launch the Canadian Community Projects and, together with the Department of History, also provided some relief from teaching. The Office of the Vice-

President (Research and External Affairs) provided some additional funding. The Alberta Historical Resources Foundation generously provided travel money. The University of Alberta Press would also like to acknowledge the financial support of the Alberta 2005 Centennial History Society for this publication as part of Alberta Reflections. Additional funding for the Society's series has come from the Alberta Historical Resources Foundation. We appreciate the continuing interest of Carl Betke, President, Alberta 2005 Centennial History Society and Les Hurt, Alberta Historic Sites Service in the Alberta Reflections series.

INTRODUCTION
THE PURPOSE OF A RURAL WEEKLY NEWSPAPER

ANY INQUIRY INTO THE PURPOSE of rural weekly newspapers immediately raises a broader question: what is the purpose of newspapers generally? The answer has changed significantly since newspapers first appeared in British North America in the late eighteenth century. The earliest ones survived by securing government contracts, and colonial administrations told them what to print. Although the cherished notion of "freedom of the press" arose in conjunction with Enlightenment thought about free speech during the American and French revolutions, it did not prevail in the loyal colonies of British North America where authorities worked to suppress revolutionary ideas.[1]

Newspapers that did not rely on government contracts but on subscriptions and advertising first appeared in the early nineteenth century. Some editors even attacked government, although doing so risked sedition charges and jail sentences. As elected assemblies demanded more power from appointed officials, many newspapers began to align themselves with political groups. (True political parties had not yet emerged). No pretence of objective reporting existed, as editors indulged freely in sharp opinions and vicious attacks on their political enemies. In consequence, editors faced endless libel suits and even physical threats. Sometimes thugs from the political opposition destroyed presses and beat editors; chopping their ears off became one means of registering dissatisfaction with their views.[2]

In the mid-nineteenth century, industrialization brought enormous changes. Cheap methods of mass producing paper, steam-driven presses, and the rapid flow of information through telegraph lines gave rise to city dailies, which thrived on growing urban markets, rising literacy rates, and increased advertising. Political parties still financed many newspapers or otherwise formed alliances with them. Some defended their coloured reporting in terms of the new British liberalism. John Stuart Mill's *On Liberty* (1859) advanced the notion that a free press spawning a plethora of viewpoints and vigorous debate served freedom and democracy by ultimately revealing truth. Conveniently, such a viewpoint also served as a defence against libel charges.[3]

As the century ended, political parties no longer monopolized the press. With substantial investments to protect, some publishers no longer wished to deliberately offend a significant portion of the reading public. By 1900, 37 dailies had broken free of party relationships, and their combined circulation rivalled that of the 77 papers that still maintained political alliances.[4] In the nonpartisan press, no great commitment to objectivity resulted, as editors freely slanted the news to suit their views, but they became more concerned with accuracy—with getting the facts. The distinction between "factual" news stories and "opinionated" editorials grew sharper, but the editorials became more moderate in tone and increasingly presented information rather than opinion. Even the advertising grew tamer and subtler as its more outrageous claims came under attack.[5]

All the dailies, partisan and nonpartisan alike, sought to broaden their readership and advertising base by providing a host of features: business news, sports, culture, and fashion. They sensationalized reports of accidents and crime, accounts of bizarre events, and other "human interest" stories. Newspapers presented serialized novels, poetry, humour, gossip, reviews of books and entertainment, and helpful hints related to health, gardening, housekeeping, and other matters. The proliferation of this variety continued into the twentieth century with the growth of regular columns and even whole sections devoted exclusively to specialized interests. In the struggle to attract readers and advertisers, the daily newspaper evolved into the multi-purpose medium that it remains today. Most of its many functions can be grouped into three large categories: information, education, and entertainment.

The emergence of the metropolitan daily also permitted the weeklies to evolve into a distinct genre. Weeklies first proliferated in nineteenth-century Ontario where they presented a counterpoint to the vision of metropolitan dominance propagated by the dailies.[6] By 1911 more than half of Canada's population still lived in rural municipalities. Over a thousand incorporated villages and towns ranging in size from several hundred to several thousand people serviced this population, and at one time or another, the weekly press appeared in virtually all of them. Alberta alone supported 94 weeklies by 1920 and still boasted 77 in 1951.[7]

Among them, the High River Times occupied a proud position. It began in 1905 in an established ranching community 38 miles south of Calgary. Its appearance signified the rapid change that swept the community in the first decade of the new century when agricultural settlers invaded the ranchlands and stimulated the growth of the town. Over the next six decades, the Times would serve a community of small town advertisers and an extensive hinterland of ranchers and farmers. Throughout that period, it remained a family owned and operated business. Charles Clark founded the newspaper and remained active in its operation until his death in 1949. His son, Charles A. Clark, ran it until 1966 when he sold the business. (The younger Charles did not favour the appellation "Junior" and always used his middle initial to distinguish himself from his father.)

Under the ownership of the Clark family, the High River Times came to epitomize the nature of the rural weekly press. Its peers in the business recognized the excellence of the Times by repeatedly awarding it prizes in various categories of competition sponsored by the Canadian Weekly Newspapers Association or its Alberta Division. The most spectacular string of victories came between 1927 and 1930 when the Association crowned it the best overall weekly newspaper in its circulation category in all Canada for three consecutive years.[8] In 1936 John Casey, Professor of Journalism at the University of Oklahoma, included the High River Times in his "all star team" of outstanding North American weeklies—the only Canadian newspaper so honoured.[9] The Times also served as the basis for the fictional novel Roses are Difficult Here, written by the prominent Canadian novelist and High River resident W.O. Mitchell. The Times is therefore more than merely another example of the rural weekly: it is a model of the genre that others aspired to emulate. From its pages, one can probe the nature of the rural weekly and unravel its purpose.

The rural weeklies insisted that they differed from the dailies in important ways. They formally announced their distinctiveness in 1919 when they withdrew from the Canadian Newspapers Association to form their own trade organization. The Canadian Weekly Newspapers Association never tired of reminding members of their unique identity. "The weekly...is different from the daily," it often intoned, "and hardly the twain shall meet."[10] Weeklies embraced this declaration with such confidence that they did not even regard dailies as competitors. On 3 March 1927, a *Times* editorial argued that the rural citizen needed both a daily and a weekly paper. Like many weeklies, the *Times* often teamed with city dailies, offering joint subscriptions at reduced rates.[11] Joe Clark, who worked for the *Times* as a boy, also delivered the *Calgary Herald* to High River homes.[12]

How did the weekly differ from the daily? First and foremost, it did not attempt to present news. The *Times* often admitted as much: "The local paper does not exist to tell you what the world is doing," it wrote on 14 December 1916, "nor to discuss matters touching the affairs of nations." In turn, readers did not expect to find such news in the rural weekly. As one subscriber to the *Times* confessed in the 14 January 1943 issue, "It is a nice feeling to pick up a newspaper in which the front page isn't covered with war news." The *Times* provided some coverage of international, national, and provincial events, but usually did so only when they directly affected the local community. Even stale news about legislation, foreign treaties, or wars could become relevant if it affected the newspaper's readership. When news did not directly affect the local community, such items appeared in brief snippets and often served as filler. On 6 May 1909, for example, the *Times* observed that: "There is a real resemblance in appearance between Premier Rutherford and the new Sultan of Turkey."

To explain the neglect of outside news by the weekly, one must consider the scale of its business operations and its publication schedule. Weeklies simply could not compete with the metropolitan press, which could afford to buy news from the wire services or dispatch reporters to distant locations. The rural weekly possessed no such resources. None, for example, held a seat in the Parliamentary Press Gallery of Ottawa before the 1970s.[13] And in the railway age, most rural communities could obtain a daily newspaper within one to three days of its publication. Since the weekly only appeared once every seven days, any distant news it contained would already be dated. The advent of other media rendered any attempt at providing outside news even more futile. Radio penetrated most rural communities in Canada during the 1920s and television arrived in the 1950s. Indeed, these new technologies even beat the dailies in supplying fresh information.

One might surmise, therefore, that the rural weekly fulfilled its mission by providing news of a purely local nature. But such a presumption would be mistaken, for although the weekly presented a plethora of local items, they were rarely "news" to its readers. In rural communities where "everyone knows everyone," word of mouth effectively relayed recent events, especially after telephone lines invaded the countryside. Most people already knew about the big fire, the grisly accident, or the birth of twins before reading about it in the local weekly. Even the hermit, who went nowhere and spoke to no one, learned nothing from reading that "a heavy snowfall blanketed the district last Saturday," or that "crops are looking good this year." Still, the weekly faithfully supplied such information issue after issue, and often in fine detail. Paradoxically, it deliberately excluded other sorts of local news.

One form of local news often did inform readers: the proceedings and rulings of local governments. The number of such jurisdictions within the reporting area of the *Times* shifted whenever the province created new entities or amalgamated others, but included the town council of High River, the councils of nearby villages that had no weekly presses of their own, and various rural municipalities in the adjacent countryside. News from these administrative units made dreary reading and interested only those directly affected by their rulings. A meeting of the rural Municipal District of Sheep Creek, reported in the *Times* on 15 November 1928, is typical of these local government notices. The report included an account of bills received and paid, a discussion of tax arrears, and reports on road work completed or planned. A farm couple appeared before the council to complain about a neighbour who dumped garbage on the public road. The councillors also discussed letters and complaints from other ratepayers, virtually all of them concerned in one way or another with road conditions or property taxes.

News from the High River town council provided more variety, if scarcely more excitement. On 15 May 1941, for example, subscribers learned that "Early this year dog taxes were lowered in the expectation that this concession would be met by prompter payment of dog taxes. This result has not been realized. Dog taxes are now overdue and unless owners come through with payments shortly, strict action will have to be taken." Still, such notices made more compelling copy than the one and one half pages of dense print required to list all 35 clauses for the "Notice of Voting on Electric Light By-law" that appeared on 15 July 1926.

While presenting current information did not constitute a major function of the weekly press, it did share with the dailies a growing propensity to educate its readers. The *Times* offered advice on a host of topics from housekeeping to health to gardening. On 21 February 1929, for example, it informed parents that adolescents required a variety of good food, regular and plentiful sleep, exercise and good posture, and not so much smoking as to impair the appetite. On 27 June of the same year it informed readers that "Iodine stains may be removed by holding over the steam of a kettle." Since the *Times* served a large farm and ranch hinterland, it naturally offered much advice and information related to farming and ranching. Issues published in March 1921, for example, offered tips on livestock feeding and the elimination of stinkweed and Canadian thistles. After World War II, the *Times* featured regular columns from the provincially-sponsored District Agriculturalist and the Home Economist. But again, it could not match competitors in supplying such information, especially the many specialized magazines that focused advice squarely on particular interests. Anyone craving agricultural information could and did subscribe to such publications as the *Farm and Ranch Review* or *Canadian Cattlemen*, to cite just two popular periodicals published in Calgary that dealt specifically with conditions in southern Alberta.

As for written entertainment, the weekly again faced overwhelming competition from the dailies, magazines, and books. Compared to the typical daily, the *Times* rarely published fiction, humour, cartoons, comic strips, crossword puzzles, horoscopes, or other amusements. By the twentieth century, many of those features had become syndicated and too costly for the weekly to buy.

Compared to the city daily, then, the rural weekly did not inform, educate, or entertain. But before we can ascertain what it did do, it is necessary to note another important difference between the rural weekly and the city daily. People read the weekly in an entirely different manner. Rural editors had long made this claim, but assembled no hard evidence until 1960. Following a preliminary study of an Ontario weekly in 1956, the Canadian Weekly Newspapers Association and its Alberta Division hired a sociologist from the University of Alberta and commissioned an empirical study of the readership of Alberta's *Lacombe Globe*. The study confirmed that readers did not rely on their rural weekly for news, as three quarters of them also took a daily, and all consumed general interest magazines, farm magazines, and radio and television news. But they also read the *Globe* much more thoroughly than the dailies. The study even noted that subscribers read the advertisements in a weekly more frequently, and more often accepted them as credible. Readers of weeklies even read the classified ads, something no reader of a daily would ever do except to satisfy a specific need. The *Globe* study also revealed what weekly editors had long told advertisers: readership extended beyond listed circulation since subscribers often passed the newspaper to other households, something rarely done with dailies. The study concluded that "Weekly readership would appear to differ considerably from daily readership," a finding that investigations of American weeklies also revealed.[14]

Since reading a weekly differed from reading a daily, it followed that the format and style of the weekly also differed. While city editors thought about the appropriate length of a story, the heading it should receive, the page it should appear on, and its placement on the page, these considerations scarcely troubled the weekly editor who knew that everything in the paper would be read anyway. Sometimes, articles with a local appeal would take precedence over what would appear to be more important news. For example, the front page of the 30 October 1952 issue of the *Times* read: "C. Stroud Wins Big Freezer At Rotary-Active Carnival," while the presumably more important story, "District Convention of Farmers Union," received a smaller heading. The writing style of the weeklies also differed from that of the dailies. The metropolitan press developed the "inverted pyramid," whereby the first paragraph provided only the most essential, basic facts of a story, while each succeeding paragraph retold the story with increasingly more detail and context. The technique permitted readers to quickly scan for items that interested them, and it permitted editors to fit any story into any given space by simply chopping as many paragraphs off the bottom as necessary.[15] But since readers consumed weeklies in their entirety, editors found such a style neither necessary nor desirable, and an unrestrained breeziness billowed through many stories.

Now the mystery deepens: readers avidly devoured newspapers that served no apparent purpose. Pragmatic considerations are of some importance. No one reads a daily completely because it is too thick and includes a smorgasbord of items that cannot all appeal to every individual. Readers scan the dailies for items of interest and often read only a paragraph or two of some stories. Moreover, the daily is rarely kept for more than a day or two because it is continually replaced by the next issue. By contrast, the slender rural newspaper can easily be consumed, especially since readers kept it day after day and read it piecemeal over the course of a week.

Still, readers did not consume weeklies simply because they found it possible to do so. The rural press apparently satisfied psychological and social longings that other forms of media did not. The *Globe* study did not probe the reasons for the popularity of the weekly, and plunging into the ocean of literature related to journalism and communications yields surprisingly few clues. The weekly press is rarely the focus of scholarly examination, and when it is analyzed, it is for reasons other than determining its distinctive character.[16] Nonetheless, one avenue of interpretation about the relationship between newspapers and readers is helpful. The earliest analysts insisted that the press possessed immense power to influence people, but for a long time nobody actually bothered to study newspaper readers. When social scientists first tackled this problem empirically, they came to the opposite conclusion. The press did not influence anyone. People simply took the information and opinions provided and slotted them into their own preexisting prejudices.[17]

The most recent and currently fashionable interpretation is that the media largely reflects and reinforces the deeply ingrained values and views of its audience. It articulates bias, but does not create it.[18] This interpretation seems especially valid for the rural weekly. As a *Times* editorial on 5 March 1925 admitted, the paper existed "to voice correctly the public opinion of the community." In effect, then, activities and ideas current in the High River district found articulation in the Times, and then subsequently provoked a corresponding response in the community. A feedback system evolved whereby the community and the newspaper danced together in close consort. They responded to each other's motion, but the community led the dance.

More city dailies began behaving in a similar fashion by the opening of the twentieth century, seeking to find common denominators that would maximize readership and advertising revenue, but the goal remained far more important to the rural weekly because of its precarious financial position. Whereas the metropolitan daily might offend a segment of the community and still remain profitable, the rural weekly could not take such risks when the loss of even 200 readers might sink the business. Thus, a first rule for the weekly: avoid controversy. As one veteran publisher quoted in the Times of 27 November 1947 stated, "it is the policy of almost all weekly editors not to launch into print with little local controversies." Readers agreed. In a survey conducted in one small town in the early 1960s, community leaders thought that the weekly should shun divisive issues.[19]

Avoiding controversy meant adhering even more rigidly to the trend in dailies towards political nonpartisanship. As early as 1910, most Alberta weekly editors strongly agreed with this notion, including Times founder Charles Clark who in the first issue on 7 December 1905 pledged that "In politics it is our purpose to pursue a strictly non-partisan course."[20] The Times reiterated this principle often, noting on 25 August 1921 that the success of the weekly "financially and morally is measured by the degree in which it supports not a party, but the people." This policy prevailed in spite of Clark's ties to the Conservative Party. His brother Hugh served as a Conservative in the Ontario legislature and later as a Member of Parliament in Ottawa. Indeed, the Conservative Party gene passed from generation to generation, for son Charles A. also became a loyal Conservative, and grandson Joe rose within the party ranks to become leader and Prime Minister. But operating as a voice for the party would surely have sunk the paper in a region of southern Alberta where Conservatives often ranked near the bottom in popularity. The Times found political safety in general tirades against government corruption, waste, and inefficiency regardless of party, but more often it ignored politics entirely. Only once did the Times violate its nonpartisan rule. In the late 1930s it joined virtually all Alberta newspapers in launching an attack on Alberta's Social Credit government, an anomaly that will be examined in due course.

Religion also provided an obvious topic to avoid. Although overwhelmingly Protestant, at least fifteen denominations established themselves in the High River district over the years, including "controversial" groups such as Jehovah's Witness, Mormons, Christian Science, and the Salvation Army. Roman Catholics also maintained a steady presence in this sea of Protestantism. The *Times* did not hesitate to provide announcements about upcoming church services and events, or bland descriptions of church social functions. Sometimes it even permitted clergymen to pen innocuous messages, but it never plunged into the heart of religious turmoil. Happily, few conflicts erupted. The most conspicuous rift occurred when some of the local Presbyterians refused to join with the Methodists in the creation of the United Church of Canada in 1925. They stubbornly maintained a local congregation in the traditional faith. Avoiding religious debate no doubt came more naturally to *Times* founder Charles Clark than to most newspaper editors. As a Protestant who married a Roman Catholic, he had powerful reasons to avoid wars of religion.[21]

Aside from party politics, plenty of other controversies arose for the rural weekly to avoid: town-country conflicts, land use disputes, and contentious single issues, such as prohibition or military conscription. Any conflict that divided the local community signalled extreme caution, even on the editorial page. If editorials grew increasingly less opinionated in the twentieth-century dailies compared to their nineteenth century counterparts, the weeklies virtually abandoned opinion whenever it involved contentious local issues. A 1922 bulletin of the Canadian Weekly Newspapers Association declared that the "best editorials of today...are informative rather than argumentative."[22] Safe topics included commentaries on the weather, the changing of the seasons, and the significance of national holidays. The *Times* expressed itself on all these matters and many others unlikely to cause trouble. An editorial on 5 August 1915 focused on weeds and cut worms, and another on 18 February 1932 stressed the importance of sleep.

On one occasion a *Times* editorial even complained about the lack of suitable topics for editorials. "There may be controversial issues in this and other neighbourhoods," it wrote on 3 August 1950, but the wise editor resisted them and turned "to writing about nature, bees, birds and such, saving himself a headache, and perhaps serving his district as well as if he went threshing about, having opinions." Others concurred with the weekly's assessment of itself. "The Times is no thunderer; no crusader mounting its editorial steed and galloping off in every direction," observed the Calgary Herald in 1964.[23] The Times not only avoided controversy; it often maintained that it never existed. "It has been remarked by more than one visitor to the town and district," it noted on 10 December 1936, "that we seem singularly free from feuds and hostilities amongst ourselves."

One controversial theme vexed weekly editors. Crime and scandal became popular staples of the city daily and many wallowed in its sordid details. Rural readers enjoyed reading such material as much as urbanities, but only if it did not impinge on their own reputations. Editors of weeklies disagreed on whether or not to publish the names of local offenders since it would upset and humiliate their families. A speaker at the Alberta Division of the Canadian Weekly Newspapers Association convention in 1920 reminded editors about the "grief and sorrow" they might inflict on the innocent.[24] From its inception, the Times decided to publish news from the local police court, but handled the subject delicately. It usually published the names of itinerants involved in local crime, but not those of established residents. The Times once received a lesson in this regard from a merchant who sold the paper in her store. She pestered the editor to carry more court news, but when the Times reported that her own son had organized an illegal gambling operation, the indignant merchant henceforth refused to sell the paper.[25]

Besides sparing the sensibilities of innocent relatives, who undoubtedly appeared on the subscription list and might even be advertisers, weekly editors discovered other reasons to avoid finger pointing. As Charles A. Clark confided in an interview: "It was pretty difficult to come out and criticize a mayor or a councillor or a situation because you were living beside them. They're people you've known all your life, and you're friends with them."[26] His son Joe concurred:

The perspective of a community newspaper was that you are part of that which you are assessing. You don't have a judgmental role, you don't stand apart. That fails some of the strict tests of objective journalism, but it means that things that are said and noted are said and noted with more care than is the case in other kinds of journalism.[27]

These comments reiterated what a *Times* editorial had once explained concerning the position of the small town editor. He was "not secluded in a skyscraper office behind a barricade of secretaries," it wrote on 9 February 1933, and local people "know exactly where he is and can talk to him almost any hour."

Sensitive to giving offence, weeklies disliked letters to the editor. They tended to publish few of them, and often severely cut or edited them.[28] "Avoid sarcasm," the *Times* instructed letter writers on 21 April 1966, "You make a bad impression and we don't like to hurt people's feelings." Compared to the inflammatory prose sometimes published in dailies, letters to the weeklies usually consisted of bland commentary when they appeared at all. The *Times* even offered letters to the editor as a platform for people to defend their reputations against any real or imagined slight that may have arisen against them in the community.

But the *Times* did not merely avoid community conflict; it did everything in its power to actively promote social cohesion. Reflecting on fifty years of publication in the 18 August 1955 issue, it stated: "One of the ideals of the *Times* has been to maintain harmony, rather than encourage or record contention....[T]he accent has been on the good and the positive." The *Times* achieved this goal by acting as cheerleader for the community, encouraging, supporting, and praising every local event, activity, and organization. "[E]very moment of the dance was enjoyed by all," read a typical report on 29 November 1913. "Bouquets are pleasanter than brick bats," the *Times* explained on 21 March 1929, "and as a rule, convey more nearly the real sentiment of people generally." The paper found this expression appealing enough to repeat it verbatim on 14 February 1952. Even events that kindness itself might consider social disasters received tender treatment in the *Times*. A typical example appeared on 3 April 1930:

The tea given on Saturday afternoon by the Women's Guild of St. Benedicts, in the parish hall, was unfortunate in its choice of weather. Despite the raging storm, however, many visited the tea room in the course of the afternoon and although the event was not the financial success it would have been under kinder skies, the ladies were well satisfied with the result.

Sharp criticism did appear in the paper, but the *Times* directed it towards outsiders: itinerant troublemakers, rival towns, or distant corporations and governments who threatened the community in some manner. The *Times* may have insisted on a policy of political nonpartisanship, but it was not devoid of ideology and it strongly supported the aspirations of the farmers, ranchers, merchants, and self-employed tradesmen who provided its advertising and its readership. In defending these small capitalists, the *Times* often attacked both big business and organized labour. At the same time, the paper always insisted that no serious disagreements arose among the dominant social groups of the district. "In any agricultural community," it wrote on 30 October 1952, "the ranch, farm and town interests are for the most part identical."

The way in which the *Times* promoted the High River community varied over time. When settlers poured into the district early in the twentieth century, High River thrived by supplying them with goods and services. Like other boom towns, it launched promotional campaigns to stimulate further growth. The *Times* played an aggressive role in this crusade, serving as the chief organ of local boosterism and fashioning a vision of High River as an emerging city commanding a vast hinterland of resource development, railways, and industry.

After the Great War when the settlement boom ended, and drought and recession gripped Western Canada, urban growth fizzled in most prairie towns, including High River. It soon faced the reality that it would long remain a small town servicing a hinterland of farmers and ranchers. The *Times* now began to promote small town and rural life as a virtue, and contrasted it favourably with the trouble-plagued big city. It cleverly combined this new vision with a campaign to promote tourism as the catalyst for future economic growth by emphasizing such pastoral attractions as the scenery of the foothills and mountains, hunting and fishing, and dude ranches. The Great Depression ensured that the town would remain small, the district rural, and the wilderness unspoiled.

World War II and the post-war era brought renewed prosperity to the community, but the spectre of rural depopulation threatened to undermine growth, a troubling development that received considerable attention in the *Times*. Moreover, the roads and automobiles that once promised to bring visitors to the district now whisked them to the city. Faced with commercial decline, High River sought to make a virtue of its very obsolescence. The *Times* now presented the district as a living relic of the old Wild West, and it promoted rodeo, chuckwagon racing, and other cowtown attractions designed to attract tourists. A town that once presented itself as "bustling and modern," and then "small and friendly," now prided itself on being "old-fashioned," and with the help of the *Times*, constructed a mythical past to fit the image.

Before these various eras in the history of High River and the *Times* can be explored, it is necessary to review the district's development prior to the establishment of the weekly press. The paper always remained conscious of its role as a recorder of history and its interpretation and reinterpretation of the district's past contributed significantly to the contemporary images it attempted to shape.

PART I

TO **1918**

Overleaf: The varied terrain of the High River district: plains, foothills, mountains.
Glenbow Archives NA–67–6.

1 | HIGH RIVER
BEFORE THE *TIMES*

THE HIGHWOOD RIVER collects its water from snow melt high in the Rocky Mountains, then tumbles and twists through the foothills where tributaries rush to join it. When the landscape finally unwrinkles and the prairie commences, the river hesitates in a shallow pan. Normally it bends north and flows to the Bow River, but in springtime when it frequently floods it also spills to the southeast, swelling the Little Bow River. These floods occur when heavy flows of snow melt and spring rains encounter heaps of ice and gravel deposited in the shallow pan. "High River" would be an apt name for the future settlement, and flooding would continue to plague the town in spite of endless projects to tame the river.

That a town should arise on such a hazardous site seems curious but not uncommon in the history of human habitation where countless settlements arose on perilous ground, usually because their locations afforded some compensating advantage. So it was at High River. When the floods subsided and the dry summers advanced, the location offered an easy ford across the Highwood River. For that reason, the nomadic Blackfoot often camped there when hunting buffalo or gathering Saskatoon berries. These visits brought the Blackfoot close to the territory of the Stoney, an Assiniboine people who occupied the foothills. Europeans appeared occasionally, but established most of their fur trading posts much further north where a myriad of rivers and lakes facilitated transportation and supported larger numbers of the prized beaver.

By the early 1870s, independent American traders operating out of Fort Benton, Montana, penetrated southern Alberta and established a string of trading posts centred on Fort Whoop-Up near present day Lethbridge. One of those posts appeared near the Highwood ford: Fort Spitzee. The name may have derived from a Blackfoot word meaning "tall wood" that undoubtedly referred to the great cottonwood poplars in the flood plain, thereby giving birth to the name "Highwood River," or possibly from the Blackfoot word for "high," in reference to the flooding waters, giving birth to the name "High River."[1]

Near Fort Spitzee a collection of smaller posts and cabins also appeared, occupied by "wolfers" rather than traders.[2] The wolfers left poisoned meat on the prairie to kill wolves and then collected their hides. Violence often erupted as a result of the interaction among Indians, traders, and wolfers. Unlike the established companies that had developed a long-term interest in furs, the independent traders cared only for immediate gain. They knew the great buffalo herds were fast disappearing. They mainly sold whisky to the Blackfoot and then often took advantage of the Indians by stealing their horses. Moreover, Indian tribes intensified their warfare against each other to capture horses and dominate the hunt of the remaining buffalo. The Blackfoot developed such a craving for alcohol that they slaughtered the buffalo relentlessly. Frequently, too, tribal members killed each other in drunken brawls. The Blackfoot also attacked the wolfers since their poison killed pack dogs as readily as wolves. The wolfers responded by forming the "Spitzee Cavalry," an armed gang intent on forcing the traders to quit selling repeating rifles to the Blackfoot. But in a confrontation with the traders at Fort Whoop-Up, the wolfers backed down.[3]

The Canadian government, which had annexed the territory north of the 49th parallel in 1870, feared the consequences of this anarchy, especially after the Cypress Hills Massacre of 1873 when wolfers killed 30 Assiniboine Indians. The government worried that the American military, already at war with plains Indians south of border, might occupy Western Canada under the pretext of protecting American citizens. The traders also mocked Canadian jurisdiction by flying American flags over their forts. In response, Ottawa

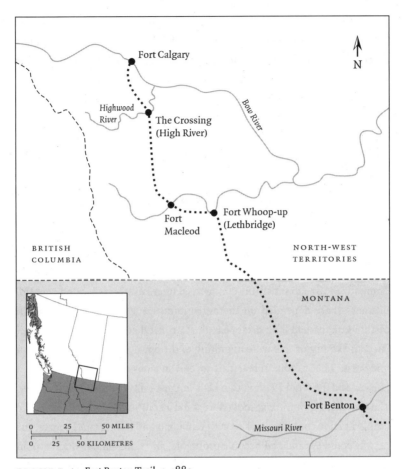

FIGURE 1: *Fort Benton Trail, c. 1880.*

created the North West Mounted Police in 1873 to eliminate the whisky traders, to consolidate Canadian jurisdiction, and to convince the Indians to sign treaties. Although the traders and wolfers abandoned their posts without a struggle, the Mounties remained, establishing headquarters at Fort Macleod in 1874 and building numerous posts, including Fort Calgary in 1875.

Although sent to rid the land of American traders, the Mounties subsequently relied on them for supplies. Ox wagons carried goods from Fort Benton to Fort Macleod and on to Fort Calgary (See Figure 1). Thirty-eight miles south of Calgary, the ford on the Highwood River acquired strategic importance. It became known simply as "The Crossing." In 1879 it spawned a stopping house owned by Lafayette French and O.H. Smith—the first in a succession of crude inns erected for the convenience (or more often the inconvenience) of travelers between Fort Calgary and Fort Macleod.[4] A tiny settlement appeared near the ford. The bull trains from Fort Benton ended when the Canadian Pacific Railway reached Calgary in 1883. The Mounties could now buy directly from eastern Canada, but wagons still moved south to supply Fort Macleod, and The Crossing retained its importance.

RANCHING SOON PROVIDED the district with a new purpose. It developed as a stepchild of preferred Canadian policy. The government had wrestled control of the vast North-West from the jurisdiction of the Hudson's Bay Company in 1870 to satisfy the commercial interests of Quebec and Ontario. Business there depended on the agricultural trade, but frontier lands in eastern Canada had long disappeared. Many rural areas became overpopulated and young people were migrating to the empty lands of the American mid-west. This exodus threatened to end business expansion in eastern Canada and the Grand Trunk, Canada's longest railway, steadily lost money. The Canadian government looked west for a solution to its problems. The untilled plains could be stocked with Canadian and immigrant farmers, the railway could expand and become profitable, and Canadian business would thrive by exporting western produce and by selling manufactured goods to westerners.

The Canadian government expended considerable effort and money to implement this plan. It created a political entity called the North-West Territories and appointed a governor and council to carry out Ottawa's wishes. It established the Mounted Police. It signed treaties with the plains Indians, culminating in Treaty Seven with the Blackfoot Confederacy of southern Alberta in 1877, and it established Indian reserves. It surveyed the remaining land, creating townships measuring six miles by six, each containing 36 sections. It reserved most of the even-numbered sections for the famous homestead system whereby one quarter-section, or 160 acres, could be given freely to any settler who lived on the land and tilled it. It reserved most of the odd-numbered sections for railway companies, ostensibly to help them finance construction through land sales. The government also launched a massive advertising campaign to lure settlers from eastern Canada and abroad. It established a tariff to protect the anticipated market from foreign manufacturers, provided massive support for the building of a transcontinental railway, and quelled an uprising of Metis and Indians in the Saskatchewan district in 1885.

In spite of these exertions, few people came west. By 1891, the entire population of the North-West Territories remained less than 100,000—far short of the expectations of eastern Canadian politicians and businessmen. A host of problems limited settlement, including recurring financial depressions and the greater attraction of the American west, which still offered quality frontier land better served by railways. Settlers who braved the Canadian west faced low grain prices, early frosts, and drought. Many failed, giving the region bad publicity in spite of the government's promotional efforts.

Near The Crossing, government surveyors had measured the land as early as 1883, which attracted a few more pioneers, but severe drought from 1889 to 1896 discouraged further settlement. Those who remained led a precarious, largely subsistent existence. They sometimes sold wheat and bought supplies in Calgary, but a wagon trip could take 24 hours, including an overnight stop. Instead, they raised food for their own consumption, mostly root vegetables, wheat, and oats. They cut wild hay to feed a few head of livestock. They hunted and fished, and gathered wild duck eggs and berries. They built log cabins from trees along the river. They bartered with each other for their needs.[5]

Some of the settlers turned to ranching rather than farming. It did not require as much rainfall, machinery, or labour. George Emerson and Tom Lynch established the first substantial herd in the area by importing 1,000 cattle from the United States in 1879.[6] The environment favoured this new venture. An abundance of streams spilled from the mountains, providing cattle with water. Heavy erosion carved sheltered valleys where stock could find refuge from storms. Most importantly, the chinook winds melted the snow in winter, exposing the native grasses for grazing. Cured in the autumn sunshine, the grass retained nutritional value throughout the winter.

Cattle roundup southwest of High River. Glenbow Archives NA-3697-1.

The Mounted Police forts provided the first markets for beef and horses. In return, the Mounties furnished protection against cattle rustling. Moreover, many officers quit the force after serving three-year stints and became ranchers themselves. The Indian reserves provided another early market. When they failed to establish viable farms, the reserves relied on the relief food promised to treaty Indians in times of famine. The construction gangs building the Canadian Pacific Railway provided yet another market. But the real value of the railway lay in the access it provided to eastern Canada and beyond, to Britain. Such a distant market could be profitable. The cattle ate grass on land that cost nothing, and they could be herded to the railway over long distances. Although their subsequent movement by rail and steamship entailed considerable expense, western cattle had an important advantage upon reaching Britain. Fearing the importation of disease, Britain placed an embargo on live American cattle in 1879. They had to be slaughtered immediately upon arrival, thus leaving the feeder market open to Canada.[7]

Under the impact of the British market, cattle ranching grew rapidly. By 1885, over 100,000 head grazed the Western Canadian range. Ranchers soon discovered that British breeds could best withstand the winters and fend for themselves, especially Herefords, but also Shorthorns and Aberdeen Angus. Initially, most of this British stock came from the United States. The ranchers also imported the free grass tradition of the American west. Cattlemen ran their herds into any suitable river valley that they found vacant. Whoever arrived in the valley first had unofficial claim and subsequent arrivals were expected to push on to unoccupied lands. While this informal system continued in the United States, it soon ended in Canada. The government had committed itself to agricultural settlement, but when settlers failed to arrive, interested parties convinced the government that some benefit should be wrung from the land by conferring legal status on ranching. Ranchers would eliminate the reliance on Fort Benton merchants for beef, and their presence would help consolidate Canadian sovereignty. In 1881, the Canadian government announced its policy. Land could be leased up to 100,000 acres in extent for a period of 21 years for one cent per acre per year. The rancher could also buy a small amount of land within the lease in order to erect buildings. The leases could be cancelled with two years notice should a rush of agricultural settlers suddenly appear. Only leaseholders could import cattle duty-free from the United States to stock their ranges.

Since the cabinet awarded all leases by order-in-council, prospective ranchers needed connections to the ruling Conservative Party. In turn, it encouraged the creation of huge enterprises owned by members of the eastern business establishment, but some aristocrats who operated stock-feeding estates in Britain also received leases. So too, did some retired Mounted Police officers, but they also came from prominent Conservative families. Matthew Cochrane typified the sort of individual who could acquire a lease. Cochrane was not only a Conservative, but a member of the Senate, and a big stock feeder in Quebec's eastern townships. Indeed, Cochrane authored the government's ranchland policy and became its first beneficiary, establishing the giant Cochrane Ranch Company west of Calgary in 1881.[8]

Less than a dozen huge ranches soon dominated the foothills region. Northwest of the High River crossing, the British-owned Quorn ranch dominated the Sheep Creek watershed. To the southwest, the Oxley, another British-owned ranch, controlled the Mosquito Creek area. On the open plains to the east of High River, the Circle Ranch—the only huge American

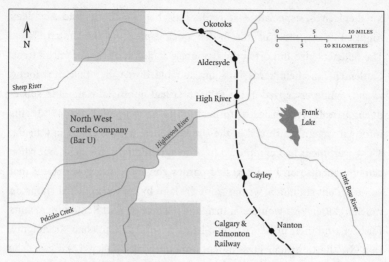

FIGURE 2: *High River Area, 1892.*

ranch in southern Alberta—ran its cattle between the Bow and Little Bow Rivers. But the most dominant ranch in the High River district, and the one most intimately associated with it, was the North West Cattle Company, better known by its cattle brand (and subsequent name) as the Bar U. Montreal capital organized this mammoth outfit. Major investors included Hugh and Andrew Allan, who were already prominent in railway, steamship, and industrial development. Fred Stimson became the most active partner. Like Matthew Cochrane, he was a merchant and stockraiser in the eastern townships of Quebec and he became the on-site ranch manager. Incorporated in 1882, the Bar U initially leased 59,000 acres in the Highwood watershed, but quickly expanded by combining with Stimson's personal leases, and by buying out the British-owned Mount Head Ranch in 1886, effectively extending its range to 158,000 acres (See Figure 2). By 1890, the initial herd of 3,000 cattle that had been imported from Idaho had grown to 10,400, plus 832 horses.[9]

The government's lease policy has led some historians to draw sharp contrasts between ranching in Canada and the United States. South of the border, they claim, unregulated frontier conditions produced a ranching culture more open and democratic, but also more raw and violent, particularly since it did not have the Mounted Police to patrol the range. By contrast,

Canadian policy created mammoth ranches run by an elite who imparted a conservative, aristocratic tone to social life. The nature of ranch work left the managers with much leisure time and they devoted it to genteel pursuits, such as attending functions at the Anglican churches, and hosting teas, bridge parties, elaborate dinners, and formal balls. They favoured British sporting activities: horse racing, lawn tennis, cricket, and especially polo. They also recreated the English foxhunt, often using the prairie coyote or wolf as a substitute for the fox. They built large ranch houses staffed with cooks and servants, and they frequently vacationed in eastern Canada, Britain, or California.[10]

Many of the examples offered in this historical literature are drawn from the High River district, and local sources also support such a view of ranching society. The district became especially known for its elite sporting events. Horse races sponsored by the High River Turf Association, formed in 1892, routinely drew contestants and spectators from Calgary and as far afield as the American border. High River polo teams traveled far and won often. A Montreal team recruited one player as its manager, while another subsequently managed a club in California.[11]

The literature also stresses that working cowboys contributed to this tradition. Often the sons of prominent eastern families or British aristocrats and gentlemen, they came west in search of adventure and supplemented their meagre pay with allowances from home. Many of these remittance men appear in published biographical sketches of early High River area residents. Thomas Robertson, for instance, worked in the British diplomatic service in Germany and Russia before seeking adventure in Colorado at the British-owned Powder River Cattle Company in 1886. Following a cattle drive to Alberta, he worked as cowboy in the foothills until 1890 when he opened a store a High River. Four years later he acquired his own ranch.[12]

Not all historians favour this portrayal of an elite British-Canadian ranching frontier. Some contend that Americans and American influences are often slighted in the dominant literature, particularly by ignoring their presence outside the foothills country, but also within it. They contend that frontier circumstances and environmental conditions similar to the northern American plains produced similar techniques in range management that were best understood by American cowhands. The big ranches

Branding Bar U calves. *Glenbow Archives NB–16–260.*

therefore often hired Americans, and Americans also acquired many small ranches of their own in the foothills, and especially on the open plains to the east.[13]

Americans appear to be of little consequence in the official population statistics. An analysis of 1891 manuscript returns for 657 ranch owners and cowhands in the foothills reveals that the American-born comprised only 17 percent of the total, and only 16 percent of those in the High River district, proportions that had changed little by 1901.[14] Nonetheless, the statistical profile understates the importance of the Americans, since they often occupied the critical positions of managers or foremen where their ranching knowledge could be transmitted to Canadian and British greenhorns. George Lane provides a striking example. Born in Iowa, he had acquired considerable expertise in open range ranching in Montana when the stock association there recommended him to the North West Cattle Company as a foreman for the Bar U. After his arrival, Lane also served as trail boss for the cooperative roundups with other ranches. He left the Bar U in 1889 to buy and sell cattle on his own account, and he soon began acquiring ranches in his own name. In 1902, he bought out his former employers to become the largest and most prominent rancher in the High River district.[15]

Lane's early career also illustrates the geographical and social mobility of the cattle frontier, a product of the nature of open range ranching. At first, cattle simply ran like wild animals to breed and survive as best they could. With no fences to contain them, they did not respect the boundaries of the leases and roamed across vast areas, mixing freely with the cattle of other ranches. In summer they migrated to the open plains to enjoy the seasonal growth of rich grass. In winter they drifted back to the foothills, seeking shelter from storms and benefiting from the magnified effect of the chinooks. Each year predators killed some of them, while others died from exposure, disease, and accident, but natural increase in the herd provided ample compensation.

Most of the labour required under such a system came during the semi-annual roundups. In spring, cowboys from the various ranches combed the range to identify newborn calves, to give them the same brand as their mothers, and to castrate the males. The fall roundup largely culled fat four-year olds to ship to market. At other times of the year, few chores occupied the ranchers. More work became necessary after the harsh winter of 1886–87 when the chinooks refused to blow, and perhaps 50 percent of the range cattle died. After that, the ranchers introduced winter feeding in a modest way, collecting hay for the weaker calves and cows, and bringing them to fenced pastures with shelter sheds after the fall roundup. Running cattle through dipping vats to chemically treat the skin parasite known as mange also required labour. Nonetheless, ranch work remained highly seasonal and big spreads like the Bar U retained only their most skilled cowhands on a year-round basis.[16]

Biographical sketches of people in the High River district before 1900 identify many who worked as casual labourers on the ranches. They appeared in the district at busy times and then disappeared, sometimes for years in succession. These "drifters" came from the United States, giving Americans a significantly greater presence than an analysis of the permanent population indicates. Philip Weinard, who arrived in the High River area in 1882, later recalled: "On the fall roundup of '86 there were about 75 men in the saddle. Most of them were from across the line and had worked on all different cattle ranges from Texas to Alberta."[17] Aside from the Anglo population that dominated it, this floating labour force also included continental Europeans, Indians, Metis, and American blacks.[18] Although a skilled craft, cowpunching drew from a potentially large talent pool. Anyone who could ride well (and that included many rural British and North Americans) might become a cowboy so long as he also learned the use of a rope and the basics of cattle behaviour.

Some of these paid workers eventually acquired their own small ranches. Typically, they applied for a 160-acre homestead outside the boundaries of the great leases, bought small herds, and let them run loose. The small ranchers simultaneously irritated and assisted big spreads like the Bar U. It resented the homestead cattle drifting onto the lease land, especially the inferior bulls who enjoyed impregnating Bar U cows. At the same time, these small ranchers often filled the seasonal labour needs of the big ranches, contracting to provide hay and fencing, assisting in the roundups on their own account, and helping to kill wolves, cougars, and other predators.

Many small ranchers in the High River district first learned the cattle business as Bar U employees before striking out on their own. Numerous examples abound, including the legendary black American cowboy, John Ware. Every account of him attests to his extraordinary skill as a horseman and cattleman, and after working the Bar U for two years, and then the Quorn, he acquired his own ranch in 1888.[19] In spite of his illiteracy and intense prejudice against blacks, he demonstrated that social mobility in the ranch country remained a real possibility so long as unoccupied land remained plentiful. And if John Ware represented a cowboy from the lower social strata of North American society, he often worked side by side with well-educated cowboys of the genteel class.

What difference did the presence of American cowboys and ranchers make to the social life of the High River district? According to wild west mythology, the American tradition meant high stakes poker, heavy drinking, hard brawling, gunfights, lynchings, and a limited, if colourful, vocabulary delivered in faulty diction. Such depictions of ranch society in the High River district are also abundant.[20] But drawing a sharp contrast between Canadian and American ranching traditions does not always match the evidence.

Cowhands from prominent British and Canadian families also succumbed to boozing, brawling, and gambling. Moreover, some American cowboys contributed to the genteel ranching tradition. In spite of polo's aristocratic reputation, and the fact that a quintessential British remittance man managed High River's team for many years, the sport attracted players from various social classes and nationalities. Anyone skilled in horsemanship could and did play.[21]

Moreover, in identifying a distinct American ranching tradition, the British-Canadian school ignores the fact that British capitalists also owned and managed many of the great ranches in the United States. As well, the Canadian literature makes little effort to distinguish between the imagined American ranching tradition portrayed in dime novels and Hollywood productions, and its actual history, which was certainly less raw and violent. There is also the problem of determining the "real" history of American ranching. One major study argues convincingly that several distinct ranching traditions emerged.[22] And the literature on both sides of the border often slights Mexican contributions to ranching techniques and traditions—a legacy that still echoes in such words as ranch, lariat, chaparral, and rodeo, which are all Spanish in origin.

Many of the social activities described as American had more to do with the demographic structure of ranch society than with nationality per se, for it consisted overwhelmingly of single young men. Of the seventeen people living on the Bar U in 1891, only three were women: Stimson's wife, his unmarried cousin, and a maid. The twelve bunkhouse men averaged 31 years of age. Only one had a wife and she was not present.[23] Most women in the ranch country were the wives or daughters of the owners and managers. This tiny group included such cultured individuals as Agnes Skrine, who with her husband Walter, emigrated from Ireland to establish the Bar S west of High River. Already a published writer, she described the lot of the genteel British frontier woman in "A Lady's Life on a Ranche," which appeared in Edinburgh's *Blackwood's Magazine* in 1898 under the pen name Moira O'Neill.[24] Although few in number, such women contributed much to a social existence centred on church, teas, dinners, and balls.

As for unmarried women, almost none appeared. High River rancher Fred Ings later recalled that "In all frontier countries, girls are scarce, and so it was here. Hardly had a visiting sister, niece, or friend arrived, than she was besieged with suitors. Practically every girl or young woman who came in married at once."[25] Lula Short's diary from the 1880s recorded that she almost never sat out a dance. She later recalled, "there were few ladies and so many cowboys that half-grown girls and even younger ones were in great demand."[26]

One consequence of the extreme imbalances of age and sex on the ranching frontier was a greater tendency towards drinking, gambling, and brawling—activities often noted in studies of frontier bachelor societies. In the High River district, young men frequently indulged in these activities regardless of their national origins. Prostitution also commonly appeared in such communities. High River did not acquire brothels until after the turn of the century, but the Stoney Indians who occupied reserves in the foothills often provided the Bar U with prostitutes. According to one cowhand, ranch manager Fred Stimson even encouraged his men to engage their services.[27]

Thus, the ranching society of the High River area represented a complex blend of several national traditions and social classes. It included a mammoth ranch, but also many small and intermediate-sized ones. Its social hierarchy included ranch barons, middle managers, and paid labourers. Nonetheless, it was also a fluid society with considerable mobility. It was overwhelmingly young, male, and single. The nature of this tiny community and its varied elements would assume tremendous significance in later years when High River and its weekly newspaper, the *Times*, attempted to define a community identity based upon the district's early history.

FOR ALL THE ATTENTION it would later receive, the golden age of ranching soon faded in the face of political threats that arose in the 1890s. At first the big ranchers used their influence in the Conservative party to extract a host of favours. Initially, they pressured the government to allow the free importation of American cattle to stock their ranges. Once they had done so, they reversed position in 1886 and persuaded the government to slap stiff quarantine regulations on American cattle to prevent latecomers from enjoying the same advantage. The ranchers also used their clout to thwart unwanted competition from sheep grazers, who soon found it difficult to obtain leases and were subsequently banished from many cattle districts. They also pressured the government to expand Mounted Police patrols to check cattle rustling. The Bar U even acquired its own police outpost in 1886 and its own five-man detachment the following year.[28]

The big ranchers enjoyed less success, however, when faced with the gravest threat to open range ranching: an invasion of farmers. In sufficient numbers, they would claim all the grazing land, but even the few who appeared in the 1880s caused problems. They settled on the riverfronts and erected fences to protect their crops from the range cattle. The fences prevented cattle from reaching water and shelter. The ranchers wanted the settlers out, especially the squatters who had not taken out legal homesteads. The demand placed the Conservative government in a quandary. It had committed itself to the agricultural settlement of the west under pressure from an eastern business community that wanted a populous hinterland market. Now the ranchers formed a powerful interest group within the Conservative Party. At first the government declared southern Alberta too dry for farming, and it directed prospective settlers to the many vacant lands elsewhere. It also assisted the ranchers by evicting squatters from leased land.

As settlers continued to arrive, the ranchers took direct action. They pulled down buildings, cut fences, and trampled crops with cattle. Many cowboys willingly helped. They disdained farmers and regarded farm work as an endless round of menial tasks. They considered themselves elite workers, whose talents with a horse and rope elevated them above the lowly sodbuster.[29] Since evicting small farmers to aid big ranchers proved unpopular, the government introduced a new policy in 1886. It cancelled the leases of ranchers who failed to fulfill the lease obligations, opening some of their lands for settlement. In 1886 it also established a public water reserve system. Strategic areas along rivers could neither be homesteaded nor leased; they would remain open to all and the herds would always have access to water and shelter.[30]

These solutions only delayed the inevitable conflict. At bottom, the Conservative government remained committed to its national policy of intensive settlement. As pressure mounted to release ranch lands for agriculture, the government gave in. In 1892, it announced the cancellation of all leases within four years, although it allowed ranchers to buy one-tenth of their ranges. A second consideration prompted this change. The Calgary and Edmonton Railway, a child of the Canadian Pacific, planned to build south from Calgary to Fort Macleod. As its parent company had earlier demanded, it insisted on a generous land grant to help finance construction. To award it nearly two million acres, the government needed control over the odd-numbered sections of land. Ranchers responded to the cancellation notice by buying ten percent of their leases, and many odd-numbered sections of the railway lands. But they could not afford all the land they needed, so they continued to run cattle on their former ranges, relying on the water reserves to stay in business.

Further calamities soon struck. In 1896 the Liberals came to office in Ottawa and the big ranchers lost political influence. Indeed, the Liberals became even greater champions of farm settlement than the Conservatives, even though they awarded some new leases to Liberal ranchers. In 1901 the government announced it would sell off the water reserves, although it allowed ranchers to purchase these key sites and many did so. The Liberals did not destroy ranching, and indeed, even devised their own policies to ensure its survival, but they had delivered a clear message: ranching would not be allowed to block agricultural settlement.

Other forces wrecked havoc too. The British market became less lucrative in 1892 when Britain applied the same restrictions against Canadian cattle that it did against American cattle, and both countries soon faced competition from Argentina. The severe winter of 1906–7 killed many range cattle. The chinooks did not arrive to relieve the bitter cold and unveil the grass. By spring, perhaps half the range cattle in Alberta lay dead. The last great co-operative roundup occurred that year. Other events physically eliminated the ranchers themselves. Given their devotion to Britain and all things British, many patriotically volunteered for duty when the South African war broke out in 1899, and some died in action. Even more died fighting World War I. Between those conflicts, the invasion of farm settlers accelerated. The land owned by ranchers soared in value and it became more profitable to sell it to farmers than to keep it. The Mormon church bought the giant southern Cochrane Ranch for settlement purposes in 1905 and 1906, and the huge British-owned Walrond Ranch sold its lands in 1907. By then, many ranches in the High River district had also subdivided and sold parcels to settlers.[31]

High River's Bar U met these challenges more effectively than other big ranches. When the government permitted ranchers to buy up to ten percent of their leases in 1892, the Bar U acquired the maximum permitted— 15,800 acres purchased over several years. Since most of its leased and deeded land nestled in foothills terrain where agriculture proved difficult or impossible, it did not face an onslaught of settlers. Even so, the ranch reached a low point in 1902 when its great herd of over 10,000 cattle had been trimmed by two-thirds. In Montreal, the Allan family decided to sell the ranch over the objections of manager Fred Stimson. Ex-foreman George Lane purchased the company. After he had left the Bar U in 1889, he acquired several ranches in his name, and also bought cattle for the Winnipeg firm of Gordon, Ironside and Fares. That enterprise operated ranches and meat packing plants, and also exported live cattle. Since he was unable to finance the $220,000 deal alone, Lane bought the Bar U with the help of his Winnipeg partners. He also served as ranch manager and in 1920 he bought out his partners and became sole proprietor.[32]

Lane immediately bolstered the fortunes of the Bar U. Unlike most big ranchers, he supported the Liberals. So did another prominent High River rancher, Dan Riley. Since both men served as executives in the most important ranching associations, and since the Liberals ruled Ottawa from 1896 to 1911, they influenced policy and safeguarded their interests. Lane replaced some of the lost government land by leasing from the Calgary and Edmonton Railway, and he eventually bought much of that land. In combination with his other ranches, he established a herd of 30,000 to 40,000 cattle on the eve of the destructive winter of 1906–7.[33] After that devastating season, he intensified winter feeding and produced more hay, oats, and barley on his own grain farm east of Calgary. Although the British market became less important, compensation arrived in the way of a stronger domestic market and even exports to the United States. Lane also tapped an important new market. The homesteaders who flooded the district after 1900 needed horses to pull machinery and wagons. Lane imported heavy Percherons from France and became the major supplier of that breed.[34]

To a considerable extent, the Bar U exemplified the transformation of ranching generally. It abandoned the open plains and retreated into the foothills. It intensified cattle feeding and raised much of its own feed, often diverting creeks to irrigate meadows where workers collected hay and planted coarse grains. It sought more diversified markets for cattle and began raising more horses, and even some milk cows and hogs. It focused on selective breeding and even used the once-hated barbed wire fences to control the herds. By such means, land-extensive, open-range ranching evolved towards more labour-intensive, mixed-stock farming.[35]

CHANGES IN THE FOOTHILLS ECONOMY, however, paled in comparison to the mighty transformation on the plains to the east. There a highly commercialized wheat economy arose with astonishing speed. The grey clouds that thwarted western settlement in the late nineteenth century lifted under the sunny skies of the new century. The industrial world entered a period of robust growth. Wheat prices rose and solutions appeared for a host of technical problems associated with growing, milling, and shipping wheat. Pioneers had settled the best lands of the American frontier and now looked towards Western Canada. The Liberal government in Ottawa renewed its efforts to attract them and succeeded dramatically. Two new transcontinental railways began and branch lines penetrated new territory. Rainfall returned. The region of the North-West Territories that became the new province of Alberta soared in population from 73,000 in 1901 to 374,000 in 1911 and 588,000 in 1921. Since the newcomers were predominately young adults, high birth rates prevailed, and by 1931 the population had reached 732,000.

The High River district began receiving the new settlers by 1897, but an especially heavy influx occurred in 1903. The following year, pioneers claimed homesteads more than 30 miles east of the town. The eight rural municipal districts closest to High River contained less than 2,000 people in 1901, but by 1911, this number had increased to 7,400. Virtually all this growth occurred in prairie municipalities, while the foothill districts experienced only nominal gains.[36] Like the ranching community before it, English-speaking settlers dominated the ranks of the newcomers. Some came from Britain and eastern Canada, especially Ontario. Most came from the United States, particularly from the mid-west and the Pacific northwest where many farmers sold out for good prices and migrated to the new frontier where larger farms could be acquired cheaply. Considerable movement in and out of the district before 1920 did little to alter the national and ethnic composition of the population. Few minorities of any sort appeared, and even fewer of them settled together, although small groups of North Dakota Germans, American Mormons, and immigrants from France formed pockets of settlement in the district. Once again, young, unattached males dominated the ranks of the newcomers. In 1910, one township southeast of High River had 31 single adult men, but only one unmarried adult woman.[37]

Although most settlers took advantage of the free quarter-section offered by the government, not all of them were struggling homesteaders trying to scratch a living from a mere 160 acres. Many came with sufficient capital to buy adjacent railway lands, and some even bought large blocks for speculation. S.J. Main of Nebraska, for example, bought five sections (3,200 acres) in 1906, which he hoped to resell in smaller lots for a considerable profit.[38] Many absentee landowners also rented land to expanding farmers. As in other wheat growing communities in southern Alberta, farm size greatly exceeded the provincial average. By World War I the average farm size east of High River neared three-quarter of a section (480 acres), although a half-section remained the most common size.[39]

Large farms prevailed for many reasons. The district attracted many settlers with substantial capital. They invested heavily in horse-drawn machinery to grow wheat on an extensive scale. Although many farmers raised livestock, wheat immediately became, and remained, their dominant cash crop. With considerable numbers of draft horses to feed, settlers also required land for pasture, hay, and coarse grains. They also required more land because the dry climate demanded the practice of summer fallowing, where one-third to one-half of the field acreage would be kept out of production each year in an attempt to conserve moisture.

Many settlers did not remain in the district for long. Some started a business, proved up a homestead, or even developed a substantial farm, only to sell to later arrivals. After its establishment in 1905, the *High River Times*

The high country west of High River. Clark Family Papers.

packed its columns with the sales of town lots, businesses, and farms of various sizes in various states of development. It also marvelled at the fast-rising prices. Free homesteads still remained available in 1904, but by 1912 raw land fetched between $11 and $25 an acre depending on location and perceived quality. Improved farms ranged from $25 to $50 an acre.[40]

Escalating prices reflected good yields and high wheat grades. These did not prevail evenly across the district, which contained many distinct soil and climatic zones. In spite of plentiful rainfall, the foothills west of High River would not support wheat farming at all because of the terrain. Steep slopes and outcrops of rock increasingly prevailed as one approached the mountains. Thick stands of coniferous forest, mostly spruce, blanketed the highest foothill ridges, aspen poplars covered parts of the lower hills, while dense willow and huge cottonwood poplars prevailed in the river bottoms. Thin or rocky soil covered much of the foothills. Fertile, open meadows could be found, but the high elevation imposed a short growing season. On some meadows, ranchers could raise fast-maturing plants like hay, oats, and barley, crops of little commercial value, but useful for feeding cattle in winter. Although the foothills were wetter, cooler, and more frost-prone than the open prairie in summer, they were actually warmer in the winter because of the greater force of the chinook winds. Thus, they provided a better year round environment for cattle than the open prairie. Such a broad characterization of the foothills environment must be tempered by two considerations. The region contained pockets of land and micro-climates where unusual circumstances prevailed, and in any given year weather patterns could deviate considerably from the norm.[41]

Moving from the foothills to the plains around High River and then eastward into a sea of open grassland, the settlers encountered significant changes in environment and climate. As the elevation dropped and the terrain flattened, summer sunshine and temperatures increased, and the growing season lengthened. But rainfall also declined and evaporation intensified. Annual precipitation at High River itself averaged an ample nineteen inches annually, but declined erratically as settlement flowed eastward to the near desert environment of Palliser's Triangle. As in the foothills, extreme variations occurred from year to year, and pockets of unusual soil or climatic conditions appeared throughout the district.[42]

Drainage patterns also affected agricultural settlement. In particularly flat areas, surface water could not find a route to any river system. It collected in stagnant sloughs that bloated each spring and sometimes dried up completely by the fall. Not only did the sloughs themselves take land out of agricultural production, they also created highly alkaline, infertile soils for various distances around them. High River had to contend with a particularly large slough in its immediate hinterland. Five miles east of town, the Big Lake, or Frank Lake as it was later named, formed a huge blemish in an otherwise productive agricultural zone (See Figure 2). The slough and its alkaline ring removed about eight sections, or over 5,000 acres, from agricultural production; an area that expanded and contracted with recurring wet and dry cycles. Moreover, it forced travelers east of the slough to take a lengthy detour to reach High River.

The High River district thus presented the settlers with a wide variety of agricultural zones and conditions. Nonetheless, land seekers rapidly claimed it all and many of them enjoyed considerable prosperity until the first great agricultural crisis struck in the late 1910s. The town of High River now emerged as an important service centre for two distinct hinterlands: cattle ranching in the western foothills and wheat farming on the eastern plains.

2 | THE PRESS
COMES TO BOOMTOWN

BEFORE 1900 High River scarcely grew at all. Ranching simply did not require much of an urban structure in order to function. It demanded almost nothing in the way of production equipment or services, and its tiny labour pool presented a poor market for consumer goods. To the extent that ranching required towns, Calgary quickly emerged as the dominant centre for one overriding reason: the transcontinental railway ran through it and until 1891 no branch line penetrated the rangeland to the south. Since cattle bound for eastern and British markets had to be herded to Calgary, Pat Burns established meat slaughtering operations there to feed Canadian Pacific construction crews. In the 1890s he built a major packing plant to supply more distant markets. For many years, only Calgary offered banking services to the big ranches, and hence it became the favoured place for ranchers to buy their supplies. It also emerged as the main social centre for the cattle barons who founded the exclusive Ranchman's Club in 1891. Yet, in spite of its role as cattle capital, Calgary's population reached only 3,876 by 1891.[1]

At the High River crossing, little more than a hamlet developed. Between 1884 and 1891 it acquired a new stopping house, a general store, a blacksmith shop, a post office, a school, and a church. That such basic services appeared at all owed much to the difficulty of crossing the Highwood River to reach Calgary. Wagons originating south of the river (including those from the Bar U) had to travel east to the tiny settlement before proceeding north. A ferry service supplemented the ford at High River in 1886, followed by a bridge in 1887. Surprisingly, the arrival of the Calgary and Edmonton Railway in 1892 did not lead to much greater urban development. Even though it eliminated the necessity of herding High River cattle to Calgary, the railway built its major stockyards at Cayley, an even smaller siding nine miles to the south (See Figure 2). Nonetheless, the mere addition of a railway and train station encouraged the High River Trading Company to build a new stone store in 1893. The railway also stimulated a novel, if short-lived, activity: bones could be sold to fertilizer and sugar refining companies, and the remains of the extinct buffalo littered the prairie around High River. In a brief flurry of activity, collectors gathered them in wagons and hauled them to the railway.[2]

High River did not grow vigorously until commercial wheat farming created the demand for an array of goods and services. New enterprises sprouted to supply the first big influx of settlers in 1903 and a decade later, 89 businesses operated in the town, including half a dozen general stores and many specialized retailers.[3] Some sold consumer goods, while others catered directly to agricultural production: machinery dealers, hardware stores, fencing and lumber suppliers. A wide assortment of service businesses appeared, including banks, livery stables, hotels, cafes, a pool hall, a theatre, and shops for blacksmiths, tinsmiths, and other tradesmen. Professionals also flooded the town: doctors, dentists, lawyers, accountants, realtors, insurance agents, and a veterinarian. The duplication that appeared in nearly every line of business expanded consumer choices and introduced a degree of competition, making the town attractive to outlying settlers. Five grain elevators drew people from the east country as distant as 30 miles, exposing them to High River's array of stores and services.

Although pre-eminently a prairie shipping and distribution point, High River did acquire one important manufacturing establishment. The John Lineham Company had operated a lumber mill at Okotoks on Sheep Creek thirteen miles north of High River since 1891, and in 1903 it opened a second mill in High River to tap alpine timber in the Highwood watershed. Strong local markets existed because the settlers and townspeople immediately

Logs on the Highwood River. Glenbow Archives NA–695–33.

needed lumber for new buildings and fencing. A demand for telephone poles and railway ties for branch line construction subsequently emerged. The company often hired local homesteaders to cut timber in winter and float it to the mill each spring. By 1907, it employed 80 men in two shifts at the mill itself, and perhaps a like number of cutters in the foothills in winter, making it by far High River's largest employer.[4] Given a ready supply of lumber and an instant market for prefabricated windows and doors, a planing mill opened. A small brickworks, creamery, and grist mill also appeared in the town, but no other manufacturing concern matched lumber in scale and importance.

The town also acquired modern utilities. By 1913 it boasted a telephone exchange, an electric power plant, a water and sewage system, and such civic amenities as gravelled streets, concrete sidewalks, a park, and a "cottage" hospital. High River incorporated as a village in 1901 and advanced to town status in 1906. In 1912 a new, two-storey, brick town hall provided a council chamber, municipal offices, a police court and jail, a fire department, and a meeting hall. Half a dozen churches appeared. Voluntary associations proliferated like gophers: service organizations, fraternities and sororities, social clubs, sports and recreational associations.

From a population of 153 in 1901 High River may have surged to 1,500 by 1907, although the official census of 1911 pegged it at 1,182.[5] Certainly, the town experienced a wild construction boom in 1906 and 1907, and faced a severe shortage of carpenters and other building tradesmen. As in the countryside, speculation gripped the populace. One downtown lot, worth almost nothing in 1901, fetched $3,755 in 1906, and the following spring a subdivision known as "Park View" sprang to life.[6] Escalating rural and town land prices, combined with the frantic movement of people in and out of the district, gave rise to no less than 42 real estate agents in High River, although nearly all of them only worked part-time at this occupation. As one of them recalled half a century later: "there was keen competition to meet and keep one's prospective buyers. We saw them to bed and were on hand to greet them when they rose in the morning. Real estate was no dignified profession in those days."[7]

THE SUDDEN AND DRAMATIC GROWTH of High River and district after 1900 meant that the community could support one other specialized business: a weekly newspaper. The first such enterprise in High River, however, could hardly be described as a typical weekly, or even a typical newspaper. It was the product of Bob Edwards, a Scottish immigrant who dabbled in publishing in Wetaskiwin and Strathcona before moving to High River in 1902. There he launched the *Chinook*, a paper that later acquired notoriety after changing its name to the *Eye Opener*. The newspaper appeared irregularly, a frequent casualty of Edwards's drinking binges. Nonetheless, he was a creative writer who mocked social pretension with biting satire. He often invented fictitious characters and reported on their activities as though they were real people. By such means he lampooned politicians, clergymen, and other respectable citizens, portraying them as hypocrites who often succumbed to his own vice, drunkenness. As one biographer noted, "In truth, the *Eye Opener* was not a newspaper, but Bob Edwards's personal platform for social comment and humour."[8]

Edwards would spend much of his career fighting libel suits, and he soon offended the new residents of High River by indulging in what *Times* later described as "brilliant though erratic attacks on all and sundry."[9] His most scandalous story involved a traveling gramophone salesman who supposedly sold recordings of hymns to the Methodist minister. When played in church, however, bawdy dance hall songs bombarded the congregation.

To the relief of local residents, Bob Edwards moved the *Eye Opener* to Calgary in 1905 where it achieved a degree of national and even international fame. His departure opened a journalistic void in High River, and Charles Clark moved quickly to fill it. Born in 1869 and raised on a farm near Kincardine in Bruce County, Ontario, Clark learned the weekly newspaper business from his older brother Hugh, who published the *Kincardine Review*. Although Charles eventually became a partner in the business, he first nurtured youthful ambitions to visit two exotic locales, the Rocky Mountains and Africa. He realized the first goal in 1899 when he traveled on a press excursion from Toronto to Victoria. The second became possible with the outbreak of the South African War in 1899. Traveling at his own expense, he joined Canadian troops as a civilian clerk in a noncombatant role.[10]

After returning to Canada, he recalled falling victim to "propaganda extolling the West as the land of opportunity."[11] In 1903 he arrived in Calgary, where he began trading horses and cattle, and even considered claiming a homestead. While scouting for land in 1904, someone suggested that the town of Okotoks needed a newspaper, since the local weekly had ceased publication. Clark would have preferred to operate in the more promising town of High River, but with Bob Edwards already there, he bought the defunct *Okotoks Review* and began publication. The following year Edwards told him about the decision to move the *Eye Opener* to Calgary, thus providing Clark with the opportunity to transfer to High River before rivals appeared. He seized the chance and published the first issue of the *High River Times* on 7 December 1905. He sold the *Okotoks Review* the following year.

Clark quickly sunk roots in the new community. Already 36 and still a bachelor, he returned east in 1906 to wed Mary Elizabeth McDonell of Bay City, Michigan. The couple had met when her family visited Kincardine. Returning to High River, the newlyweds commissioned the building of a spacious new house, finished in 1909. Children soon arrived: Mary Margaret (Marnie) in 1908 and Charles Archibald in 1910.

IN ITS FIRST YEARS OF PUBLICATION, the *Times* greeted its public with a drab face. Advertising cluttered the front page. Few headings appeared and stories of all sorts competed for attention beneath them. The paper presented almost no photographs or illustrations since the engraved plates needed for their reproduction had to be made in Calgary, and this entailed considerable time, trouble, and expense. As a result, the *Times* rarely bothered with photographs, unless itinerant entertainers or politicians traveled with their own ready-made plates. No ready solution to the problem would appear until the 1960s.

Unimpressive as it might appear to modern readers, the *Times* resembled other rural weeklies of the day. Charles Clark fretted more about the content and he issued an apology in the inaugural issue:

> It is with considerable diffidence that we present this, our first issue to our readers and subscribers because we feel that High River is worthy of the best that can be produced and must have something far superior to the ordinary run of country newspapers such as are so frequently found throughout the West. We can safely promise readers that future issues of the *Times* will be more interesting than the one we now present to you.

Clark apologized, in part, for the paucity of local material. While the earliest issues of the *Times* consisted of eight pages, half of them came from an insert known as "ready-made print," sometimes referred to as "boiler plate." Obtained from Winnipeg, and likely written and printed by the Toronto Type Foundry Company (which sold much equipment to weekly newspapers), boiler plate provided a means for small weeklies to augment their meagre offering of original material. Most often, patent medicine advertisers paid for these inserts that ran "news stories" about the miraculous cures produced by their products. The boiler plate that appeared in the

Front page, 23 May 1912. High River Times photo.

first issue of the *Times* included a testimonial from a man "rescued from the Deadly Clutches of Bright's disease by Dodd's Kidney Pills." Subsequent issues of the boiler plate featured stories about "Dr. Chase's Syrup of Linseed and Turpentine," and its marvellous effect on croupy babies and "A Mother's Duty," in which a woman saves her daughter's blood by administering Dr. Williams's Pink Pills.[12] Although dominated by such material, the boiler plate also offered stories of the "human interest" variety, as well as humour and fiction. Most readers did not like ready-print, and even the advertising business considered its ads scandalous. Weekly publishers did not like it either. They suspected it garnered national advertising revenues that might otherwise go to themselves. Most rural weeklies dumped boiler plate during the 1920s, but the *Times* dispensed of it within a year.[13]

In spite of Clark's apology, the four pages of material actually produced by the *Times* staff during the first year of operation introduced many features that would endure for decades: local advertising, notices of upcoming events, reports on the activities of local organizations and institutions, and snippets about the doings of local residents presented in a column entitled "Town Topics Tersely Told." Similar items appeared in reports from various rural neighbourhoods in the High River area.

As for news from outside the district, the *Times* quickly established the tradition of largely ignoring it. It had no intention of competing with city dailies that had infiltrated the district long before the *Times* appeared. From its beginnings, the ranching community had received newspapers from London and other British cities, or from Chicago, Montreal, or Winnipeg. "Our relatives in Ontario and New York had by nearly every mail kept us well supplied with papers and magazines," recalled one woman.[14] This news arrived belatedly. Before the building of the Canadian Pacific Railway, all mail came via the United States with other freight in the bull trains that ran from Fort Benton to Calgary. The mail was simply dumped at the High River stopping house, and cowboys rummaged through an open box to retrieve items for their ranches.

The completion of the transcontinental railway to Calgary in 1883 brought these distant newspapers to the ranching frontier more quickly, even though they still traveled south by stage. At High River, a post office replaced the open box in 1884. The North West Cattle Company wielded enough political clout to acquire its own post office in 1886. Named Pekisko after the Highwood tributary that flowed past the Bar U, Mrs. Stimson served as postmistress. By 1889 it handled mail for 55 people in the surrounding foothills. At first, a horse rider carried it from High River to Pekisko, but since the volume of newspapers sometimes reached 75 to 100 pounds in weight, the ranch soon petitioned the government for wagon delivery.[15]

The *Calgary Herald*, which began publication in 1883, contributed to that bulk. Its founder recalled that during the first year of operation, he sold about a dozen subscriptions in the High River district.[16] To win more readers, the *Herald* provided some coverage of the district, mostly social notes on the coming and goings of visitors, and the results of horse races. By 1886 it also carried advertisements for the Smith and Chambers stopping house. The *Herald* added considerably to the stock of outside information since it utilized the new telegraph line to obtain national and international stories. The *Herald* arrived with greater speed once the Calgary and Edmonton Railway reached High River in 1892. The rush of settlement by 1903, the inauguration of twice daily train service from Calgary, and the establishment of retail stores that carried newspapers and magazines all made timely outside news readily available to anyone who desired it. In addition, the High River Club, a social organization for men founded in 1905, maintained subscriptions to many publications, including British newspapers.[17] Moreover, rural post offices rapidly proliferated in the new settlements east of town, bringing news within miles of nearly every pioneer.

What the *Times* offered in the way of outside news largely consisted of unrelated tidbits and curious oddities, particularly regarding international affairs. On 11 April 1907, readers learned that "King Alfonso of Spain is suffering from tuberculosis and the Spanish counts are extremely uneasy about his condition." Occasionally an international story carried enough interest to make it worthy of many retellings and additional details no matter how often it had appeared in the dailies. The *Times* treated readers to many stories about the sinking of the Titanic throughout 1912. Outside news also appeared whenever local residents visited distant locales and conveyed their (often detailed) impressions to the *Times*.

The paper most often reported outside events whenever they exerted a direct impact on the local community. The outbreak of the Great War provides a prime example. The Times could not provide fresh news from the front, but it did assess how the war drove wheat prices skyward and sustained prosperity in the district just as the settlement boom ended. An editorial on 17 May 1917 assured farmers that planting more wheat did not indicate greed, but only a desire to feed the Allies and aid their victory. The Times also covered local, war-related projects, particularly money-raising efforts for the Patriotic Fund, the Red Cross, and other wartime charities. It also attempted to provide coverage about the local boys who enlisted, seeking their families' permission to print whatever information they conveyed in letters home. Details about their whereabouts, their safety, and their activities appeared in a regular column entitled "Military Men and Matters."[18]

Regardless of the geographical origins of any story, the Times studiously adopted the weeklies' tradition of avoiding controversy. In its inaugural issue, it announced a policy of political nonpartisanship in spite of Charles Clark's personal leanings. Although one letter to the editor in 24 April 1913 accused the Times of Conservative bias, the paper routinely praised all local politicians regardless of party affiliation. It flattered its readers on 30 January 1908 by congratulating both the Liberals and Conservatives in the local riding for nominating farmers as candidates since Ottawa desperately needed "shrewd, clear-minded, level-headed farmers." It supported Liberal Dan Riley's successful bid as High River's first town mayor in 1906, but hastened to add that the other candidates would also make excellent choices.[19] Liberals from outside the district sometimes received praise too, as on 3 October 1907, when the Times applauded the Dominion Minister of the Interior, Frank Oliver, for having the best interests of Western Canada at heart. Usually, however, the Times preferred to quote others on political matters instead of offering its own views.

The Times found plenty of other controversies to avoid, including the clash between ranchers and settlers over land use. When compelled to choose between them, the Times sided with the farmers, who represented a vastly larger pool of potential subscribers, but did so in a manner designed to placate the ranchers. "Of course this [agricultural settlement] cannot be effected without...disturbing the status quo...of the big ranchers," it wrote on 15 February 1906:

but they will consult and conserve their best interests by accepting with good grace the inevitable altered conditions...and cooperate with the new settlers in developing the country for the good of the commonwealth, and while their freedom and privileges of the past may be somewhat curtailed by the fencing of the homestead and purchased railway lands, they will be more than compensated by the enhanced value of their tilled lands...created by the demands and requirements of the new comers.

During the Great War when controversy raged locally, as well as nationally, about the conscription of men for overseas military duty, the Times discovered another subject to avoid. When it finally decided to introduce the debate, it proceeded cautiously, publishing an anticonscription letter on 13 April 1916 and a proconscription one on 27 April. It penned a neutral editorial on 11 January 1917. After conscription became a reality, the Times finally lent support to the matter, relieved that it exempted farmers as producers of goods essential for the war effort.

In its quest to avoid opinion, the Times made an exception when it solicited contributions from Robert J.C. Stead. Born in Ontario in 1880 and raised on a Manitoba farm, Stead ran his own newspaper and acquired a modest reputation as a writer with the publication of his first book, The Empire Builders and Other Poems, in 1908. He moved to High River in 1909 to join in partnership with his brother, who had founded the Alberta Automobile Company, agents for McLaughlin and Buick cars. Charles Clark immediately recognized Stead's talent. He praised The Empire Builders and offered a free copy to anyone taking out a new subscription to the Times. In 1911 he persuaded Stead to become a columnist. His "Observations" appeared on the front page of each issue where the paper provided ample space for his thoughts—frequently two full columns or more. No one else on the Times received a by-line, not even Clark.

"Observations" provided the Times with its closest approximation of a true editorial column since Stead seemed to have free reign to write as he wished. Topics ranged widely from the farm co-operative movement to British colonial rule in India to the art of tipping. While Stead's frank opinions broke with the cautious tradition of the rural weekly, he rarely expressed views repugnant to his local audience. He believed that Western Canada represented a clean slate for the creation of a new and improved agrarian society. He did not oppose urban ideas or modern technology, but believed they could enhance rural life. His vision was more spiritual than materialistic and his idealism remained intact until the Great War. Unfortunately for the *Times*, Stead's tenure with the newspaper ended in 1913 when he accepted a position in Calgary. Stead subsequently wrote thirteen more books, establishing his reputation as an important figure in the development of Western Canadian literature. His most popular novel, *The Cowpuncher*, appeared in 1918 and his most critically acclaimed one, *Grain*, in 1926, books based in part on his observations of ranch and farm life in the High River area.[20]

The riskiest position the *Times* took was the decision to report local court cases. Many rural newspapers refused to do so because it would embarrass the families of the accused—a position that the *Times* itself would later take. In its early years, however, it covered local crimes and usually named the perpetrators. Sometimes it even offered commentary on the court proceedings and occasionally disagreed with rulings of the local magistrate. Reporting on a case of unpaid debt on 28 June 1910, the *Times* noted that "Mr. Middleditch was well known and though he was considered peculiar and rather unbusiness-like in his methods, still dishonesty was never considered one of his characteristics...We trust that even yet some evidence may be found which will tend to explain or justify his conduct." A notable tendency here was to extend some understanding or even sympathy towards the local perpetrator. But the *Times* did not always print names. In cases involving raids on brothels, for example, it commonly named the prostitutes, but not their local clients.

Crimes committed by transients against established local citizens made the best material for reporting purposes. In such cases, the criminal could be named and his crime vigorously deplored without any danger of offending a subscriber. Indeed, suspicious drifters could be condemned even if they had not been arrested for any offence. The *Times* warned residents on 21 March 1912 that "the town is again infested with night prowlers and objectionable persons who have no visible means of support." On 23 July 1914 it mercilessly denounced a "disreputable band of four-flushers and cutthroats ...touts and harlots," who appeared at the summer fair. Sometimes the distinction between outside criminals and established citizens could be blurred, as in the case of High River's first murder, which involved the death of a woman at the hands of her husband. The Times feared that it would harm the town's reputation, but the paper took some solace in the fact that both murderer and victim were not really local residents since they had lived in the town for "a very short time."[21]

ASIDE FROM THE RISKS it took in reporting crime, the Times sidestepped controversy most effectively by focusing relentlessly on themes that virtually all its advertisers and readers could endorse. Nativism offered a prime example. The great boom years brought unprecedented numbers of foreign language immigrants to Canada, including many from peasant cultures in central and eastern Europe. The dominant English-speaking groups disdained them. Many people simply harboured a crude prejudice against the unknown and the different. The educated upheld sophisticated theories of racism such as social Darwinism that ranked races and ethnic groups in order of their superiority. Labour hated immigrants for working as strike breakers and lowering wages generally. Others considered them a threat to British culture and morality. Many called for greater restrictions on immigration, and virtually everyone demanded that the educational system and the immigrants themselves embrace cultural assimilation.[22]

The response to immigrants became known as nativism and newspapers across Canada wallowed in its rhetoric. In 1907, the Alberta and Eastern British Columbia Press Association formally adopted cultural assimilation as a campaign worthy of support in their newspapers.[23] Although the High River district received few foreign language immigrants, the Times joined the nativist chorus. On 11 November 1909, for example, it deplored the appearance of Bulgarian fortune tellers in the town. "The Gypsies are a motley bunch," it warned, "they are, to say the least, a very undesirable bunch of immigrants." Anyone distinctive in culture, and particularly race, received the sharpest condemnation. "The appearance of several Jap women in High River," noted the Times on 5 August 1909, "is a matter to be deplored."

The small contingent of Chinese immigrants in High River received most of the critical attention. A story on 15 February 1906 typified the reaction to them and established a pattern for years to come. A fight erupted between a Chinese café owner and a white patron when the customer refused to pay an old debt before ordering his next meal. The court found the Caucasian guilty and fined him two dollars and costs. Nonetheless, the Times argued:

> It is a peculiar thing, but nevertheless a fact that some people, in their sober moments refuse to patronize the wily Mongolian, but while in their cups drift into any old Chinese restaurant and invariably get into trouble. With so many first-class restaurants in town, conducted by respectable white men, there is no reason why the Chinese restaurants should not be boycotted. When that is done there will be no further trouble.

It is perhaps relevant to note that the Chinese had not yet begun advertising in the Times, and that in the same issue, a notice for the Astoria Cafe assured customers: "No Chinese Employed Here." In any event, the Chinese soon began to place advertisements in the Times. In a curious example of cross-cultural fertilization, Hong Sing may have thought that a hint of old Ireland would soften the mood of white customers when he advertised his Shamrock Restaurant on 4 October 1906. Such patronage seemed to soften the journalistic blows, for on 12 November 1908, the Times rewarded the advertising loyalty of the Royal Restaurant: "The place is kept immaculately clean and excellent meals are provided. Sing Lung, the proprietor, is to be congratulated and he deserves to be patronized by the people of High River." The advertisement also assured customers that "A white waitress will attend to your wants."

On other occasions, the Times demonstrated begrudging respect for the hard work, thrift, and business acumen of the Chinese. "In High River the celestial is quietly forging to the front," it wrote on 4 June 1908, "and we have in town many well-to-do Chinamen who own buildings on our principal streets. The average Chinaman is a money maker, or to be more accurate, a money saver." On another occasion the *Times* expressed sympathy for a Chinese man who committed suicide, and it condemned the rioting "hoodlums" that destroyed property in Vancouver's Chinatown in 1907. But while the *Times* established limits to racism, it condemned the Chinese in general and urged that they be barred from entering the country.[24]

Reports on the Chinese clearly mirrored attitudes embedded in local society and in the nation at large.[25] Once, however, the *Times* misread local opinion on the nativism issue. On 9 April 1908 it attacked the French immigrants in the district for speaking their mother tongue. An editorial insisted that they "must come here with the firm purpose and desire to conform to the customs and manners of the country of their adoption." If they did so, they would be welcome, but "if it is their desire to remain French, then they should have stayed in France." The *Times* seemed surprised to receive letters of protest and on 16 April it published two of them: one from a French-speaking resident and another from a English-speaking one. Both expressed astonishment at the attack and argued that it was not unreasonable for recent immigrants to speak their native language amongst themselves. The letter writers insisted that the French immigrants constituted valuable and welcome settlers in the community. On 23 April the *Times* announced that it would not raise the matter again, and it never did. When the *Times* misread local opinion and inadvertently sparked controversy, it retreated rather than offend a segment of its readers and advertisers.

By way of contrast, the American Mormons at the Frankburg settlement never received an unfavourable notice in the *Times*, even though some clergymen of the dominant churches in Western Canadian feared Mormonism and openly attacked it. On 31 July 1913, the Frankburg settlers received accolades for their celebration commemorating the nineteenth-century trek of the Mormons from Missouri to Utah. Their kindly treatment reflected the high approval rating that the *Times* accorded Americans generally. As the largest national group in the High River district, and the one arriving with the most capital and agricultural knowledge, their desirability became an established fact in the pages in the *Times*. The comment on 8 February 1906 is typical: "It is very gratifying to note the excellent class of American settlers who have located in the district of High River. Possessed of sufficient of this world's goods they have cast in their lot with Alberta and are a most cheerful and optimistic people and very progressive."

THE *TIMES* ALSO SOUGHT to insure social cohesion by defending and promoting the economic interests of the self-employed groups that dominated its subscription list. The grievances of prairie settlers are well documented. They criticized the manufacturers of farm implements, hardware, and supplies for colluding to create virtual monopolies, thereby eliminating competition and raising the costs of producing wheat. They condemned banks for high interest rates and credit practices that did not readily accommodate agriculture. They denounced railways for high freight rates, and elevator companies for low grain prices. And they opposed Dominion government policies that protected corporate interests, particularly the high tariffs on imported manufactured goods that eliminated foreign competition and allowed domestic producers to dominate the market.

The *Times* did not hesitate to articulate these grievances. In a single issue on 4 October 1906 it called the Canadian Pacific Railway a "parasite and leech," "a financial octopus...sapping the vitality of the country," "a corporation of graft and greed," and a "hog corporation." It routinely blasted the railway for exorbitant freight rates, for the dangerous condition of its roadbed, for poor passenger service, for delays in installing a new railway crossing in town, for failing to provide sufficient boxcars at harvest time, for its ownership of local farm land, for stifling competition, and for ignoring High River in the construction of branch lines. It even blamed the railway for the spread of dandelions in the town.

Other corporate interests despised by farmers received their share of venom. When local elevator agents complained to the editor that many of the farmers' accusations against the grain companies were unfounded, the *Times* declared its allegiance on 31 October 1907: "anything we published was done solely for the protection of the farmers whose interests we will always uphold, come what may." Needless to say, the *Times* heartily supported every organizational attempt by farmers to advance their interests, including the formation of co-operative enterprises and lobby groups such as the Grain Growers' Associations and the United Farmers of Alberta.

The *Times* also backed the farmers' war against the high tariffs that protected corporations from cheaper American competition. It launched tirades of its own and often borrowed antiprotectionist material from other publications. The tariff issue even threatened the nonpartisan policy of the *Times* when the Liberal government negotiated a trade agreement with the United States that became known as "reciprocity." The deal included modest reductions on agricultural machinery tariffs and the Liberal government prepared to fight an election on the issue in 1911. The Conservative party opposed the measure and thereby won the support of Canadian manufacturers. Although the *Times* presented some Conservative viewpoints in its pages, it refused to publish the "daily flow of anti-reciprocity material coming into this office" that it considered nothing more than vile propaganda.[26] The *Times* readily supported reciprocity because of its great popularity in the High River district. Even the local Conservative candidate, John Herron, broke with his own party over the issue, and claimed to be more committed to free trade than his Liberal rival. Even so, Herron lost by a wide margin.[27]

In supporting local producers, the *Times* did not befriend organized labour. Even though farmers and workers routinely condemned the same business corporations, often in the same way, and sometimes for the same reasons, farmers rarely sympathized with the working class. Higher pay in industry and transportation meant higher production and transportation charges for farmers. The 1906 coal mining strike disrupted grain shipments and left farmers shivering without heating fuel. Moreover, farmers employed labour themselves. The largest farms and ranches hired year-round hands and extra help in the summer. All farmers depended heavily on labour in the fall when they paid threshing contractors to harvest their grain. In turn, the contractors hired gangs of temporary labourers, many brought in from eastern Canada just for the harvest.

Like all employers, farmers wanted labour as cheaply as possible and cringed at the thought that vital operations might be disrupted by strikes. The *Times* readily supported local employers in this regard. A typical response appeared on 11 April 1912, when an editorial denounced union organizers as "floaters," and "trouble-makers." The local community especially feared the Industrial Workers of the World, a radical, Marxist organization that sought to unite all unskilled workers and that advocated militant tactics like industrial sabotage. Fearing that it would attempt to organize harvesting crews, the *Times* borrowed a vicious anti-IWW story for its main editorial on 22 February 1912. In response to a local report about an IWW harvester who caused an accident by tampering with a farm wagon, the *Times* suggested on 21 August 1913 that "A sound flogging is in order for such a man."

The *Times* also disdained those who would not work. "Don't give any able-bodied man a penny or a mouthful unless he works for it," it warned on 25 September 1908. "By this the man retains self respect and the profession of the tramp is not encouraged." Like most of society, the *Times* believed charity should only be extended to the "deserving poor," those mired in circumstances clearly not of their own making and who had little chance to rectify their situation. Thus, on 3 January 1907, the paper appealed to readers to assist a local family who lost its sole breadwinner in a threshing accident: "Mrs. Bannon is an aged and pathetic invalid utterly incapable of keeping herself and her daughters, who are compelled to remain at home to care for their mother, and so prevented from adding to their maintenance."

Most of the ideological positions taken by the *Times* to advance the economic interests of farmers also appealed to other self-employed groups in the district: ranchers, tradesmen, professionals, and merchants. But all of them hoped to benefit more from one other crusade launched by the *Times*, the one that consumed most of its journalistic energies and enjoyed the most enthusiastic local support: the great booster campaign.

3

BOOSTING
THE EMERGING METROPOLIS

BOOSTERISM ATTEMPTED TO STIMULATE economic and population growth by offering railways, industries, and government institutions incentives to locate in a particular community. These incentives often took the form of free or cheap building sites and utility connections, tax exemptions, or even cash bonuses. Promotional pamphlets published by municipal governments and boards-of-trade advertised these rewards, praised the virtues of the community generally, and discredited rival towns.[1]

Newspapers across Canada have always acted as boosters for their communities, but particularly so in the early twentieth century West when lightning growth fuelled grand ambitions and when decisions about the location of many economic facilities remained unsettled.[2] The *Times* declared town promotion as its primary mandate in the inaugural issue of 7 December 1905:

> ...we will bend all our energies towards the advancement of the interests of High River and her people. We have established ourselves here because we have been watching the development of High River for some time past and judging from the wonderful progress it has made, the character of the men who are taking their part in its construction,

and the splendid country of which it is the center, we are confident that it is destined to rank among the leading cities of Alberta.
...one dare not assume to limit its possibilities.

While virtually every subsequent issue extolled the virtues of High River in some way, the *Times* also published special promotional issues, such as the "Immigration Number" of 9 September 1909 and the "Homeseekers Number" of 16 May 1912. Planned far in advance, these issues offered readers 24-page editions of the *Times* and the rare treat of many local photographs. Every page and picture single-mindedly promoted the town and district.

Neither the rhetoric nor the message of local boosterism was unique. Every town argued that settlers should come to its district because of the outstanding potential for agriculture. Oblivious to the climatic variations throughout the High River district, and to the wild swings in yearly and even daily weather patterns, the *Times* insisted on 1 August 1907 that the climate was perfect for agriculture and "never extreme in any way." The special "Immigration Number" provided more details: "Moderate and timely showers seem never to fail us, and although never excessive, appear to be always adequate to the requirements of our moisture retaining soil." In describing the bounty that sprang from this nourishment, poetic rhapsody overtook the *Times*:

> First, we notice in early summer the drill rows of vivid green, reaching in unbroken lines from half a mile to a mile and sometimes further, in pleasing contrast to the dark, chocolate colored soil that brought them forth and will nourish and sustain them to fruitful maturity; then in a short time—it seems almost a miracle—we see the fields transformed to a solid sheet of living green.

Testimonials from local settlers buttressed these descriptions of nirvana, and biographical profiles provided the financial details of their success. "The above reads like a fairy tale," concluded the *Times* after presenting one such story on 15 July 1909, "but it is absolutely true and only goes to demonstrate what a young man with a little industry and common sense can do in a few short years in this wonderful land of opportunities."

The Times also threw its support behind promotional schemes to demonstrate productivity, such as High River's first fair in 1907 and the creation of an Agricultural Society in 1909 to organize fairs annually. Although High River considered itself the greatest cattle and wheat district in Western Canada, these fairs also sought to confirm its suitability for a wide variety of mixed farm products. Commenting on the fair in the 28 October 1909 issue, the Times noted that "High River has thus demonstrated to the rest of the province her capabilities as a district pre-eminent in the production of high class stock, dairy products, cereals, vegetables, and fancy work."

Not only did the Times exaggerate agricultural potential, it also ignored real problems and even denied their existence. When one farmer complained that the Times had not reported the damages caused by a killing spring frost, the paper responded angrily on 3 June 1909: "We may say that it is our intention to boost the country notwithstanding the efforts of a few so-called farmers who have made a failure of farming." In any event, the Times argued on 11 September 1913, early frosts would magically disappear as the country became more settled. When widespread crop failure in 1910 belied any report to the contrary, the Times put the best possible face on the disaster. It admitted on 4 August that farmers suffered from "one of the most severe droughts that southern Alberta has ever experienced, and many have lost their entire crop." Nonetheless, it added, "there are numerous excellent fields."

The Times recognized that the foothills west of town would not support farming, but it praised those districts as unsurpassed grazing lands that offered cattle bountiful grass, comforting shelter, plentiful water, and balmy chinooks. Again, it minimized problems. Although historians estimate that ranchers lost 50 percent of their stock in the devastating winter of 1906–7, the Times insisted on 16 May 1907 that losses did not exceed fifteen percent. It made this pronouncement before the spring roundup could provide more accurate estimates, and after the roundup it ignored the question of losses entirely.

The wheat lands east of High River. Clark Family Papers.

LURING MORE SETTLERS to the district promised to enrich existing residents. Farmers and land speculators would enjoy a rise in the value of their holdings and the town would gain more customers. But that advantage would be lost if the settlers shopped elsewhere, and the *Times* worked feverishly persuading them to patronize its High River advertisers. It worked just as energetically to discredit rival towns and other shopping alternatives.

Railway companies attempted to determine the distribution of new towns in Western Canada through the placement of sidings and stations. They relied on past experience and took into account the feasibility of frequent train stops, the size and distribution of elevators preferred by grain companies, and the distances farmers might reasonably be expected to haul crops, but the lure of real estate profits often undermined these considerations.[3] Railways invariably established sidings and stations on odd-numbered sections that constituted part of their Dominion government land grants, thereby monopolizing all initial town lot sales. They also co-operated with town-building speculators who promised to buy railway lands adjacent to the track if the railways agreed to provide sidings. As a result, more town sites appeared than economics and geography warranted.

The Calgary and Edmonton Railway built sidings every five to ten miles between Calgary and Fort Macleod, but most of them never became towns. In 1906 it sold land to H.R. Moore, who surveyed 200 lots for the new town site of Norma only six miles from High River. A few businesses established themselves, but when lot sales collapsed, they abandoned the site.[4] Other town sites never grew beyond hamlets. In 1908, Aldersyde, situated seven miles north of High River, consisted of one grain elevator, one general store, one lumberyard, one machinery and harness shop, a post office, and a few residences.[5] Two other town sites reached populations between 100 and 500 by 1911, three more reached the 500 to 1,000 range, but only two exceeded 1,000: High River and Fort Macleod.

These results suggest that farmers did not always patronize the nearest town, but favoured particular ones, thus contributing to differential rates of growth. Distance and travel time influenced their choices since any trip by horse and wagon proceeded slowly. The survey system that blanketed the west wisely made provision for road allowances, thus avoiding the need to appropriate land for future road construction. These road allowances ran every mile north and south, and every two miles east and west. Every quarter-section therefore bordered on at least one road allowance, but for many years, rural municipalities had no funds to actually construct and maintain roads. The allowances remained nothing more than dirt trails and wagons broke down frequently as they bounced over the rough terrain. Rain or snow often rendered the trails impassable. Ravines and creeks necessitated risky fords and lengthy detours since municipalities often failed to build bridges.

Travel time varied with luck and road conditions as much as with distance. One farm family that lived eight-and-a-half miles east of High River usually needed two hours to reach town by wagon in 1903.[6] A shopping trip often consumed an entire day and could not be justified for the frequent purchase of a few routine supplies. To meet that demand, enterprising pioneers opened general stores in the countryside. They often secured post office contracts that drew surrounding farmers to their stores. Sometimes a blacksmith opened a shop beside such a store and an off-railway hamlet developed.

While settlers patronized country stores frequently, only railway towns could satisfy many of their crucial needs, including the provision of grain elevators. After the harvest, the lengthy grain-hauling season commenced. Horse-drawn wagons held little grain, necessitating many trips. In 1908 one outlying pioneer discovered that it took one and a half days to haul a single load of wheat 45 miles to High River.[7] Such trips entailed considerable expense since the farmer needed to feed and board both his horses and himself overnight. Settlers situated far from the railway considered their destination carefully. They wanted a town that offered competing grain companies (even through farmers argued that they all conspired to eliminate competition). They also wanted a town where many merchants offered a wide selection of supplies and services. Since they would find themselves with empty wagons after unloading their crops, grain hauling presented a convenient opportunity to stock up on goods. As one High River hardware merchant later recalled, distant country people did not come to town often, but when they did come, "they bought supplies by the wagon load to last for months ahead."[8]

The *Times* tried to convince farmers to make High River their preferred destination. It did not fret about competition from country stores and off-rail hamlets. They did not offer the range of goods and services available in High River, and without rail connections, they never would. Nor could they compete with High River prices since the goods they sold had to be transported from the railway at considerable expense. And since they had no newspapers of their own, they often advertised in the *Times*. Moreover, High River merchants owned some of the country stores; E.E. Thompson opened a huge branch store in the off-railway hamlet of Brant fourteen miles east of town. For all those reasons, the *Times* regarded these outlying communities as part of High River's trade hinterland, and the newspaper maintained district correspondents in many of them.

Other railway towns presented High River with serious competition, especially Okotoks, twelve miles to the north, and Nanton, eighteen miles to the south (See Figure 2). Both had populations exceeding 500 in 1911 and both offered a wide range of goods and services. They also sustained weekly newspapers that carried the advertisements of their merchants. To the west, the three towns faced no competition at all since no railway existed between them and the summit of the Rockies. Before 1913, one could travel 25 miles east of High River before reaching a point equidistant to Gleichen, the next railway town with over 500 people.

Comparing High River to its rivals, the Times boasted about the vast selection of goods, the low prices, and the outstanding service provided by its business community. It also bragged about the special attractions that High River offered the visiting farm family: agricultural fairs, horse shows, sporting events, holiday celebrations, and by 1908, motion pictures, as well as touring circuses, musicians, theatre companies, chautauquas, and other professional entertainment that stopped at the larger towns. In covering special events that might draw rural dwellers to High River, the Times almost never delivered a negative review, and often posted positive ones in advance.[9] The paper also became a tireless crusader for transportation improvements that would whisk farmers into town more quickly and reliably. It nagged rural municipalities in the district to build and maintain decent roads and bridges. Without them, it warned on 10 June 1909 "much business will be lost to our town."

Rival towns and their newspapers employed similar tactics and it became necessary on occasion to discredit them directly. When the Gleichen Call claimed that its town offered lower prices than High River, the Times indignantly confronted the outrage in several issues in December 1908. When the southern Alberta town of Claresholm crowned itself the greatest wheat shipping point in Western Canada, the Times unleashed an avalanche of statistical evidence to bury the lie and claim the title for High River on 6 May 1909. But the nastiest exchange began on 22 February 1906 when the Times accused Okotoks fans of misconduct at a hockey game. The incident quickly escalated into a war with the Okotoks Review over the relative merits of each town generally. Exasperated by one attack, the 5 April issue of the Times denounced a Review article as "a tirade of personal abuse...to a great extent false...also low and vulgar." On 12 April, it reprinted a Review article that was sure to enrage local sensibilities:

> The Times only makes itself ridiculous when it speaks of High River taking its place as one of the metropolis" [sic] of the great empire. Its versatile editor should come down from the clouds and take a prac-

tical common sense view of matters as they stand at the present day, and not be exposing himself, his paper and his town to the laughter of the public by the rapsodical flights of fancy he takes when prophesying the future greatness of High River.

Calgary, which offered far more selection and price competition than any town in southern Alberta could hope to provide, constituted a special rival. It did not threaten to steal the trade of High River's rural hinterland, but enticed the townsfolk themselves. By 1908 the railway offered twice daily passenger service to Calgary. Even with various stops, it took one hour and forty minutes to travel the 38 miles, making it possible to visit Calgary, shop, and return to High River in a single day.[10] The *Times* routinely condemned the practice and in an editorial tirade on 26 July 1906 argued that: "the person who does almost his entire buying...with an outside town simply because he can save a few dollars a year is a mighty poor citizen to any town, and not possessed of the spirit of loyalty which goes to make an enterprising citizen."

As it had with Okotoks, the *Times* seized any weapon, including sports rivalry, to discredit the city. Reporting on 16 June 1910 about a lacrosse game, the *Times* claimed that Calgary resorted to its usual bully tactics when it fell behind. One Calgary player knocked the teeth out of a High River player and another, "nasty McDonnel, very deliberately fouled Adams with a vicious smash in the face." At that point High River spectators poured onto the playing field, forcing the game to end early and preserving the win for High River. The *Times* also attacked the *Calgary Albertan* for criticizing High River fans and for its biased report of the game. "The town with the loud talk has been beaten to a whimper," crowed the *Times*, "and High River did it, and did it right."

High River confronted another potent enemy of the small town merchant: the mail order catalogue issued by Eaton's or some other metropolitan department store. To combat this menace, the *Times* sponsored numerous "trade-at-home" campaigns. The paper insisted that local stores often carried goods superior in quality and lower in price than the catalogues. As for selection, local merchants would happily order any item not in stock. Even when catalogues offered cheaper prices, the local merchant always provided superior service. His goods could be inspected before purchase; mail order goods could not. Local merchants extended credit and some even took farm produce in trade; the catalogues required cash in advance and also charged postage and shipping. Local purchases could be taken home immediately; mail order entailed a two-week wait. Moreover, local merchants deserved patronage because they paid local taxes and supported local institutions and charities; the mail order firms gave the community nothing.[11]

The last argument could also be raised against the itinerant peddlers who prowled the High River district by wagon, and later by truck, selling everything from books to stoves.[12] The local merchant could do little to stop the flow of catalogues, but they could, and did, take action against peddlers by convincing town council to charge them hefty license fees, and by urging the provincial government to restrict their activities or even regulate them out of existence.[13] The Times gleefully reported every instance of peddlers caught and fined for evading the local license, and it supported every new attempt to curb them. On 22 May 1913 it cheered Lane Photography when that local business asked the town council to add "tramp photographers" to the list of those requiring licenses. In denouncing outside merchandisers, the Times often resorted to a favourite argument: a dollar sent out of the community was gone forever, but one spent in the community would circulate locally and eventually come back to the spender. This curious logic seemed to deny the legitimacy of long distance trade, and apparently it did not apply to those who sent money to High River to buy wheat and cattle.

ATTRACTING NEW SETTLERS, luring country trade, and ensuring the loyalty of local shoppers would all stimulate High River's growth, but other developments promised much more. Explosive growth would ensue when developers unlocked a veritable treasure house of resources in High River's hinterland. The Times reviewed these golden opportunities in its special "Homeseekers Number" of 16 May 1912. Timber cut in the upper watershed of the Highwood represented the mere beginning of a great forestry industry. A few coal mines that supplied low-grade fuel for home heating hinted at the extensive mineral wealth awaiting discovery, especially oil and gas. High River businessmen formed an exploration company as early as 1907, and in 1913 another local company actually struck gas within the town limits. The *Times* announced on 30 October that "it is practically certain that within a short time High River will be known as a gas city." The petroleum strike at Turner Valley the following year generated great excitement. Since it occurred only 21 miles northwest of High River, it bolstered the notion that similar vast reserves lay underfoot. The High River Oil and Gas Company sprang to life and on 25 June 1914 the *Times* urged local investors to consider the future: "With innumerable oil wells about to be drilled in this district the question of making High River an oil refining centre should not be overlooked by our citizens."

Given the vast energy sources at hand—coal, oil, gas, and numerous hydro-electric sites on the Highwood River—extensive manufacturing would arise, and the "Homeseekers Number" predicted High River would become "another Pittsburgh." No less than four railway lines would serve this vast industrial complex. These included projects by all three transcontinental companies, as well as a grand scheme by local businessmen to build a railway that would tap the riches of the Highwood watershed, bringing them to High River for processing and manufacturing. Subsequently, the goods would be transported across the prairies to Hudson Bay, from where they would move on to overseas markets. The High River and Hudson Bay Rail Road sought incorporation in the provincial legislature in 1910, received a charter in 1913, raised capital in Britain, commissioned a survey, and even began construction when the outbreak of the Great War made it impossible to raise further funds. Nonetheless, the *Times* expressed every confidence that the line would be completed.[14]

The *Times* realized that all these tremendous developments would not succeed without local support. "The town of High River has a brilliant future," it predicted on 19 August 1909, but it required "the citizens to rise as one man and use every legitimate and proper means to forge the place ahead." Unity provided the key to success, and its importance could be worked into any story. In urging residents to support the local Choral Society on 14 January 1909, for example, the *Times* launched a passionate plea: "Remember that unity is strength, by unity we mean oneness, concord, conjunction, and unless, as a town, we acquire unity and stand by our town together and put it ahead, we stand a very good chance of seeing it deteriorate into one of those one horse towns." The *Times* identified the enemies of solidarity as "knockers" or "kickers," people who criticized projects to advance the town or even mocked boosterism entirely. "Let the knockers get out," it cried on 1 June 1911, "We don't want them. They are no good to themselves, their fellow men, or to this country."

The *Times* cheered any organization that generated publicity for the district, including local sports teams. "The boys deserve a right royal welcome," wrote the *Times* on 5 September 1907 after the polo team won a tournament in Winnipeg, "for they have done much to advertise High River."[15] Similarly, the *Times* trumpeted the High River Real Estate Association that was formed in 1906 to promote the district in eastern Canada and the United States.[16] It also pressed for the creation of a board of trade and urged everyone to join: "if you are a true and loyal citizen you will not fail to become a member," it declared on 20 September 1906. When the response did not meet expectations, the *Times* pleaded with residents on 18 October: "shall we lie upon our backs hugging the delusive phantom of hope while less favoured localities capture all the advantages that belong to us?" The *Times* also praised outside agencies whenever they included High River in campaigns to promote Alberta or Western Canada generally. The Dominion Department of the Interior, for example, often treated members of the American press to agricultural tours, and in 1908 it arranged for 21 traveling reporters from Minnesota to spend a day at High River. The Board of Trade fed and entertained them, and took them into the countryside to examine the crops.[17]

The *Times* not only stirred local enthusiasm for boosterism; it also aimed its message at distant investors. In the first year of operation, 159 subscribers, representing a quarter of the total, lived beyond the *Times*'s reporting area. Of those, 25 lived in Ontario and 38 in the United States.[18] Most were absentee landlords who wished to monitor local developments affecting their holdings. The paper provided extensive coverage of weather and crop conditions largely for their benefit. The *Times* hoped its messages would entice these speculators to invest more and to interest others in the district. Similarly, the *Times* urged local subscribers to send copies to family and friends in their former communities. According to the paper, these strategies often led to further inquiries, such as the one by a Dr. Billig of Chicago that appeared on 26 December 1907: "I am deeply interested in the development of the High River district," he wrote in a letter requesting a subscription to the Times.

The Times soon emerged as the principal medium for advertising High River. Instead of publishing its own brochures, the Board of Trade usually joined forces with the newspaper. In 1908, for example, it agreed to buy 1,000 copies of a promotional issue for distant distribution.[19] As the Lethbridge Herald noted in 1912, the Times routinely provided High River with "valuable publicity."[20] Few other outlets presented themselves. Small towns could advertise in the city dailies, but always at considerable cost. In 1906, for example, the Calgary Herald invited towns to submit one-page spreads for a special issue on southern Alberta, but it charged $200 for the privilege.[21]

MUNICIPAL GOVERNMENT FURNISHED boosterism with another potent weapon, for it had the authority and borrowing power to entertain more costly schemes. It could entice industry with free land, property tax exemptions, loans, bond guarantees, or even cash bonuses—rewards offered by urban centres throughout Western Canada and elsewhere. The Times urged High River to abandon its village status and seek incorporation as a town in 1906 precisely because of this enhanced capacity to snare industries: "it is only by going after them with every effort that we can ever hope to get them," it argued on 13 September 1906. It also urged the municipality to lobby senior governments for public institutions, notably a provincial court and an agricultural college.[22]

A town council could also furnish modern utilities and services. The Times endorsed dozens of ideas for civic improvement between 1905 and 1913, embracing everything from the establishment of a fire department to the provision of a band stand. Such facilities would contribute to the health, protection, comfort, or enjoyment of existing residents, and also promised to lure new investment. In pleading for a modern water and sewage system on 17 March 1910, the Times argued that "We must have a healthy town, otherwise people with capital will give us the go by and go to some other

High River business street, 1907. *Museum of the Highwood 977–65–5.*

town." Utilities and amenities also promised to raise property values. "It is a well known fact," the Times stated on 22 February 1906, "that with the introduction of a telephone system, the country through which the line is established appears attractive to the prospective land buyer, and as a result, the price of land begins to rise rapidly."

Utilities such as the costly waterworks and electrical system required municipal action, but voluntary effort sufficed for other improvements. The Times often complained about the accumulation of garbage in the alleys, the dilapidated condition of poorly constructed buildings, and peeling paint. In response, the paper sponsored spring clean-up campaigns. It urged everyone to paint all buildings in the town and countryside, least any visitor mistakenly think that "hard times" prevailed in the district.[23] The Times also advocated tree and flower planting. On 9 January 1913 it combined all these ideas by suggesting that High River adopt the urban reform known as "City Beautiful." While often boasting about High River's magnificent natural setting, it admitted that "the development of the artistic had been lost in the struggle for the practical and commercial." And since both sexes believed that women possessed superior artistic sensibilities, the Times suggested that they take a leading role. The publisher's wife, Mary Clark, promptly organized the High River Civic League to promote town beautification.[24]

In its original conception, City Beautiful advocated a complete rebuilding of cities according to a master plan with strict architectural guidelines. Big cities made little headway in implementing such expensive and disruptive schemes, and the High River Civic League pursued more modest goals: it planted flowers and lawns at some public buildings and encouraged residents to beautify their property by offering prizes for the best yards and gardens. In August 1913 it sponsored its first competitive flower show. While the Civic League hoped to beautify High River for the enjoyment of the residents, it did not overlook the impact on potential investors.[25] In that respect, it represented a unique instrument of boosterism, the only one dominated by women.

Other attractions of the town and district included less tangible amenities such as good churches and schools, and a wonderful array of cultural, fraternal, and sporting organizations. Most important of all, the district had wonderful people. Not only were they progressive, intelligent, and civic-minded, but also honest, decent, and law-abiding. The Times declared in the "Homeseekers Number" of 16 May 1912 that "brawling, fighting, or disorderly conduct on the streets or in public places are entirely unknown." This bold assertion directly contradicted dozens of stories that routinely appeared about the prevalence of such activities. Rowdiness persisted because the rush of settlers and labourers into the district did nothing to rectify the demographic imbalance of the old ranch community. An army of single young men still surged through the town in search of excitement. The Times worried about their effect on High River's reputation and its ability to attract prospective investors and newcomers.

Newspapers in big cities and small towns alike expressed alarm about the "unsavoury element" and virtually all them became staunch defenders of social order.[26] The Times called for a crackdown on rowdy behaviour and on 2 May 1912, it applauded the town council for hiring a night policeman. It especially demanded the closing of brothels and gambling dens, and expressed frustration when periodic raids failed to prevent their re-emergence.[27] Like reformers elsewhere, the Times came to believe that liquor fuelled most social and moral problems. It condemned drunkenness and welcomed the arrival of the Temperance and Moral Reform League and the Women's Christian Temperance Union in High River. It even gave the latter organization its own column in 1912.

In its quest for social order, the *Times* confronted the political question of prohibiting liquor sales—exactly the sort of controversial topic that the paper preferred to avoid. It struggled for a middle ground, supporting temperance but not prohibition, which, it argued on 31 October 1913, "results in the silent growth of places of far more sinister purpose." Certainly the *Times* did not wish to close the High River Club. It featured both drinking and gambling, but prided itself on a membership of well-behaved, respectable men. Charles Clark himself belonged.[28] The loyal advertising of the hotels contributed to the dilemma, and the *Times* and often complimented them on many aspects of their business, including their saloons. In a profile of the St. George Hotel on 9 March 1911, for example, the *Times* wrote: "In the bar there is stocked a splendid assortment of wines, liquors, ales and lager, together with a supply of really high grade cigars." Pool halls also developed a reputation as unsavoury hang outs that sold liquor illegally, tolerated gambling, and encouraged foul language, but they also advertised and the *Times* defended them against the threat of new provincial restrictions.[29]

When the Great War erupted, prohibition rose in popularity. Alcohol wasted grain needed for the war effort and did not exemplify the spirit of sacrifice. It undermined efficiency since drunken troops, farmers, and workers could not contribute effectively to victory. Prohibition also became a way to punish those hard-drinking immigrants born in enemy lands.[30] As happened elsewhere, these new considerations lent considerable force to the prohibitionist argument in High River. When the district voted two to one in its favour in the provincial referendum of 1915, the *Times* finally lent its approval on 22 and 29 July. In spite of the rise of bootlegging, it admitted on 5 July 1917 that local conditions had improved "from a moral point of view." The *Times* thus reflected community opinion, even though editor Clark privately disagreed with it.[31]

Prohibition had always been closely associated with women's suffrage, another potentially divisive topic that the *Times* studiously avoided. But the popularity of that measure rose steadily in the district as boosters realized the value of women's votes in the campaign for respectability and order.

Farmers increasingly regarded women as partners in the development of the agrarian economy and especially as allies in their fight against corporations and governments. As with prohibition, the outbreak of war also gave this reform a substantial boost. Propaganda presented the war as a crusade to save democracy abroad, which heightened the crusade to expand democracy at home. Women sacrificed the lives of their husbands and sons. They played a crucial role in the wartime economy, including the munitions industry. They voluntarily worked for a host of war-related charities, sold war bonds, and helped recruit soldiers. Their votes would also counter the influence of immigrants born in enemy lands.[32] Recognizing the rising local demand for women's suffrage, the Times lent its support on 22 October 1914, a year before the Alberta government granted women the right to vote and three years before the Dominion government did so. Thus, by indirect means, boosterism led the Times to champion a series of positions it might otherwise have ignored.

4 | BOOSTERISM
AND THE NEWSPAPER BUSINESS

THE *TIMES* EAGERLY BECAME A TOOL for boosterism because it reflected the attitudes and hopes of its readers and advertisers. In addition, the newspaper itself stood to gain as much from promotional success as any other local business. An increase in economic activity meant more advertising and printing jobs, while an increase in population meant more subscribers, which in turn, permitted advertising rates to rise. Launching a weekly required little capital when Clark founded the *Times*—perhaps $500 or $600 cash and some financing by the Toronto Type Foundry for equipment purchases.[1] Surviving presented a more formidable challenge and many weeklies succumbed to bankruptcy.

Compared to many small businesses, the rural press was labour intensive.[2] Its workforce divided into two groups: the "front shop" which sold advertising, collected news and wrote copy; and the "back shop" which actually printed the newspaper and special job orders. The publisher often controlled costs in the front shop by working long hours and by acting as chief reporter and writer. He also solicited advertising and printing jobs while simultaneously serving as general manager. Charles Clark laboured at all these tasks. Like many other small town publishers, he joined a multitude of local organizations, several as a charter member. In this way, the publisher established himself as a solid member of the community, deeply involved and interested in its activities and welfare. It plunged him into settings where news circulated and it cemented relationships with advertisers.[3] It also committed most evenings to attending meetings and taking notes after a full day's work.

While Clark maintained this gruelling schedule for many months at a time, he sometimes escaped the business entirely, as in the winter of 1911 when he vacationed in California.[4] On such occasions, he relied on a trusted employee to assume managerial responsibility. It is difficult to determine how many full-time reporters the Times employed in its early years—at least one and perhaps more—but as many businesses discovered during the settlement boom, employees came and went at a brisk pace. The outbreak of war contributed to this instability; on 21 January 1915 the Times reported that three employees had already enlisted.

The rural weeklies did not rely heavily on costly reporters, and instead discovered many ways to obtain copy cheaply. The district correspondents they maintained in outlying communities received little reward for their weekly columns. There is no record of how the Times remunerated them in the early years, but rural weeklies typically offered token sums for each line of type published, perhaps a free subscription, or even small commissions for any subscriptions or advertising sold. Most country stringers were women who did not perform their journalistic duties for the meagre material rewards, but because they satisfied creative urges and offered a modicum of local status.[5]

The rural weeklies also shaved expenses by relying on volunteer reporters. "It has always been our policy," the Times stated on 27 February 1908, "to have our readers furnish us with news and reports of any events which they want published...." Over the years, the Times often repeated the request and suggested that every local organization appoint a press secretary to pass along news. Rural weeklies relied on another popular means to slash costs: they plagiarized each other. To facilitate this practice, they agreed to freely swap subscriptions to their newspapers. Between 1905 and 1909 the Times arranged exchanges with no less than 23 other newspapers, most of them in Alberta, but some from neighbouring provinces.[6] In addition, it acquired its random selection of national and international news by reprinting items from a variety of eastern Canadian and American newspapers. In 1915 the

Times began to plagiarize itself by reprinting stories from the earliest issues, a practice that would prevail for decades.

If front shop costs could be controlled in a variety of imaginative ways, less flexibility prevailed in the back shop. Steam-driven equipment had permitted the rise of fat metropolitan dailies by the mid-nineteenth century, but rural weeklies could neither afford nor fully utilize this technological revolution for their own small runs. Most of the weeklies relied on outmoded equipment that broke down frequently. They bought much of it from the Toronto Type Foundry that offered new, used and reconditioned machinery; most importantly, it extended credit to the weeklies.[7] In most shops, the printer selected individual metal letters of various sizes from bins and arranged them by hand in a form that would print one page. He then fixed the form into a press, applied ink with a hand roller, and used levers or foot pedals to print one side of one sheet of newsprint. Using this method, three or four workers could generate about 250 sheets per hour. The *Times* no doubt sped up the procedure in 1910 when it announced the acquisition of a gasoline-powered Babcock press.[8] After printing, workers cleaned the forms, separated the letters, and laboriously sorted them into the correct bins. One long-time employee recalled that the *Times* required eight or nine people to handset and print the newspaper in the 1910s, "half throwing in type, and the other half...setting up the next run."[9] Once finished, they assembled and folded the newspaper by hand.

TO COVER ITS COSTS and generate profits, the weekly relied on three sources of revenue: subscriptions, advertising, and custom print jobs. The *Times* initially set its subscription rate at $1.50 per year, but on many occasions it offered special reductions. In any event, subscriptions provided little income.[10] The important task was to raise circulation in order to boost advertising rates. The *Times* sought to do so by relentlessly promoting itself. It often listed reasons why residents needed the local paper: to keep abreast of municipal government, to receive announcements of upcoming events, to apprise themselves of the tremendous values announced in the advertisements, to entertain themselves, to support their home community in general. "The man who does not assist and does not see the benefits arising from a local paper is about as much value to a town as a delinquent tax list," lectured the Times on 22 April 1909. It frequently attacked the common habit in rural areas of passing the newspaper from family to family, insisting that every household needed its own copy.[11] The Times expected that its columns from district correspondents would build circulation in the outlying communities, and it urged residents to give subscriptions as gifts, even for distant relatives, or for friends who had left the district. It also launched promotional schemes. In conjunction with advertising from a local merchant, new subscribers in 1912 could win a piano.[12]

It is impossible to gauge the effect of these campaigns. Circulation did rise quickly, but perhaps because the population of the district itself climbed rapidly. Within months of its founding, the Times had managed to build a respectable circulation of 624. Half the newspapers went to townspeople and farmers with High River addresses, 133 to farmers in outlying postal districts, and 63 to distant subscribers, including those in Ontario and the United States.[13] The Times claimed that circulation soared to 1,000 by 1906, and to 1,500 by 1908.[14]

Like all small town businesses, the Times extended credit to its customers. Farmers insisted on it, arguing that they only received income at highly irregular intervals. Collecting the money owed for subscriptions presented the publisher with a perpetual headache and notices about arrears often appeared. Sometimes the paper appealed to the delinquents' sense of fairness, sometimes it pleaded with them, and sometimes it threatened them. As the Times once warned, it could employ the cold-hearted tactics of a city daily by publishing debtors' names or cancelling their delivery, but it hesitated to do so because its subscribers were also "personal friends." More importantly, the delinquents might eventually pay, and building circulation counted for more than the subscription money itself. In the end, the Times simply continued to remind and cajole readers about their debts.[15]

The Times expended even more energy securing advertising. In its first year, the weekly devoted approximately 60 percent of its space to paid advertisements, a ratio that varied from issue to issue, but remained a rough standard for decades. The amount of advertising sold therefore dictated the overall size of the newspaper.[16] Except for its special booster issues, the *Times* normally issued eight pages. Like all newspapers, it presented both news and advertisements on most of those pages to enhance the exposure each received.

The *Times* printed several distinct kinds of advertising. People who did not normally advertise bought lines in the classifieds in order to buy, sell, or rent particular items; or to recover lost possessions or announce found ones; or to find work or hired help. Whenever these advertisements brought results, the *Times* immediately alerted readers to the fact, inviting further use. But although the classifieds provided the weeklies with a steady diet, their cheap rates earned little revenue.

The most lucrative accounts remained the most difficult ones for the rural weekly to capture: advertisements for brand name products sold nationally. The *Times* began operating in the wake of a massive transformation in consumer advertising. Throughout much of the nineteenth century, few goods carried brand names. A trip to a general store revealed barrels and bins and stacks of bulk products that lacked both packaging and brand names. Customers did not know, or much care, who made the nails and crackers and cloth they bought, and advertising offered no clues. Retailers simply provided the press with lists of goods recently received, their price, and bland assurances of quality and satisfaction. They rarely provided illustrations or photos.

In the late nineteenth century, merchandising began a dramatic transformation. Expanding railway networks created national markets, leading to business consolidation and centralized manufacturing. The big firms now sought to secure and expand their markets through national advertising, and the packaging of products became an essential aspect of this process. It began with patent medicines because they had to be placed in containers in order to be shipped and sold, and the need to label the bottles provided the opportunity to give the products names, and consequently to advertise those names. By the 1890s, individual packaging and brand name advertising characterized virtually all consumer goods sold to mass markets, including drugs, tobacco, soaps, cooking and baking supplies, ready made foods and drinks, and finished clothing.[17]

At first, manufacturers penned their own advertising, but as it grew in importance specialized agencies arose. Canada's first advertising agency, based on American models, opened in Montreal in 1889 and when the *Times* began publication in 1905, agencies handled virtually all the sales promotion for big manufacturers. They wrote and formatted the copy and began transforming advertising from "information" to "persuasion." They decided where to place the advertisements; they paid the costs and billed the manufacturers.[18] Newspapers hated the agencies. With their huge accounts, they could impose discounts. In addition, they charged what they euphemistically referred to as a "commission," a kickback from the newspapers for providing them with advertising. The commission usually amounted to twenty percent of the value of the contract. The press begrudgingly acquiesced to this system when it became virtually impossible to acquire brand name advertising without the agencies.[19]

Rural weeklies faced an additional problem. The agencies preferred to deal with the metropolitan dailies where the placement of a single advertisement would reach many consumers. Advertising in the weeklies meant dealing with countless independent publishers to reach fewer people, many of whom had little money to spend. The rural press fought back. It argued that subscribers read the weeklies more thoroughly than the dailies, that readership surpassed subscription lists because of the practice of passing the newspaper from household to household, and that farmers and townspeople had much more money to spend than the agencies appreciated. Arguments over these matters persisted for decades.[20] At the same time, the weeklies tried to impose standard advertising rates and to eliminate or cut the agency commissions, but they rarely succeeded.

Like other rural papers, the *Times* most often landed brand name advertisements for farm equipment and supplies. In a five-month period from 21 February to 18 July 1907, it advertised various Massey-Harris and Deering implements, Standard Plows, Canton Plows, Fairbanks Morse gas engines, and U.S. Cream Separators. With many buildings under construction in the town and district, it also obtained advertisements for Sherwin-Williams Paints and Sunshine Furnaces. Small notices also appeared for banks and insurance companies. Sometimes the paper secured advertisements for clothing manufacturers: Fit-Rite, Twentieth Century Brand, and D&A Corsets.

But the paper usually failed to land the biggest consumer advertisers of all: the food, drug, and tobacco companies. In the 26 July 1906 issue only a single item of this type appeared—an engraved illustration of "John Bull" smoking a Shield Brand pipe. In all of August 1908 advertisements appeared for only two brand name consumer goods: Ram Lal's Pure Tea and Blue Ribbon food products. The agencies seldom committed themselves to a weekly paper for more than a month or two, and securing long-term contracts presented another problem.

The *Times* did not control the format and wording of a brand name advertisement; the agency simply supplied a plate for the entire spread. In virtually all cases, the name of the local store that sold the product appeared beneath the advertisement, enhancing the exposure of both sellers. Although usually smaller than the advertisements of local retailers, agency plates were far more attractive since they featured intriguing designs and illustrations. The most elaborate plates came from traveling entertainers, especially circuses, whose large, illustrated advertisements justly qualify as pop art.

Governments constituted a special category of big advertisers that also frustrated the weeklies. Every level of public administration bombarded them with endless notices relating to new laws, regulations, research, and other announcements. Governments regarded these items as "news" that the press would naturally wish to publish freely. The press regarded them as "advertisements" that governments ought to pay for. An uneasy compromise ensued. Governments sometimes paid advertising rates for some kinds of information, but not others. In turn, the press often refused to print much of the unpaid government output, but just as often it felt obliged to freely print material of importance or interest to readers.[21]

While the rural press continued its quest for big advertisers, it relied most heavily on local businesses. Professionals, tradesmen, and service businesses typically placed small advertisements that conveyed virtually no information except to state that they existed. By contrast, auctioneers ran large spreads, frequently listing all the items for sale in upcoming auctions. Most of the big advertisers sold goods: the larger general stores and retailers in hardware, lumber, dry goods, clothing, furniture, and groceries. The High River Trading Company spent $178 on advertising during the *Times*'s first year of operation—the equivalent of collecting 118 subscription fees.[22]

Such businesses often took out half- or full-page advertisements in large type, but they lacked both illustrations and the psychological guile of the advertising agencies since the merchants usually wrote their own copy. Many still relied on the nineteenth century tradition of largely providing information about goods and prices. Creative impulses compelled some of them to engage in the literary practice known as "wordsmithing." The J.A. Gillis Company, dealers in dry goods and groceries, promised on 22 March 1906 to sell silk and satin "as soft as the cheeks of a woman," to wrap it in paper "as strong as the hide of an elephant," and to deliver it "with the speed of a cannon ball." On 10 July 1913 the Little Bow Trading Company held a "Gigantic Slaughter Sale" with "Bargains that Beggar Description and Stagger Belief." Such outbursts of literary endeavour apparently exhausted local merchants, as they often ran the same advertisements month after month without alteration.

The *Times* relentlessly advertised the value of advertising. Issue after issue chronicled its crucial importance to the successful business and urged merchants (usually without success) to change advertisements frequently to keep the readers' attention. At the same time, it urged readers to patronize only those businesses that advertised in the *Times*. Often it ran stories with no purpose except to encourage local advertising. On 8 August 1912, the *Times* ran a story about a local merchant who spied a farmer taking delivery of a load of mail order goods. When the merchant indignantly informed the farmer that all the goods ordered were available in his own store, the surprised farmer replied that he would have gladly bought from the merchant, but had not realized that he carried the goods since he had not seen a line of advertising in the *Times*. On 4 December 1913 the *Times* claimed that local merchants actually sold goods more cheaply than peddlers and mail order catalogues, but that people did not realize it because local merchants failed to advertise sufficiently. The *Times* also encouraged merchants to begin, continue, or expand their advertising by occasionally tossing them free publicity. One such "news" story appeared on 11 February 1909 and informed readers that "Mr. Austin Francis of Winnipeg has opened up a new drug store. The fixtures are very attractive and up-to-date and with the new stock neatly displayed, the store presents a splendid appearance."

Printing jobs provided another stream of revenue. Some of the smaller rural newspapers largely survived as print shops that only published newspapers as a sideline.²³ The *Times* relied more heavily on advertising, but job printing may have accounted for one third of revenues in some years, and remained important until the advent of desktop publishing on personal computers.²⁴ Print jobs also contributed to the efficient use of the back shop labour force. Printing with handset type was a labour intensive operation that needed to be performed quickly just prior to the appearance of each week's issue. It generally took two or three days to set the weekly, and contract printing thus became an important means of utilizing back shop labour for the remainder of the week. The *Times* accepted virtually any job that required attaching words to paper—from tickets to menus to posters. It also sold a wide variety of stationery supplies and continually discovered new reasons for local businesses to expand their use of printed material. On 27 June 1912 it insisted that merchants use printed letterheads and envelopes instead of rubber stamps, a shoddy substitute that made them look like amateurs doing business in a "one horse town." It even urged rural people to christen their farms with names, a custom well established among ranchers, thereby creating a need for printed stationery from the *Times*.²⁵

The *Times* most often discussed print jobs when it warned against awarding them to out of town firms. On 27 June 1907, the *Times* relayed the sad tale of the local professional who ordered letterheads from Toronto, paid more than the *Times* charged, and had his name misspelled besides. "Why not support a local institution?" implored the paper, "we pay taxes and are doing our utmost to boost High River and yet there are people who support outside institutions in preference to home industry. We may say that the aforesaid professional man swears by all that's good that he will never again bite or give orders to outside houses when he can get better at home." When the *Times* discovered an outside printer canvassing the town, it demanded his immediate arrest for failing to take out a peddler's license.²⁶

When advertising on its own behalf, the *Times* presumed that a covenant with the community existed. It agreed to boost the district vigorously; in return, it expected everyone to subscribe to the newspaper, to advertise heavily, and to award it all printing jobs. The *Times* emphasized the point when it quoted another weekly on 5 September 1907: "When a newspaper man has to yell himself hoarse to patronize home merchants, and then accidentally stumbles onto the fact that one of the men he is trying to protect had sent away for his job printing, it rather shakes his faith in mankind." The newspaper revealed on 1 November 1906 that it had turned down lucrative advertising contracts from mail order houses in order to support local merchants. On 4 June 1908 the *Times* claimed that it paid out $335 a month in wages and that virtually all it of it was spent in the town, but people who failed to support the newspaper threatened to reduce that total because it would force the weekly to fire an employee for lack of work. "It is only common fairness for you to support your local paper," it insisted on 12 November 1908, since "we have been doing our utmost to build up this part of the country." Perhaps Clark also valued loyalty beyond its commercial utility. After his death, eulogies emphasized his intense devotion to friends.[27]

ASIDE FROM DIRECT APPEALS for patronage, many of the editorial positions taken by the *Times* on behalf of the community also served the specific interests of the newspaper. Its criticism of labour unions on behalf of small, independent businesses, for example, also reflected the fact that rural weeklies could not afford to pay the same wages or provide the same working conditions as the dailies, and they sought (successfully) to keep unions out of their shops.[28] Similarly, aspects of boosterism trumpeted for the progress of the entire district promised concrete advantages for the *Times*. The paper often listed the numerous benefits of telephone service: it would cut business and farm costs by eliminating unnecessary travel; aid in soliciting help in the event of illness, accident, or other emergencies; and enhance rural life by breaking down social isolation. The advantage to the *Times* appeared less often in print, but the telephones saved much legwork in gathering information, particularly from outlying districts. On 7 September 1916, it celebrated the fact that seventeen rural circuits in the High River district provided service to 196 farms and connected them to 175 phones in the town.

Similarly, the *Times* pushed aggressively for more country post offices, cheaper postal rates, and more frequent and free direct farm delivery, citing immense advantages for the district as a whole when in fact such postal reforms particularly served the *Times* in providing more copies of the paper more cheaply and more quickly to more farmers. Mail bound for outlying districts moved by wagon from High River to rural post offices where farmers collected it. Like all rural weeklies, the Times selected a mid-week publication day to ensure that outlying districts received the paper by Friday. This meant that farm families could consult the advertisements for the Saturday sales, the biggest shopping day of the week for rural people. On 26 March 1908, the Times complained bitterly that some rural post offices received mail on a day that delayed receipt of the newspaper by a full week, thus making it impossible for readers to take advantage of advertised sales. The Times periodically juggled its mid-week publication day to secure better connections with rural mail routes. On 20 August 1914 it cheered the inauguration of direct delivery to individual farms, which provided a more reliable schedule for the Times to follow.

The specific interests of the press also led to the formation of trade associations not unlike those created by farmers and ranchers for the purposes of mutual self help and political lobbying. Charles Clark became a founding member and the first treasurer of the Alberta and British Columbia Press Association, established in 1905.[29] It joined the Canadian Press Association in 1912, which led to the creation of separate provincial branches. These organizations offered members advice on a host of press-related problems and lobbied government for better and cheaper postal service, for lower tariffs on imported newspaper equipment, for less stringent libel laws, and other advantages. The list of activities specifically tailored to the interests of the rural press would expand tremendously when the weeklies created their own organization in 1919.

IT IS DIFFICULT TO MEASURE the effectiveness of the booster campaign launched by the Times, either on its own behalf, or that of the High River district in general. Many new settlers flooded the district, but perhaps they would have done so even in the absence of promotional schemes. Clearly boosterism failed to achieve its loftier goals since High River did not blossom into a hub of industry and resource development. Some tools of boosterism were simply too expensive for a small town to provide. In 1907 the town acquired a planing mill that made sashes, windows, and doors by offering the company cheap land and property tax exemptions.[30] Those incentives involved little or no outlays of money, but most prospective industries asked for much more: free or cheap utilities, loans, and cash bonuses.

Costly demands repeatedly frustrated attempts to secure a flour mill, an industry that the *Times* believed naturally suited a wheat-growing district like High River. The paper championed various schemes to secure one, from suggesting that local farmers build it themselves to supporting the Board of Trade in lobbying the Quaker Oats Company of Chicago.[31] From time to time intriguing offers surfaced, but in each case, the prospective company wanted something expensive from the town council. In 1906 one Mr. McDonald promised to build a mill in conjunction with an elevator and warehouse, but only if the town lent him $10,000 interest free for ten years. Although the *Times* supported the plan, a local businessman suspected a scam and exposed it in a letter to the editor on 21 November.

Many unscrupulous entrepreneurs devised schemes to collect bonuses without any intention of establishing industries. Urban centres countered with performance clauses whereby construction had to commence before a bonus could be collected. The promoter often responded that he could not start building unless he first secured the bonus. Quite aside from the question of legitimate intentions, bonuses threatened to saddle young towns with burdens they could not bear, especially when they also struggled to provide new utilities and services. For that reason the High River council refused to guarantee $6,000 in bonds for a company that promised to establish a door factory.[32] Because the council wisely (or luckily) avoided such commitments, it never acquired insurmountable debt and it met every debenture payment for its infrastructure projects.[33] Since small towns could not compete with cities that attracted industry with cash, the *Times* eventually condemned the practice of bonusing and urged the provincial government to ban it. Alarmed by the staggering debt incurred by many Alberta municipalities, the province did outlaw many booster incentives in the Town Act of 1912, including bonusing, bond guarantees, buying stock in companies, and property tax exemptions.[34]

Sometimes prospective industries demanded incentives directly from the residents instead of town council. One visiting entrepreneur promised to build a flour mill if local people would invest in it. The *Times* urged them to do so on 28 December 1905 lest "one of the neighbouring towns... capture the prize," but local money thought the project unworthy. Similarly, the *Times* expressed high hopes for the establishment of a sugar factory that wanted nothing from the town, but asked that a sufficient number of local farmers sign contracts to grow sugar beets. Farmers found the contracts highly unfavourable and refused to sign them.[35]

Beyond providing incentives, small towns like High River lacked other prerequisites for industry: an array of supporting service businesses, an abundance of cheap labour, and convenient access to important markets. Even the largest cities of Western Canada failed to match their eastern counterparts on those criteria. Within Western Canada, any hope of achieving metropolitan status depended on winning crucial railway advantages. Aspiring towns needed to become divisional points, places every hundred miles or so where trains switched running crews. Many benefits ensued. Railway employees would live in such centres and contribute to their growth. Divisional points also became logical places to install maintenance shops, adding more railway employees to the town. With their various rail facilities, divisional points became logical centres for the construction of branch lines. These tentacles encouraged wholesaling, which might benefit from yet another blessing conferred by railways: special freight rates permitted favoured cities to receive goods at lower per mile rates than nearby rivals. Discriminatory rates helped determine which towns became wholesaling centres and which remained retailers. The railways benefited from preferential rates too, since they could assemble high volume long distance trains untroubled by the continuous handling and storage of small consignments. Calgary, only 38 miles away, acquired all these advantages before High River even entered the booster game, and it continued to expand them thereafter.[36]

High River never realized its dreams for railway development. The *Times* expressed excitement whenever a company commissioned a survey or purchased a right of way into town. After the Canadian Northern did so, the *Times* declared construction "an established fact" on 20 November 1911. But railways typically planned far more projects than they ever started, and the Canadian Northern never built the line. Similarly, the grandiose High River and Hudson Bay Rail Road, organized by local businessmen, never materialized. The one new railway built in the district actually hurt High River instead of helping it. As early as 21 October 1907, the *Times* began agitating for a branch line into the wheat country east of town. The Canadian Pacific Railway subsequently planned a route that would begin near Lethbridge and connect with the Calgary and Edmonton line. High River assumed that it would be the natural terminus for this new extension, but the *Times* and the Board of Trade expressed outrage in 1910 when the railway decided to connect at Aldersyde, the insignificant hamlet seven miles north of town. The reason? The Canadian Pacific already owned land at Aldersyde but not at High River.[37]

The Kipp-Aldersyde line dealt High River a more serious blow. It spawned new town sites, all on land owned by the Canadian Pacific Railway, and all promoted by the advertising arm of that giant corporation. The new towns threatened to rob High River of considerable farm business in the eastern hinterland. In response, some merchants planned to open branch stores in the new town sites, especially at Blackie, twelve miles east of town; or at Vulcan, 36 miles by road to the southeast (See Figure 3). When the latter town quickly emerged as the dominant centre on the new line, some merchants even abandoned High River and relocated in Vulcan.[38] Although boosterism implied an intense loyalty to a particular place, loyalty proved to be as transferable as the people themselves. Whenever townspeople or farmers moved to seek new opportunities, they immediately proclaimed the virtues of their new locale.

Charles Clark also feared the emergence of Vulcan and decided to hedge his bets by establishing a second newspaper in the rival town. Corporate chains would not devour rural weeklies until well in the future, but some publishers owned two or more papers. Although a newspaper called the *Vulcan Review* appeared in 1912, Clark established the rival *Advocate* the following year. On 7 August 1913, the *Times* cheered its appearance and argued that "it should receive the support and patronage of every loyal citizen," in the Vulcan area, but did not mention Clark's ownership.[39] The *Advocate* thrived and the *Review* disappeared in 1914.

Just as it failed to monopolize the trade of the east country, High River also encountered trouble securing the loyalty of those closer to town. Farmers and townspeople alike continued to find value in mail order cata-

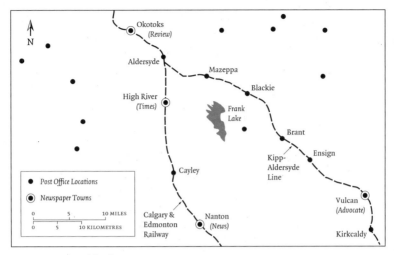

FIGURE 3: *High River Area, 1919.*

logues, and their use is legion in pioneer memoirs. As one member of a family living only five miles from the stores of High River recalled: "Eaton's catalogue was the standard reference for supplies of all kinds from clothing and books to such things as an Edison phonograph with large horn and cylindrical records. Once or twice a year, an order was sent to Eaton's and the shipment eagerly awaited by the family."[40] Some consumers even boldly declared that they had the right to shop wherever they wanted, and one letter to the *Times* even claimed that Board of Trade members sometimes shopped out of town.[41]

ALTHOUGH BOOSTERISM SEEMED TO SCORE few solid victories in the High River district, it undoubtedly contributed to the rampant speculation in farmland and town lots during the settlement boom. Robert Stead even ventured the opinion that boosterism sprang almost entirely from land owners who burned with the "desire to make money without earning it."[42] The *Times* often published stories about real estate ventures. A typical example appeared on 12 April 1906:

Mrs. J.J. Sullivan is displaying great faith in the future of the town by investing heavily in real estate. Last week she purchased Mr. Blaylock's residence and three lots for the handsome sum of $5300. On Tuesday she purchased a block of lots, 32 in number on Saratoga Avenue near the school which she will place on the market. Being the owner of a 100 acres just east of the town she leased 6 acres to a party recently who proposes commencing the manufacture of bricks at once.

In spite of all difficulties, High River enjoyed modest success in promoting itself. It failed woefully to match Calgary's population of 44,000 by 1911, a number that continued to climb sharply, but it still experienced growth that hundreds of towns might envy. By 1911 Alberta had produced 109 incorporated urban places, of which only 19 boasted populations of 1,000 or more. High River appeared in that select company.[43] The success of the *Times* itself paralleled this modest achievement. In 1908 the R.G. Dun credit rating agency valued the business in its $3,000 to $5,000 category and rated its credit "fair." By 1912 it had elevated the valuation to the $5,000 to 10,000 category and advanced the credit rating to "good."[44]

Beyond any economic or population growth it might have encouraged, the boosterism expressed in the pages of the *Times* served other functions. It helped create a sense of community. Reports from outlying districts gave concrete names and firm identities to loosely-defined rural neighbourhoods while simultaneously creating the idea of a greater High River district centred on the dominant railway town. The promotional campaign also imparted a particular self image to the new settlers in both town and country. Words like "modern," "up-to-date," and "progressive" peppered the vocabulary of boosterism and evoked an urban perspective. On 1 March 1906, the *Times* campaigned to banish wandering cattle from the streets because "It reminds us too much of the country village, and we of High River, would like to pride ourselves on the progressiveness of the town." Other references in the *Times* more explicitly established the city as an accepted standard of measurement. Writing about the winter carnival on 18 January 1906, the *Times* concluded: "Altogether it was an evening of which many a large city might be proud and would find difficult to eclipse." Similarly, the *Times* observed that the two-storey building built and owned by rancher George Lane to house professional offices in High River "would be a credit to a large city."

Scholars have often regarded the small town as a lynchpin between city and country, metropolis and frontier. Dominated by merchants that tried to emulate their urban counterparts, they transmitted urban values, ideas, and fashions to the countryside.[45] This role seemed particularly strong in an era when booming frontier growth promised limitless possibilities. An urban ethos also appealed to the well-capitalized commercial farmers that settled the High River district. They regarded themselves as agrarian entrepreneurs who intelligently applied business principles, technology and science to agricultural production, and who rebelled against images of farmers as clodhoppers, hicks and hayseeds. Their attitude reflected the country life movement that swept North America in the early twentieth century, seeking to bring the advantages and amenities of the city to the countryside.[46]

A forward-thinking society that pinned its hopes on a glorious future had no use for a rustic frontier past. Although colourful, a history filled with Indians and whiskey traders and cowboys evoked outmoded and irrelevant ways of life that could not contribute to High River's bright destiny. The old-timer might be praised for his initial pioneering efforts, but as the Times explained on 14 April 1910, he was "an awful nuisance to advancement." Insisting that "everything is good enough the way it is," he often opposed the introduction of piped water, electricity, and other improvements essential to a modern city. History, therefore, became important only as a measuring stick for progress. As the Times noted on 12 April 1906: "Not very long ago the site of High River was a pasture field, and today we find a thriving, energetic town, bustling with business and rapidly developing into a young city." On 26 March 1908 the Times decided that historical progress began sometime around 1902 when High River was merely "a store or two, a few dwellings, and a decrepit saloon." Thereafter, however, it became a "thoroughly up-to-date town [with] spacious graded streets with wide sidewalks [and] business places laid out on metropolitan lines." The Times presented yet another rendition of this history for the special "Immigration Number" of 9 September 1909: "Six years ago the town of High River was a small hamlet of about 150 population; today it is a bustling town of over 1800 population which is destined as the years go by to greatly increase in size and commercial importance."

The community at large seemed to share this view of history with the *Times*. In 1905 the High River School sponsored a competition among senior students for the best essay on the history of the district, and the *Times* agreed to print the winning work. When Catherine Boyd's essay appeared on 25 January 1906 it was perhaps the first history of High River ever printed. It said virtually nothing about the history of ranching aside from noting that "In those days ministers, as well as others, were obliged to carry six-shooters." Instead, it chronicled the appearance of every institution, facility, and technology associated with growth and progress, and thereby established an historical tradition for the *Times* to follow.

Unknown to the *Times* and its readers, their vision of High River's past and future was little more than a transitory historical phase. Boosterism and the mentality it produced soon faced new realities that eroded its utility as a dominant theme in the pages of the *Times*. In replacing it with a new ethos to reflect altered circumstances in the community, the *Times* would eventually repudiate boosterism's most cherished notions.

PART II

1918 to 1940

Overleaf: Fishing on the Highwood River. Glenbow Archives NA–2772–10.

5 | THE COMMUNITY
IN TROUBLED TIMES

BOOSTERISM IN THE HIGH RIVER DISTRICT and throughout Western Canada received its first blow with the collapse of the urban real estate market in 1913. Property financing grew scarce, whole subdivisions sat vacant, and speculators stopped paying taxes.[1] The entire economy subsequently tumbled, but the outbreak of war revived it. With the disruption of European agriculture, wheat prices soared. Farmers expanded by buying the last of the unbroken railway lands and some experimented with the new lightweight gasoline tractors that replaced horses and thereby freed pasture and coarse grain fields for wheat production. Farmers also harvested huge yields in 1915 and 1916.[2] Land prices soared once more. On 10 May 1917, the *Times* announced a sale of seeded land for $45.00 an acre. Ranchers profited less from the British market, which had been declining for years in the face of Argentinean competition, but they suddenly enjoyed brisk sales in Chicago. Although the United States sustained a substantial beef industry, the American population grew faster than its cattle herds.[3] Surprisingly, the world's first great industrial war still required horses to pull artillery and haul supplies, and some local ranchers sent horses to the front.

In spite of wartime prosperity in the High River district, the town itself stopped growing. Established farmers spent money, but no new settlers arrived who required great quantities of lumber, machinery, hardware, and supplies to begin farming. As merchants feared, the new towns of the Kipp-Aldersyde branch line captured much of the trade that formerly went to High River. Moreover, the war-induced boom soon ended and a serious drought engulfed southern Alberta in 1917. At first, rising wheat prices compensated for falling yields, but when the war ended prices collapsed and the drought continued. On 16 February 1922, the *Times* admitted that "conditions have given us several successive years of crop failures."

Farm income evaporated, but farmers still owed money for land and machinery. Refinancing became impossible when the banks curtailed new lending to curb post-war inflation. Farmers faced their worst crisis since arriving in the district and many went bankrupt. The 29 September 1921 issue of the *Times* featured long lists of farm lands seized by adjacent rural municipalities for nonpayment of taxes. The town had seized 149 lots for nonpayment of taxes by 1920 and most of them remained unsold by 1924.[4] In place of promotional stories designed to draw settlers to the district, a *Times* editorial on 8 June 1922 urged people not to move away. Even so, the district escaped the worst of the post-war calamity. In the infamous Palliser's Triangle of southeastern Alberta, drought and depression led to the abandonment of entire communities.[5]

Ranching also suffered in the post-war years when the harsh winter of 1919–20 imposed heavy losses just as cattle prices collapsed. The United States introduced stiff new tariffs in 1921 and neither domestic nor British markets compensated for declining American sales. The mammoth Bar U suffered a further blow as the advent of gasoline tractors cut into the demand for its Percheron horses, but the agricultural depression posed a greater problem. Although great workers, Percherons cost more than other breeds and farmers no longer bought them. The Bar U herd of over 400 breeding horses dwindled to 288 by 1927.[6] George Lane, sole owner of the ranch after 1921, died in 1925 and two years later his estate sold the historic spread to Burns Ranches of Calgary. Although still a huge enterprise with 37,000 acres of deeded land, 58,000 acres of leased land, and 6,500 head of livestock, the Bar U had deteriorated and outstanding mortgages remained. Nonetheless, Pat Burns had built a vertically integrated empire in which his own ranches supplied cattle to his meat packing plants and ultimately to his string of retail stores. He needed another huge ranch to maintain his supply line and so added the Bar U to his collection.[7]

In spite of many problems, cattle ranching advanced on several fronts in the post-war era. It focused on developing superior purebred stock, especially Herefords, Shorthorns, and Aberdeen Angus, and on producing hay, oats, and barley to fatten them once grass-fed cattle no longer commanded high prices. High River cattle continued to win praise for their quality and they captured many awards at competitive shows. Ranchers also continued to produce excellent horses. The Agricultural Society sponsored annual horse shows from 1925 to 1936 that attracted national and international buyers.[8] Yet, despite these accomplishments, ranchers earned little profit in the face of weak markets and low prices.

Other pillars of the economy faltered in response to the agricultural crisis. Two transcontinental railways, the Canadian Northern and the Grand Trunk, plunged into bankruptcy. New projects screeched to a halt, including the visionary High River and Hudson Bay line. On 10 May 1923 the *Times* finally acknowledged that the era of utopian railway schemes had ended: "During the past years we have had innumerable charters issued for the construction of railways throughout this district, which have been renewed from time to time, but, we understand, these have at last all been allowed to lapse." Without a rising demand for steam locomotives, coal mining languished. Five mines remained in operation west of High River in the 1920s, but the industry suffered from oversupply and low prices and soon faced competition from natural gas in the home heating market. High River's hopes for petroleum also withered. They had been fuelled by the 1914 discovery at nearby Turner Valley, but the wells drilled closer to town failed to yield satisfactory returns.

Lumbering had stimulated the local economy before 1914, but it too faced shrivelled markets since there were no longer many incoming settlers, who needed lumber and fence posts immediately. An already constructed town no longer grew and railways no longer bought ties. The Lineham Company stumbled into receivership in 1914 and control passed to the Union Bank. When the demand for telephone poles increased, T.R. Wilson purchased the company in 1918 and employed 40 to 60 cutters in the foothills during the

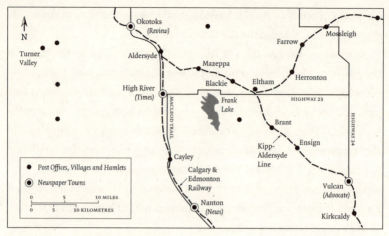

FIGURE 4: *High River Area, 1939.*

winters of the early 1920s. But the company soon abandoned cutting and milling entirely, and restricted itself to lumber retailing. The deserted mill burned down in 1928, and in 1936 High River acquired all 80 acres of its property within the town limits. That same year Wilson built a much smaller new mill up the Highwood River, but the glory days of lumbering had long since passed.[9]

The economy enjoyed a vigorous, if brief, recovery in the mid-1920s. Cattle and wheat prices improved and crop yields rose. Farmers started buying machinery again, especially tractors, as well as more trucks and automobiles. The agrarian recovery revitalized the town and on 4 August 1927 the *Times* reported the construction of new businesses and homes for the first time in many years. Calgary Power bought the municipal electrical system in 1926 and upgraded the service by linking it to a newly completed transmission line from Calgary. The following year, the Canadian Western Natural Gas Company supplied the town with a new source of heat. These utilities permitted homeowners to buy an array of consumer appliances, especially after Calgary Power opened a retail store in town.[10] The recovery even revived hopes for new railway projects. Local businessmen now proposed a far more modest enterprise than the failed High River and Hudson Bay line. The Highwood Western Railway planned only to link the town with coal mining sites upriver, but this scheme never materialized.[11] The Canadian Pacific Railway constructed a new branch line fourteen miles east of High River, but it did little to alter High River's trade hinterland (See Figure 4).

The economic revival did not last long and the local economy sank with the advent of the Great Depression. Wheat prices plunged even more dramatically than after the war, establishing record lows by 1933. The export market for cattle virtually disappeared following another sharp American tariff increase in 1930, and eating meat became more of a luxury for urban people.[12] Once more, severe drought returned. On 17 August 1933 the *Times* announced that Big Lake east of the town had dried up entirely for the first time since the 1890s. Repeatedly hammered by depression, hail, frost, drought, and soil erosion, the nearby settlement of Frankburg, a centralized village of 25 Mormon families, disbanded. In 1936, the dismantling of the meeting hall removed every trace of the community save the cemetery.[13] Soil drifting accompanied the drought. On 3 June 1937 the *Times* described how high winds whipped the parched topsoil into furious dust storms: "From brilliant sunlight to black night within the space of less than two minutes was the alarming experience of this district on Wednesday evening at 7:00 p.m. To those out of doors, it was a terrifying spectacle." The foothills received more rain than the plains, but the grass grew less vigorously and ranchers harvested lower yields on feed grains.

Once again municipal governments in the district found it increasingly difficult to collect taxes, but they no longer seized property for nonpayment since it had become impossible to sell the land. Municipal revenues declined just as a major obligation increased. At that time, responsibility for the destitute rested with local governments, who dispensed what was then known as "relief." These costs escalated as farms and businesses failed, and unemployment climbed. The town of High River spent only $350 on relief in 1926, but $8,267 in 1936, a year when the town managed to collect only twenty percent of the taxes owing.[14] To meet such crushing burdens, municipal governments begged the province for funding, and in turn the province badgered the Dominion government. The town postponed many projects and compelled the relief recipients to undertake the routine maintenance of streets, sidewalks, and parks. Many hobos passed through the district, but they did not meet the residency requirements established for obtaining relief. Although the *Times* had long feared transients, it now urged local residents to extend sympathy to the "hordes of men, drifting helplessly from town to town, looking for work."[15]

FACED WITH THE GRIM REALITIES of the interwar period, boosterism faded like a sunset over the mountains. "It's a long jump, and a hard one, from optimism to pessimism," a *Times* editorial brooded on 10 July 1919, "but there are occasions when it is necessary." Municipal affairs fell victim to apathy, and as early as 7 December 1916, the *Times* noticed that councillors began to win seats by acclamation, an increasingly common occurrence in the interwar years. Almost no one attended ratepayers' meetings. The Board of Trade grew increasingly inactive and had virtually disintegrated by 1921. A new version emerged in 1926 that eventually became the Chamber of Commerce, but like many others in the province, it concerned itself less with economic growth and fixed its attention on social and recreational facilities. Raising funds for a war memorial became its first major project.[16] The High River Agricultural Society, responsible for fairs and shows to advertise the district, lingered much longer, but finally became inactive by 1937 and remained so until 1944.

The *Times* still allowed itself a flush of excitement whenever rumours circulated about the establishment of new industries, but such stories arose much less often. It no longer spoke of industry as an inevitable step towards metropolitan grandeur, but as a lifeline for mere survival; a factory would provide a regular payroll that would prevent young people from leaving.[17] Often the *Times* set its sights on more modest prizes. After Alberta's experiment to prohibit liquor sales ended, the paper backed a petition urging the provincial government to establish one of its new liquor stores in town. Merchants hoped it would draw more country shoppers.[18]

New petroleum strikes in Turner Valley in the mid-1920s and 1930s rekindled loftier aspirations. The *Times* introduced regular weekly reports on exploration and drilling, carefully noting the formation of local companies and scrutinizing all local projects. When these endeavours again failed to ignite a boom, the *Times* focused on how High River might emerge as the dominant service centre for the existing Turner Valley fields. It occasionally printed rumours that a refinery might be constructed at High River, and in 1938 the British America Oil Company actually considered building one. Mayor Frank Watt immediately alerted the company to the town's ready labour, cheap land, and low taxes. In his capacity as reigning president of the Chamber of Commerce, Charles Clark also lobbied the company.[19]

Although British America decided to locate its refinery in Calgary, the *Times* continued to hope that High River might service the Turner Valley fields in other ways, providing it with wholesale supplies or even housing the families of camp workers. The *Times* itself attempted to become the dominant newspaper of the oil fields, and in August 1929 it began to insert a new page in the paper entitled "The Turner Valley News." Shack towns appeared and disappeared as drilling activity moved around the valley, and strikes at the southern end of the field produced new boomtowns. By 1938, Little New York and Little Chicago boasted populations of 600 and 1,000 respectively.[20] Since no railway extended to these outposts, High River seemed destined to become their supply centre. But a crucial obstacle remained. In the Depression, rural municipalities could not provide a graded and gravelled route to the oil fields, even after the town of High River offered to pay some of the cost. The *Times* joined local governments in a spirited campaign that urged the province to build a highway, but to no avail. No direct, all-weather road appeared until after World War II when production in the Turner Valley field began a steep and permanent decline. In the end, petroleum brought no direct economic benefit to High River; at best it provided employment for some young men from the district during the Depression.[21] Meanwhile, Calgary virtually monopolized the servicing of the oil fields.

Petroleum also thrust the *Times* into one of those thorny controversies that it liked to avoid. While drilling activity raised hopes for the local economy, it also angered ranchers and farmers. Few of them held the mineral rights to their own property, and the law compelled them to offer the petroleum companies access in order explore, drill, and produce. The law also compelled the companies to pay compensation for surface damage and for the use of land for roads and well sites. Farmers and ranchers considered these payments inadequate. Compelled as always to support its rural readers, the *Times* argued for increased compensation, while simultaneously urging the companies to expand their work locally.[22]

Throughout the turbulent interwar era, the *Times* discovered plenty of reasons for the lack of economic development in the High River district. International and national economic conditions shouldered much of the blame, but so too did the neglect of corporations and senior levels of government. Drought received considerable attention in the *Times*, but another environmental culprit also emerged. Every spring the Highwood River threatened to flood the town. At first many believed that the problem resulted from an irrigation ditch built by a rancher in the 1890s across the area where the town developed. A court ruling in 1907 allowed the town to fill in the ditch, but flooding continued.[23] Many circumstances contributed to the problem: heavy mountain snow melt, cloudbursts in the foothills, a high water table, the flat terrain of the town, shifting gravel deposits which redirected the flow of water, and bridge supports that blocked the movement of logs and ice.[24] The *Times* believed that the threat of floods dissuaded industries from building in High River. The municipal council itself hesitated to subdivide parts of the town because of flooding, and a substantial parcel of wilderness land remained within the corporate limits.

To correct the river's misbehaviour, the *Times* led a battle to convince the Dominion and provincial governments and the Canadian Pacific Railway to pay for preventative measures. In 1917, the three institutions spent $125,000 on dikes and an upstream dam, but in spite of these efforts, a cloudburst in the foothills in 1923 unleashed a torrent of water that surged through downtown High River.[25] That event led to the construction of a canal to divert water from the Highwood to another river, the Little Bow, that originated from springs in High River. Even so, catastrophe often threatened. On 16 June 1927, the *Times* reported the frantic efforts of the townspeople to pile sandbags along the swollen banks. On 13 October, the *Times* again called on the Dominion government to fix the problem, justifying any expense on the grounds that already "there is a whole lot of needless expenditure going on throughout Canada." The local authorities, with minor assistance from senior governments, attempted to heighten the river bank with driven piles, but did not prevent flooding from occurring in either 1929 or 1932, and the town again renewed its efforts to control the flooding.

The great flood of 1942. Glenbow Archives NA–67–45.

Nothing tamed the river. The great flood of 1942 transformed the business district into a lake, and in some stores water rose eighteen inches above the floors. In an editorial on 21 May, the *Times* again complained that the railway and senior governments had not done enough, and if further proof was needed, the town flooded again in 1943. The post-World War II era saw numerous floods, most notably in 1953. An engineering study in 1964 concluded that no definitive resolution of the flooding problem was possible without the construction of a huge dam in the foothills. The expense could not be justified unless the reservoir could also be used for irrigation or power generation, but neither purpose could be incorporated into the project because the great dam needed to be left nearly empty most of the time so that it could receive the massive volumes of sudden water that caused the flooding. Consequently, such a dam would never be built. Meanwhile, it would be necessary to continue with smaller diverting, damming, and diking projects. Although these measures could not eliminate flooding, they did curb the Highwood River's desire to permanently enter the Little Bow. If that happened, the rush of spring waters would destroy a major dam that lay downstream, resulting in massive flooding and extensive property damage.[26]

ASIDE FROM THE CYCLICAL UPTURN of the mid-1920s, some economic developments in the interwar period compensated for all these problems. A government blunder furnished the town with ten years of income and employment. The Canada Air Board, a Dominion agency that eventually merged with the air force, established an airbase at Morley, Alberta. When the high winds that prevailed at that location interfered with its operations, the Board transferred the airbase to High River in 1921. Over the next decade, it usually maintained ten planes and 30 to 40 employees who carried out a wide variety of functions. They tested airplanes and wireless communication systems, experimented with winter flying, provided parachute training, carried out aerial photography and mapping, patrolled for forest fires, and assessed crop conditions.[27] The government abruptly closed the airbase in 1931 as an economy measure, but the town continued to remind it that the excellent facilities remained intact and ready for any new airborne functions.[28]

A more enduring transportation revolution occurred on the ground. The increased use of automobiles and trucks promised to bring more farmers and ranchers to High River from greater distances more quickly. By 1931, perhaps three-quarters of the rural families in the district owned a motor vehicle. This fact prompted the *Times* to resume its good roads campaign with renewed intensity, since automobiles required much better roads than horses and wagons.[29] The *Times* complained endlessly about the rutted dirt trails leading to town and how they left people "marooned like Robinson Crusoe" every time it rained or snowed.[30] When rural municipalities could not afford to build roads, they called on the province to foot the bills. Sometimes the government responded by securing cost-sharing agreements with rural municipalities to build highways. The "Sunshine Trail" constituted one such project. It ran east of High River into the wheat lands for 26 miles and then swung south to Vulcan (See Figure 4). The road received a major grading and coat of gravel in 1930, and on 26 June the *Times* predicted that it would draw many farmers into town more often. But the province still refused to provide money for a highway west of the town, and the *Times* condemned it for High River's inability to supply the Turner Valley oil fields.

Automobiles and improved roads presented the town with as much danger as they did opportunity, for they could just as conveniently whisk customers to other centres. The Macleod Trail that ran roughly parallel to the railway line between Calgary and Fort Macleod, posed a particular problem. Often favoured with provincial funding, it could convey people to the rival town of Nanton to the south, or to Okotoks to the north, or even beyond to Calgary. In spite of provincial patronage, however, the highway sometimes suffered neglect. On 16 April 1936, the *Times* reported that a section north of town had collapsed in a sea of mud. Moreover, winter storms often halted motor travel entirely, as much because of frozen engine blocks as impassable snow drifts. Even in ideal weather, flat tires and mechanical failures plagued the motorist.[31] In 1927, High River residents wishing to shop in Calgary still found the 90-minute train ride more reliable.[32]

The day when motorists commonly bypassed towns for cities still lay in the future. In the interwar years, they more often bypassed country stores and villages. As a result, larger railway towns like High River that had always offered more shops and services largely benefited from the first era of auto travel.[33] The *Times* frequently commented on the traffic congestion and parking problems on Saturday night when rural people thronged the town. Another important and often ignored economic benefit of the automobile favoured High River: it led to the establishment of sales outlets, mechanics' garages, filling stations and tire shops. By 1930, the Ford dealership employed fifteen people, thus providing one of the largest payrolls in town.[34]

The services that High River provided for its motorized hinterland during the interwar period included new medical, educational and governmental functions. When the town began its vigorous growth in 1903, it immediately attracted doctors and dentists. In 1906 a tiny "cottage hospital" opened in a house leased by two doctors and staffed by two nurses and a domestic. In 1910 it moved to a larger house that accommodated twelve beds, and two years later a separate maternity house opened.[35] In 1920, provincial legislation encouraged municipalities to co-operate in the establishment of public hospital districts. With vigorous support from the *Times*, ratepayers in High River and nearby rural municipalities voted for a $55,000 debenture to begin construction of a new hospital. It opened in 1921 with eighteen beds. Subsidized by taxpayers in the hospital district, patients paid only $1.00 a day for care. A local funeral home provided ambulance service. The hospital also operated a modest training program for nurses that turned out 22 graduates by 1934. The facility expanded to 36 beds in 1930 when the hospital district embraced a 1,000 square miles of territory, including the villages of Blackie and Cayley. With another addition in 1941, it accommodated 43 patients.[36]

In 1931, another medical service appeared with the creation of the Foothills Health Unit. One of the earliest rural public health units in Canada, it covered a much larger hinterland than the hospital district. By 1938 it served 17,000 people spread across an area of 1,800 square miles that included the distant towns of Vulcan and Turner Valley. The local member of the provincial legislature, George Hoadley, promoted the hospital, and it received financing from the province, participating municipalities, and the Rockefeller Foundation. It engaged in a host of activities: providing immunizations and medical examinations of school children, controlling infectious diseases, conducting educational work on nutrition and sanitation, offering pre- and postnatal assistance, and inspecting local water, food, and milk supplies.[37]

High River also grew as an educational centre. Its first tiny school opened in 1889, but for many years it only served children living in the town or very near it. The widely-dispersed population of rural children could not travel any great distance, giving rise to one-room schools throughout the countryside. They rarely offered secondary instruction and when High River grew large enough to build a high school in 1912, it became a magnet for country children who wished to continue their education.[38] Most of them boarded in High River. Meanwhile, it became feasible in the 1920s to close some rural schools and use buses to carry children to more distant ones.

The large-scale amalgamation of schools began after the election of the new Social Credit government in 1935. Premier William Aberhart, a school principal by occupation, and the Alberta Teachers' Association argued vigorously for large, centralized schools on the grounds that financing would be more stable, equitable and fair; that supplies could be purchased more cheaply in bulk; and that teachers would encounter more uniform standards and salaries. School inspections would be easier; and pupils would receive a superior education in facilities with specialized teachers and more books and equipment. In spite of these advantages, many rural trustees in the High River area and elsewhere feared that education costs would rise and that a "distant" board would ignore local problems. Some parents worried about long bus rides and time lost for doing farm chores. The province forged ahead despite these concerns. In 1938, High River became the headquarters for the gargantuan Foothills School Division that brought 2,000 square miles and 78 disbanded school districts under its authority.[39]

The *Times* presented all points of view on the amalgamation, but announced on 20 October that it would neither endorse nor condemn the plan, hoping to sidestep yet another divisive issue amongst readers. The new board began closing schools immediately, and by 1944 it had eliminated over 50 of them, establishing instead 37 bus routes to carry 632 rural children to 23 centralized schools. Schools in High River still operated under their own board, but the high school continued to draw students from the huge rural school division. Some parents even organized car pools to transport senior students.[40]

The consolidation of rural municipal government paralleled that of school districts. The first rural governments in the area appeared simultaneously with agricultural settlement. Known as Local Improvement Districts, they encompassed small areas and concerned themselves almost exclusively with road building (or more often, with a lack of road building). During the 1910s the province merged them into larger Municipal Districts that usually comprised between nine and twelve townships in size, or 300 to 400 square miles. High River lay near the centre of five rural governments, but not all of them held deliberations in the town.[41]

On 30 June 1932 the *Times* urged the amalgamation of those units as an economy measure, but when the province proceeded with actual amalgamations ten years later, it reversed its opinion. Every rural government in the High River area protested the mergers. On 12 March 1942 and 11 February 1943 the *Times* reviewed their complaints, many of which paralleled the opposition to school consolidation: no pressing need for amalgamation had arisen; instead of saving money it would create a more expensive bureaucracy; and councillors would be less accessible to ratepayers and less sensitive to neighbourhood concerns. Moreover, the province refused to consult local governments on the matter. As a final indignity, it also refused to pay weekly newspapers for publishing boundary information and regulatory details about the new entities. The initial round of amalgamations simply united pairs of adjacent Municipal Districts. The new Municipal District of Highwood established its headquarters in High River, but the town's role as a major administrative centre for rural government would come in the post-war era with the creation of the huge Municipal District of Foothills.[42]

Initially, High River's growth as a district medical, educational, and municipal centre did not contribute much to the town in terms of employment or direct spending. It would do so after World War II when such public services experienced rampant expansion. In the meantime, they exerted an important, if indirect, economic impact: they bound the hinterland population more closely to the town. When rural people availed themselves of High River's public services, they also shopped before returning home. Developments in transportation and services therefore provided some compensation for the drought and depression that largely characterized the interwar decades, and they help explain High River's demographic stability. A town population of 1,250 in 1916 only reached 1,430 by 1941, a gain of less than eight people per year over a quarter of a century.

| 6 |

THE *TIMES*
IN TROUBLED TIMES

THE FORTUNES OF THE *TIMES* ran parallel to those of the High River district in the interwar years. In 1921, it announced a circulation of 1,380, lower than its claim of 1,500 in 1908, but sales rebounded to about 1,800 by 1930.[1] Increasing the subscription rate from $1.50 to $2.00 a year may partly explain the temporary dip, but clearly the days of escalating circulation had passed with the end of the settlement boom. Subscriptions to absentee speculators declined, and copies mailed to distant addresses increasingly went to former residents or young people temporarily absent from the district. A special arrangement with the rural Municipal District of Dinton in 1927 accounted for some new subscriptions. The municipality agreed to provide the newspaper to every property owner within its jurisdiction. In return, the *Times* sold the subscriptions at a reduced rate and also agreed to print all council minutes and regulations. Dinton sought this arrangement to guarantee that every ratepayer received notice of its rulings. Although such contracts appeared in Alberta as early as 1912, they remained uncommon until after World War II, and the *Times* waited decades before securing similar agreements with other municipalities.[2]

The *Times* also maintained its stable of about fifteen country correspondents least the outlying population begin subscribing to the *Okotoks Review* or the *Nanton News* (See Figure 4). District columns also discouraged attempts to start newspapers in the larger villages, such as the upstarts that appeared at Cayley intermittently between 1909 and 1914, at Blackie in 1917 and perhaps in 1921, and at Turner Valley from 1929 to 1931. A new paper even appeared briefly in High River itself in 1917.[3] The *Times* crushed any new arrival by maintaining a strong presence in the most susceptible locations. In the mid-1920s, it featured a regular page entitled "The Blackie Times" that contained more neighbourhood news than the usual country column and reserved advertising space for village merchants on the same page. The Turner Valley district later received the same consideration.

To the east, the *Times* worried less about competition from other weeklies because it owned the *Vulcan Advocate*. That enterprise continued to thrive and in 1917 vacated its rented quarters and moved into its own new building. In 1918 the value of the property and equipment stood at $8,161, and revenues of $8,628 yielded an impressive net profit of $3,406.[4] The *Times* played little role in directing the editorial policy or the routine business operations of the *Advocate*, except for a brief period in 1932 and 1933. Ordinarily, Charles Clark hired an editor and left him to function as he saw fit.[5]

In spite of editorial division, some close ties between the two papers developed. They freely reprinted each other's articles whenever empty space demanded a quick filler and they also shared some important technology. In 1917 Clark purchased a secondhand Intertype, a variation on the more common Linotype machine. Although it was a costly device worth over $2,000, it produced type about five times faster than the old method of selecting and setting individual letters by hand.[6] The Intertype operated like a giant typewriter: striking letters on the keyboard caused hot lead to pour into moulds, permitting an entire line of copy to be cast as a single unit. After printing, a hot pot melted the type, providing lead for the next casting. City dailies began using such machines in the 1890s, but because of their high cost, few weeklies in Alberta acquired one before the *Times*, and some did not acquire one until the 1950s. For some unknown reason, Clark installed the machine at the Vulcan office where it produced type for both the *Advocate* and the *Times* for two and half years before the equipment moved to High River. The new Intertype machine did not eliminate the need for the old loose-letter type, for the Intertype offered a limited range of large fonts and

The new building, 1928. Clark Family Papers.

the handset method remained useful for posters and other printing contracts, as well as for making headlines in the newspaper itself.[7]

In spite of the temporary drop in circulation, the *Times* probably survived the post-war depression better than most local businesses. Indeed, it may have fared better than it had during the more generally prosperous war years when labour and newsprint grew scarce and expensive, causing weekly publishers considerable anxiety. For most years from 1919 to 1932 the R.G. Dun credit agency valued the enterprise in its $10,000 to $20,000 category and rated its credit "good."[8] In 1924 Charles Clark felt prosperous enough to join the Canadian Weekly Newspapers Association when it sponsored an extensive tour of Europe.[9]

During the flush of prosperity in the late 1920s, Clark decided to move the *Times* into a new building. A visiting English publisher laid the cornerstone of the $6,000 structure in a ceremony in 1927.[10] The paper also treated itself to a new printing plant, a Franklin Optimus two-cylinder press obtained from the Toronto Type Foundry in Winnipeg for $2,300. The *Times* received an $800 allowance for an old drum cylinder, paid only $500 down, and secured credit for the remainder at $60 a month.[11] The *Times* proudly announced the acquisition on 3 November 1927: "with lightning-like swiftness, you see

Front page, 6 October 1938. Clark Family Papers.

the printed sheets flashing by the hundreds at edition time." On 6 February 1930 the *Times* announced the acquisition of a "stereo-typing" machine for "casting cuts," a device that permitted the paper to create its own illustrations for advertisements. It bragged that few weeklies possessed one. Other technologies became more common at weeklies, including power paper cutters, newspaper folding machines, and stitchers to bind booklets. Unfortunately, the fragmentary business records of the *Times* offer no clues about their acquisition.

The new equipment led to changes in the newspaper's appearance. Photographs remained as difficult to present as ever, but illustrations appeared more often. To display its front page banner, the *Times* designed a graphic panorama of mountains, foothills, and plains displaying aspects of ranching, farming, and petroleum drilling. Each story received its own heading, and bold headings spilled across two or more columns. The *Times* also complied with the modern fashion of banishing ads from the front page, while still reserving about 60 percent of the total paper for advertising. The new press permitted the *Times* to use wider sheets, and after 1927 it began printing seven columns instead of six, while still retaining a length of eight pages. On 15 December it explained that a growth in advertising dictated this modest expansion. The *Times* enjoyed more success in attracting brand names after 1927 when General Motors of Canada announced its intention to advertise in rural weeklies on a trial basis.[12] Its spreads subsequently appeared in the *Times*, including the November issues of 1928 when the paper also displayed layouts for no less than twelve national brand names.

EXPENSIVE IMPROVEMENTS at the *Times* in the late 1920s mirrored the land and machinery expansion of High River's farmers, and like them, it suffered shock when the Great Depression struck. The *Times* needed more income to retire its debts, but instead earned less. On 12 May 1932 it borrowed an editorial from another paper that issued a bleak declaration: "With a small amount of revenue from advertising and a large number of subscriptions in arrears, no business can be hit harder by the depression than that of the village or town weekly." Another calamity compounded the problem.

After two decades of use, the secondhand Intertype machine finally expired, forcing Clark to replace it in 1936. By 1937, the R.G. Dun agency had slashed the value of the *Times* to the $3,000 to $5,000 category and cut its credit rating to "fair."[13]

As the Depression deepened, the *Times* could not maintain its circulation. In 1931 it launched a contest to win new subscribers, but arrears increased instead. Frantic requests for payment appeared. On 9 July 1931 an editorial reminded readers that their $2.00 subscription more than repaid itself by alerting them to sales and bargains of all kinds. Still, the problem grew worse and by autumn the *Times* agreed to take wheat in payment if farmers delivered it to the elevators and credited the newspaper's account. It also accepted foodstuffs like chickens and eggs, which farmers deposited at local grocers. Since the merchants owed money for advertising, the newspaper staff received credits to shop at their stores, and *Times* avoided paying all its salaries in cash. A complex barter system had partly replaced monetary exchanges in the Depression's darkest hours. The story became part of the newspaper's folklore, recited often on future ceremonial occasions.[14] But in spite of such ingenious efforts, the *Times* announced on 24 September 1942 that circulation hovered around 1,600—a figure below that of 1930.

As always, circulation affected advertising rates. Not only did they decline, but many businesses reduced their advertising and some stopped entirely. The need for a seven-column newspaper evaporated; the *Times* reverted to six columns and sometimes failed to muster enough advertising to sustain its eight-page length. Big business retrenched as much as small businesses did, erasing the modest success the *Times* had enjoyed in the late 1920s by winning more brand name advertising. The war of the weeklies against the advertising agencies resumed. They revived the argument that subscription lists meant little because so many people passed the weekly on to family and friends. Indeed, the regrettable practice had actually grown during the hard times. In a curious twist of logic, the weeklies also insisted that rural people still had money to spend on products. Publishers also continued to complain about the high commissions the agencies charged for any advertisements they did place.[15]

Radio advertising constituted another unwelcome menace. Some brand name advertisers flocked to the airway because it could reach more rural consumers easily, especially those who still had money to spend, as their ownership of radios suggested. The *Times* condemned radio advertising for substituting brainless jingles for solid information, and because its fleeting messages made it impossible for consumers to scrutinize the advertisements at their leisure. When several radio stations offered free classified advertising to their listeners, the Alberta Division of the Canadian Weekly Newspapers Associations denounced the practice as "unethical."[16]

As the battle for brand name advertising raged, the *Times* resorted to various tactics to bolster revenue from local business. It disguised pleas for advertising as news stories. On 3 April 1930, for example, it wrote about the Welch Grape Juice Company and pinpointed the reason for its success: "[The product]…was firmly implanted in people's minds and business forged ahead of other competitors so fast that the debt from advertising was wiped out almost overnight." In the next issue, the *Times* insisted that "It is far more logical to advertise when sales are hard than when they are easy. When your car loses momentum on a hill, you give it more gas. Business has lost some of its momentum. The remedy is more gas—more advertising." On 26 October 1939 it warned local merchants who failed to advertise that they had no cause for complaint if residents subsequently shopped in Calgary.

The *Times* also courted the merchants by offering them more free publicity. On 10 October 1930 it published fifteen lines on the renovations at the Matthewson Brothers store and concluded with unrestrained praise: "the several departments provide a spacious, splendidly equipped store, unsurpassed by any small town in the West." The paper also invited more advertising by offering merchants tips on how to achieve better results. On 23 April 1931 it reminded them that sporadic notices did not attract as much attention as regular advertising. Cognizant of the fact that women had played a larger role in family shopping since the Great War, and that they read the weeklies even more thoroughly than men, the *Times* urged merchants to focus their messages accordingly: "the modern woman 'shops by the newspaper,'" it informed them, "she turns to it first, by intuition alone, to see what bargains she can find."[17] The *Times* also reminded merchants of the infinite uses and value of other printed items the *Times* could provide through its custom printing services, and it issued the usual stern warnings against

The back shop press, c. 1928. Clark Family Papers.

using outsider printers for these jobs. Charles Clark also attacked such intruders privately. In 1933 he wrote member of the legislature W.R. Howson, asking the province to curb itinerant salesmen who represented eastern printing houses and paid no local taxes.[18]

The Times often hinted at dire consequences should a lack of community support sink the paper. On 15 October 1936 it told the tragic tale of an Ontario weekly, the Penetang Herald, which slowly starved from the apathy of subscribers and advertisers. After its death, the local residents suddenly realized their great mistake and bemoaned their loss. Alas, it was too late to revive the corpse. Such tragedies, the Times argued, had become commonplace. It claimed that Ontario once proudly sported 408 weeklies, but thanks to amalgamations and failures, especially during the Depression, the number had fallen to 169 by 1932.[19] On a more positive note, it wrote approvingly on 22 November 1934 about the Quebec government's intention to subsidize its provincial weeklies.

In soliciting support from the community, the Times believed that the old covenant of the booster era remained intact. Some weekly editors turned away from boosterism after the Great War because they believed the merchants had failed to maintain their part of the bargain.[20] While the fanciful goals and the frothy rhetoric of boosterism had disappeared, the *Times* still continued to support the High River merchants' trade-at-home campaigns, sales carnivals, and other events intended to attract country shoppers. The *Times* continued to rail against peddlers, mail order catalogues, rival towns, and other competitive enemies of the local merchant.

To help resolve the problems of the rural press, Charles Clark continued to participate in publishers' organizations. In 1919, the weeklies split from the dailies to create the Canadian Weekly Newspapers Association and its provincial divisions. The new entity insisted that weeklies made little money. The publishers persisted because they loved their craft and their community and wished to be of service. Nonetheless, it sought to educate its members about various aspects of the business through publications and conventions. The weekly publisher valued the conventions highly. Since no one else in his community shared his profession, they provided a rare opportunity to meet and talk with one's peers.[21]

The organization also pursued a task common to all trade associations: it lobbied governments for favours and advantages. Over the years, it demanded lower postal rates, improved postal service, reduced taxes, less stringent libel laws, fewer restrictions on advertising, less government control over the press, and more remuneration for printing government notices. The Association also lobbied the national advertising agencies, simultaneously urging them to place more advertisements in the weeklies and to charge less commission when doing so. It tried to secure agreements among weeklies about how much to charge for advertising, even though the agreements inevitability collapsed whenever the weeklies faced the choice of accepting less or losing advertisers.[22]

Charles Clark played an active role in the organization, often serving as a director. Each publisher could serve only one term as president of the national association and Clark accepted the position for 1933–1934. He also participated in the annual competitions for prizes awarded to the weeklies in various categories. In 1931, after the *Times* won its third straight title as the best all around weekly in Canada in its circulation class, Clark withdrew his paper from the competition and donated the Charles Clark Cup to future winners in its category. In recognition of his contributions and long service, the

Alberta Division of the association rewarded him with a lifetime membership in 1947.[23]

NEWSPAPER FAILURES and high unemployment alleviated one problem that troubled the weeklies in prosperous times: the retention of quality employees. Throughout the 1930s, the *Times* usually retained seven full-time workers and varying numbers of part-timers, equally divided between the front and back shop.[24] The paper relied heavily on a core group of loyal employees identified in the anniversary issue of 5 December 1940. Although two workers with more than ten years service had left, Bob Bradley remained after seventeen years, and Tommy Logan after 22. Logan had actually started with the *Times* in 1913, but he enlisted in the military in 1915. After a long convalescence from war wounds, he rejoined the staff in 1920. He worked at the *Advocate* office until 1923 and began operating the Intertype in 1925. He would set the longevity record with the *Times*, serving 48 years in the backshop until the Clarks sold the enterprise in 1966.

The anniversary issue listed two other employees with more than ten years experience, and each shaped the *Times* in crucial ways. Charles Clark's namesake and only son, who called himself Charles A. rather than "Junior," joined the staff permanently in 1929. He had worked at the *Times* after school and during summers throughout his boyhood, sweeping floors, folding newspapers, cleaning type, and running errands. After attending St. Joseph's College at the University of Alberta, the nineteen-year old returned to High River where the *Times* would become his life's work. Although classified as a "cub reporter" when he began full time, he laboured at many tasks, including bookkeeping and selling advertising (which he did not like), and by the late 1930s the masthead often identified him as "business manager."[25]

Like his father, Charles A. plunged into the life of the community. He especially favoured the Rotary Club, which he joined as a charter member in 1928. For decades he arranged for the talks of its guest speakers to appear virtually unabridged in the *Times*. In 1937 he married Grace Roseline Welch of Wainwright, Alberta. They had met at the University of Alberta, but subsequently lost contact until Grace accepted a job teaching school in

High River in 1936. She readily joined her husband's active social life, a role that Charles's older sister Marnie also embraced. Marnie had graduated from the nursing program at the local hospital and married a widower, Dr. Harold W. Soby.[26] Children also occupied Grace with the birth of Charles Joseph (Joe) in 1939 and Peter MacDonell in 1942, but she eventually returned to teaching, serving intermittently at the high school from 1956 to 1972.[27]

Charles A. Clark's influence on the Times lay in the future, but the hiring of Hughena McCorquodale had an immediate impact. Born in London, Ontario, she came to Alberta to teach school, met and married High River lawyer A.Y. McCorquodale, moved to the town in 1908, and busied herself raising three sons. She joined the Times in 1927.[28] Hardly anyone attempted to pronounce her name. Acquaintances and young people simply called her "Mrs. Mac;" friends called her "Corky." An extraordinary character by all accounts, she gained notoriety for smoking hand-rolled cigarettes that were so poorly constructed that novelist W.O. Mitchell claimed they appeared in need of Band-Aids.[29] The misshapen cylinders spewed ashes and sparks, threatening to ignite her famously untidy desk. Besides her eccentricities, she also possessed talent. Under her own name and various aliases, she wrote for many newspapers and magazines, contributing with equal ease to women's publications like *Chatelaine* and to sportsmen's periodicals like *Field and Stream*. Other employees believed she could have worked elsewhere for considerably more money, but McCorquodale stayed in High River, as much out of choice as because of marriage for she remained with the Times after her husband's death in 1949.[30]

Although the paper did not list her as "associate editor" until the late 1930s, McCorquodale played a major role in the front office much earlier, usually serving as *de facto* editor and writing many of the stories and editorials herself. Corky instantly gained people's trust, and soon developed the capacity to engage in a conversation while simultaneously typing a story on an unrelated topic. She influenced younger employees at the Times, and taught them that the rural press must combine honesty with compassion. She encouraged other writers, including W.O. Mitchell. When he moved to High River and became her neighbour, a fast friendship developed and they provided each other with inspiration.

Three dominant individuals in the history of the Times. Left to right: Charles A. Clark, Hughena McCorquodale, Charles Clark. Clark Family Papers.

In hiring McCorquodale, Charles Clark utilized the same eye for talent that led him to hire Robert Stead before he became a prominent novelist. Certainly, Corky's sex did not bar her from employment or advancement at the *Times*. Society had long regarded writing as a natural pastime for an educated woman, and the writing profession accepted women more readily than most middle-class occupations. Indeed, the weekly press probably offered them more opportunity than the dailies, given the difficulty of attracting male journalists to rural areas.[31]

Besides the employees at the town office, the *Times* also retained its string of country correspondents who anonymously submitted their columns of community social notes week after week. The *Times* also acquired a new correspondent of some renown among weekly editors. Charles Clark's brother Hugh sold the *Kincardine Review* in 1925 and offered to supply the *Times* with a weekly column of observations on national and international politics. Consisting of short, snappy items, often presented in a humorous light, they appeared under various headings until the late 1930s when they acquired the title the column would retain for decades: "Pertinent Topics by H.C."[32]

LED BY CHARLES CLARK, and then Hughena McCorquodale, the employees of the *Times* found themselves writing, intertyping, and printing themes that better matched the new reality of community experience. The economic turbulence of the interwar years led to the rise of new political movements and parties in Western Canada, and their popularity in the High River district made them newsworthy topics for the *Times*. They also challenged the paper's commitment to political nonpartisanship and ultimately caused it to violate that policy.

Throughout the interwar period, the *Times* continued to reflect the ideological perspectives of small business in general and those of farmers in particular. "In suggesting policies which Western weeklies could very ably promote—and do promote," argued a *Times* editorial on 24 August 1933, "the most important are those which have to do with grain farming and the growing of livestock." The paper continued to crusade against the tariff on imported manufactured goods (an issue that dominated national politics in the 1920s), against high freight rates and other railway offences, and against banks and other corporations that exasperated farmers. It continued to condemn labour organizers and unions that threatened to raise farm production and transportation costs. The *Times* also applauded new agrarian organizations like the Wheat Pool, a marketing co-operative designed to enhance returns to farmers. "It is high time that the most wanted commodity in the world should receive its due deserts in the mercantile markets of the world," declared an editorial on 23 August 1923, "and that its producers should receive a fair compensation for their labors in raising it."

Charles Clark also championed these positions beyond the pages of the *Times*. Whenever eastern journalists or politicians visited High River, he offered them the hospitality of his home and then explained to them the problems and viewpoints of the rural west. In his capacity as president of the Canadian Weekly Newspapers Association in 1934, he delivered a speech in eastern Canada, reported in many dailies, that pleaded for policies more favourable to the primary producers of the country.[33]

When agrarian unrest also led to the creation of new political parties, the *Times* hesitated to violate its tradition of nonpartisanship, even when those parties supported the very measures advocated by the paper. It offered virtually no comment on the provincial and Dominion elections of 1921 when farmers defeated the old-line parties in the High River district. They sent a representative of the new Progressive Party to Ottawa and continued to do so in every election until 1935. They also sent a candidate from the United Farmers of Alberta (which decided to enter politics directly) to the provincial legislature in 1921 and continued to do so in every election until 1935. While the *Times* never endorsed the new parties, it continued its practice of occasionally praising local politicians regardless of affiliation. When local Progressive George Coote won his third consecutive election as Member of Parliament, the *Times* treated him to favourable editorial comment on 31 July 1930. Politicians from other parties received praise too, especially Dan Riley, High River's most prominent Liberal. As a resident of the district since 1883, an important rancher and businessman, High River's first mayor, and the long-standing president of the Western Stockgrowers' Association, he often appeared in the pages of the *Times*. Commenting on his appointment to the Canadian Senate, the *Times* noted on 1 July 1926 that he "is well equipped to fill the position with honor to himself and his province."

The rise of Social Credit presented the *Times* with a political entity that finally breached the wall of nonpartisanship. The Great Depression intensified an already keen interest in ideology and politics in the High River district. In response, the paper first presented considerable amounts of information about Social Credit, not as a political movement or party, but as an economic theory. Social Credit argued that a lack of purchasing power created poverty in the midst of plenty, a situation that government might remedy by issuing "social credit dividends" to provide consumers with more "money." The idea appealed to a population stricken by drought, collapsing wheat prices, and unemployment. Local interest escalated after Calgary high school principal and lay preacher William Aberhart introduced Social Credit into his religious radio programs in 1932. The *Times* presented little of its own opinion on the theory, but it did quote the views of others, especially after Social Credit evolved into a political movement and then a political party. It treated the new socialist political party, the Co-operative Commonwealth

Federation, the same way. Meanwhile, the Times entered into a business relationship with Aberhart's Social Credit organization in 1934 when it secured the contract to print its newspaper, the Alberta Social Credit Chronicle.[34]

Social Credit contested the provincial and Dominion elections held in 1935, and its candidates from the constituencies that included High River both won. William Aberhart did not run, but after Social Credit's landslide provincial victory, his supporters wished him to serve as Premier. William Morrison, the freshly-elected member from Okotoks-High River, agreed to resign so that Aberhart might stand in a by-election. On 10 October 1935 the Times argued that the party had paid the constituency "the highest possible honor." Since the other political parties declined to nominate candidates, Aberhart won by acclamation.

After the by-election, the Times endeavoured to maintain a benign neutrality towards Social Credit, but Aberhart's attitude towards the press soon led to trouble. From the beginning of the movement, the banks and other corporations challenged Social Credit economic theory and adamantly opposed its solutions. Alberta's two biggest dailies, the Edmonton Journal and the Calgary Herald agreed, prompting Aberhart to condemn them as tools of the financial interests that misrepresented Social Credit and deliberately lied to the public. When a Herald article annoyed Aberhart in April 1935, he asked the public to boycott all newspapers unfavourable to the movement.[35] In January 1936 the party planned to establish its own daily by taking over the Calgary Albertan and merging it with the Alberta Social Credit Chronicle. The party secured an option to buy the Albertan, which it hoped to finance by selling shares to the public, a scheme that ultimately collapsed.[36] Meanwhile, Aberhart threatened to license the press in order to prevent it from printing lies. In autumn 1936, an Order-in-Council actually did license some small Alberta print shops and it forced them to comply with a code of ethics.[37]

The dailies fought back, condemning Social Credit on many grounds: the province had no constitutional authority to deal with monetary matters; the economic theory rested on faulty premises; Aberhart's ideas for implementing it were ambiguous, contradictory, confusing, dictatorial, and ultimately impractical and unworkable; and Aberhart himself was both incompetent and autocratic. The dailies held back nothing and delivered their critiques with malicious contempt. The political cartoonist at the Calgary

Herald, a former Disney animator named Stewart Cameron, lampooned Aberhart without mercy. A new Calgary paper appeared in 1937. The *Rebel* devoted itself solely to the destruction of Social Credit in general and Aberhart in particular.[38]

In the fall of 1937 the government retaliated by passing the Accurate News and Information Act. It forced the newspapers to publish any press release issued by the Social Credit Board that corrected or amplified any newspaper statements about government policies or activities. It also forced newspapers, if asked, to reveal the names of writers and their sources for any story. Noncompliance could result in a publication ban against a writer or even the entire newspaper, as well as fines of $1,000 a day.[39] The press howled in protest. Although Aberhart insisted that newspapers could still publish anything they liked, the press believed that the legislation threatened their ability to do so. And even though no written constitution or law guaranteed freedom of the press in Alberta or Canada, they regarded it as a right deeply embedded in British tradition.

The government's actions alienated virtually all newspapers in the province, including the weeklies. The Alberta Division of the Canadian Weekly Newspapers Association began issuing formal protests when Aberhart first threatened to license the press.[40] A *Times* editorial about Social Credit on 18 April 1935 still maintained a tone of bland neutrality, but did express concern about the comments of party organizer Edith Gostick. She denounced newspapers as "the mouthpieces of the capitalist system" and urged supporters to ignore them if they criticized Social Credit. A *Times* editorial on 17 September 1936 condemned Aberhart's plan to license the press and another on 22 October condemned the licensing of small print shops.

Minor irritants also arose. The *Times* complained on 12 December 1935 when the government banned liquor advertising. It grumbled on 18 June 1936 after the *Albertan*, the new Social Credit daily, published a long story filled with inaccuracies about the High River district, the premier's own constituency. On 25 June 1936, it protested that Aberhart had not once visited the riding since his by-election victory. The government also began to discuss the amalgamation of rural school boards and municipal districts without local consultation. Meanwhile, even the supporters of Social Credit complained about the government's failure to issue the eagerly anticipated monthly dividends. Social Credit backbenchers in the legislature revolted in 1937 and threatened to topple Aberhart if action did not ensue. Uncertain about how to proceed, Aberhart received little help from the British founder of Social Credit, Major C.H. Douglas, whom Aberhart had managed to offend. The government hastily cobbled together a series of legislative measures to implement its monetary scheme.

The *Times* soon began to criticize Social Credit for all the same reasons as the city dailies. In an editorial entitled "The Alberta Circus" on 4 March 1937, the *Times* virtually declared war. "The past 18 months of Premier Aberhart's regime are littered with gravestones and disappointments, overhung with clouds of uncertainty and general business disruption," it complained, "he offers no convincing hope for the future." By 26 August words like "dictatorship" appeared in the *Times* to describe the legislative plans that would coerce everyone in the province into accepting Social Credit economic measures. That autumn the *Times* published the transcripts from a series of six broadcasts sponsored by the chartered banks entitled "The Facts About Banking in Canada." On 9 September it resumed its hostilities with Edith Gostick, who was now a member of the legislature. She claimed that reporters and editors were "paid for misinforming the public," and she singled out the *Times* for special condemnation. "I had not thought that the *High River Times* was amongst the financially-owned and controlled press, but I guess it must be," she said in issuing yet another call to control the press.[41] The *Times* responded that "licensing will be the first step to ending freedom of speech," and doing so would be "upholding fascism and fascist methods."

At that point rumours circulated that the *Times* only attacked Social Credit because it had lost the contract to print the *Alberta Social Credit Chronicle*. On 16 September, the *Times* decided to clear the air in a long editorial that reviewed its relationship with the party. The paper admitted that it had given the economic theory considerable publicity—not because of the printing contract, but because the new and unorthodox idea had stimulated local interest and people craved information. Strictly a business deal, the printing contract implied neither approval nor disapproval of the movement or its ideas. The *Times* claimed that it happily surrendered the contract because the circulation of the *Chronicle* had reached a point where it required that the *Times* buy more equipment and hire more staff—a step it decided not to take given the economic uncertainty of the times. The editorial also reminded readers that after the termination of the printing job, the *Times* had not criticized the government during its first year in office, giving it a fair chance to prove itself. Criticism only began after it inflicted disastrous legislation on the province and began to attack the press.

Less than a month after offering this explanation, the *Times* delivered its response to the Accurate News and Information Act. With as much sarcasm as it could muster, it presented readers with an "accurate" news story on 7 October:

> In Alberta everyone is very happy. The government has been busy passing bills to make everyone still happier. Members of the government are working very hard and in a truly Christian spirit to make nice kind laws, so that everyone will like his neighbor very much. It is indeed a nice thing to live in a cheerful province like Alberta.

The *Times* also indicated its willingness to reveal its sources: "It is a nice day and it is the opinion of several prominent residents of the district (whose names will be given immediately upon request) that it has been quite a good fall."

The Accurate News and Information Act never became law. The Lieutenant-Governor of Alberta refused to sign it and two other bills, and the courts soon declared the legislation *ultra vires*.[42] In the United States, the Pulitzer Prize committee, which honoured American newspapers in a variety of categories, decided to award a special prize to the newspapers of Alberta for defending the freedom of the press. The *Edmonton Journal* accepted the award on behalf of the six dailies and 90 weeklies in the province.[43]

In the same 7 October issue that lampooned the Press Act, the *Times* also reported on a rebellion in the Okotoks-High River constituency against their sitting member, William Aberhart. Farmers in Alberta had long argued for a political reform known as the recall, a mechanism that would enable voters to force the resignation of their elected member if he ignored or violated the wishes of his constituents. Shortly after its election in 1935, the Social Credit government passed a Recall Act that required two-thirds of the registered voters in a constituency to sign a petition of complaint in order to activate the recall. A petition circulated throughout Okotoks-High River and by autumn 1937, it had collected enough signatures to force Aberhart's resignation. Resentment against him no doubt stemmed from many of the issues that troubled the press generally, but also perhaps from his callous indifference to his own riding. But before Aberhart could be deposed, the government repealed the Recall Act retroactively, preserving the Premier's seat. Aberhart personally voted against repeal, but the Times regarded his gesture as a disgraceful sham since Aberhart knew the huge Social Credit majority would easily marshal enough votes to kill the act.[44]

In a curious turn of events, the Times suddenly received a new government contract to print the index of the Alberta Gazette for the provincial King's Printer. The Times announced the news on 20 January 1938, noting that the contract represented the first piece of government work it had received "for many a long year." The Times claimed that Alberta's Liberal administration, which ruled from 1905 to 1921, had spread printing contracts around the province, but complained that the United Farmers of Alberta never gave jobs to small presses (in spite of its avowed commitment to rural life). The Times applauded Social Credit for returning to an earlier tradition. It offered no explanation of why or how it received the index job. Perhaps Aberhart sought to mend fences after the recall episode by placating the most critical voice in the riding. Even so, the actions of his constituents frightened him sufficiently that he decided to contest a safer seat in Calgary in the 1940 election. The Premier probably acted shrewdly since High River became a meeting ground for "non-partisan" organizations dedicated to toppling Social Credit.[45] In the 1940 provincial election, the independent John T. Broomfield defeated the Social Credit candidate Ivan Casey in Okotoks-High River by a margin of 4,248 to 3,134. The Times congratulated both politicians on 28 March for setting "a high standard in their campaigning."

WHAT ULTIMATELY COMPELLED the Times to violate its long-standing policy of nonpartisanship? It cannot be argued that the Times simply reflected the views of its readers and advertisers. In spite of local resentment against

Aberhart, Social Credit still commanded considerable support in the district. The Dominion constituency of Macleod (which included High River) elected the same Social Credit Member of Parliament in every election from 1935 to 1958. And even though Social Credit lost the provincial seat of Okotoks-High River in 1940, Casey still collected three votes for every four obtained by the successful candidate. In the 1944 election Casey recaptured the riding for Social Credit and held the seat until 1955 when another independent won. At the very least, therefore, the stand against Social Credit embroiled the *Times* in a divisive issue that weeklies normally avoided.

What role did printing contracts play in the conflict? Aside from the *Chronicle* incident, the *Times* complained often and bitterly about the lack of paid government printing under Social Credit. It criticized the Accurate News and Information Act in part because it mandated "free space" for government use.[46] Many of these complaints reached the government through the Alberta Division of the Canadian Weekly Newspapers Association. Acting on its behalf, Charles A. Clark wrote to the publicity director of the Alberta government in 1945: "For many years the onus of informing rural Alberta of governmental plans, policies, and actions seems to have been dumped in the laps of the weekly press. For some strange reason the government believes the weeklies should do this work without remuneration."[47] But these complaints cannot explain the open attack on Social Credit. After all, the *Times*, like most other Alberta weeklies, had raised the same criticism about former administrations. On 22 October 1931 a *Times* editorial had agreed with the Weekly Newspapers Association that the United Farmers of Alberta government was the worst "free advertising" leech in the country.

Given the nature of the arguments presented in its anti-Social Credit editorials, perhaps the *Times* sincerely believed that readers needed to be warned against a madman seeking to impose a dangerous, unworkable, and illegal plan on the province. In an interview decades later, Charles A. Clark admitted that he and his father had never believed in Social Credit doctrine, even in the days when the *Times* printed the *Chronicle* and maintained editorial neutrality.[48]

More than anything, Social Credit's threats to control the press drove the *Times* to violate its nonpartisan rule. Indeed, the Accurate News and Information Act compelled virtually every newspaper in the province to attack Social Credit regardless of any view they previously held about the theory, the party, or the leader. No business would welcome such a direct assault on its integrity, or such heavy-handed and unwanted government interference in its affairs. This interpretation helps explain the curious action of the Pulitzer Prize committee. American newspapers typically ignored everything that happened in Canada, the committee never awarded prizes outside the United States, and it had no prize at all for defending freedom of the press. Perhaps it made such bold exceptions in all these cases to send a message to the United States government that it could expect a mighty battle if it ever attempted to trample on the constitutional rights of the American press. Despite its vocal opposition to Social Credit, the *Times* never became an unbridled champion of free expression. On 20 January 1955 an editorial denounced the British Broadcasting Corporation for allowing an atheist to air her views: "it goes rather far along the line of freedom of speech to turn over BBC channels to expression of opinion that is an affront to a great section of the British people."

Did violating its own taboo about political entanglements hurt the *Times*? The paper feared that it might, for avid Social Credit supporters in the district quickly expressed their anger. Charles A. Clark claimed that local organizers banned *Times* reporters from their meetings.[49] On 2 December 1937, the *Times* published a resolution passed by the Herronton Social Credit Group: "Whereas in view of the biased attitude that the *High River Times* has assumed, it wishes to go on record that it opposes the Dinton Municipal Council renewing its present contract with the *High River Times*." The secretary of the High River Social Credit Group expanded the attack by claiming in 1940 that "Every member of the present [town] council is a bitter enemy of social credit [sic]."[50] In spite of these hostilities, the paper tried to maintain a friendly relationship with Social Credit supporters in the district while simultaneously attacking the theory, the legislation, and the Premier. On 15 April 1937, the paper's society notes included the following item: "The home of Mrs. Fenton was the scene of a very enjoyable occasion when a card party and dance were held there on Friday...under the auspices of the Mazeppa Ladies' Social Credit Group."

If the Social Credit intrigue inflicted any damage on the subscription numbers or advertising revenues of the *Times* it cannot be segregated from the declines engendered by the Depression itself. Reflecting on the question years later, Charles A. Clark concluded that the *Times* probably suffered little harm.[51] This judgment suggests that the weeklies had been needlessly cautious about avoiding controversy in the past, and that readers and advertisers would have tolerated more vigorous debate on local conflicts. The *Times* did not intend to test the validity of such a notion in the High River District, for after the Press Act affair the paper reverted to its nonpartisan, noncontroversial tradition. Indeed, it began writing less about Social Credit or politics in any context. When Aberhart died, the *Times* almost paid him a tribute on 27 May 1943: "Many people did not agree with the Social Credit theories which the Premier clung to, in spite of all discouragements, but they did admire his persistence and determination." In a subsequent editorial on 3 June, however, the *Times* noted that newspapers were generally "much kinder to him after death than…during his lifetime."

The *Times* also grew less hostile about Social Credit when it shed most of its radicalism under the leadership of Ernest Manning. On 7 February 1952 the *Times* even extended him the sort of favourable comment that it had conferred on politicians in the past: "The fact that he is held in such high respect not only in Canada, but by those from other countries who have dealt with him in business should be matter of pride for all Albertans, regardless of party loyalties." Joe Clark remembered that his parents even voted for Ivan Casey in spite of their ties to other parties, and regardless of the fact that they remained suspicious and even fearful of Social Credit for many years.[52]

Another intriguing facet of the Social Credit affair emerges: if attacking the party did not materially harm the *Times*, it must also be noted that the *Times* did not materially harm Social Credit either. Indeed, a massive and increasingly vicious press assault throughout Alberta did not prevent the party from winning a landslide victory in 1935, nor from retaining power in 1940, nor from winning every provincial election before 1971, many by huge majorities. These facts ought to give pause to those who argue that the press exerts enormous influence over readers. One early student of Social Credit even argued that savage press attacks actually helped the party.[53] The attacks seemed to confirm the conspiracy theory about how financial interests controlled the press, and they enhanced Aberhart's populist appeal by thrusting him into the role of beleaguered underdog.

For all its high drama, the war against Social Credit represented a brief aberration in the history of the *Times*. In confronting the harsh difficulties that prevailed throughout most of the interwar era, the newspaper devoted much more energy to a theme far removed from the dangers of political commentary, a theme that offered solace to virtually everyone in the community.

7

RURAL
AND SMALL TOWN VIRTUE

SINCE HIGH RIVER SEEMED DESTINED to remain a small town serving a rural hinterland, the *Times* decided to embrace the new reality. Instead of endless commentaries on High River's inevitable climb to metropolitan status, it began to speak of ill of cities and soon stressed the virtue of rural and small town life. In doing so it relied on a well-worn stock of rhetoric that had circulated in North America for more than a century. Often attributed to the American statesman Thomas Jefferson, agrarian idealism stressed the nobility of agriculture and argued that farmers who tilled their own land provided the best possible citizenry for a democracy. Living and working with nature taught valuable lessons: the necessity of hard work, the importance of frugality, the virtue of self-reliance, and the dignity of independence. Agriculture engaged mind and body in healthy, invigorating labour. It filled one with reverence for God's works, inducing humility and providing inspiration. It immersed one in the most honest and honourable profession of all: providing food for others. These qualities and circumstances all contributed to a superior moral development, a condition nurtured in the bosom of a tight-knit family and a godly community insulated from the evils that flourished in the city.[1]

Critics often complained that the agrarian myth masked such unpleasant aspects of rural life as backbreaking labour, material depravation, and social and cultural isolation. In the early twentieth century, rural leaders began to reshape agrarian thought, emphasizing how science and technology would transform farming into an efficient and profitable business that would enrich rural life.[2] Such a view better suited the progressive outlook of the boom years and the *Times* incorporated it into its boosterism while retaining traces of traditional agrarian idealism. In reverting to the older mythology, the paper seemed to take a step backward, much as the community itself took a step backward after the heady expansion of the boom.

But the *Times* did not fully adopt traditional idealism. It sometimes presented ideas about the positive influence of agriculture on the individual, noting on 2 July 1936 that a child raised on the land "never goes very far wrong later in life." More often, the *Times* focused on the virtue of small communities generally for it needed to incorporate country towns into the mythology. On 21 May 1936 an editorial argued that in a world full of scheming national leaders and warmongers full of "hate, fear, distrust, and avarice...the only rest and security comes from...the little community," where kindly people lived at peace and treated each other with understanding and compassion. "There is less snobbishness and unjustness in the smaller places," argued the *Times* on 23 August 1917. "In the larger centers...people get the opportunity to avoid those they do not want to meet.... In the country and small towns you are always meeting everyone else. You can't dodge." Since small numbers forced people to mix, they soon discovered each other's finer qualities. An intimate knowledge of one's neighbours also led to a greater understanding of their problems and an enhanced capacity for compassion. "There is perhaps no sphere of life in which the essential kindliness of human beings is so evident as in a rural neighbourhood," wrote the *Times* on 2 April 1936.

Other benefits flowed from the intimacy of small places. In a rare admission that city department stores might offer cheap prices by virtue of some ruthless efficiency, the *Times* defended the small town shop for its friendly treatment of customers as individuals, which made shopping a pleasant social event instead of a mercenary commercial exchange.[3] Small places also displayed more community spirit. A person could participate in local projects and take pride in seeing the results of his efforts immediately, but the impersonal city obliterated the contribution of the individual. "Men in small towns know what they have accomplished," the Times observed on 20 January 1927, "those who live in large cities have to guess at what they have done."

People in small places also developed a superior intellect. On 20 August 1926 the Times reprinted an article by the prominent author, Bruce Hutchison, about a worldly man who decided to settle in a small community instead of a great city. His reason? The local people surpassed the city folk in intelligence and awareness. The urbanite knew of nothing beyond his big city and narrow-mindedly considered it the whole universe, whereas the small-towner remained acutely aware of the wider world. Far from a crippling handicap, rural solitude actually sharpened the mind. On 24 May 1928 the Times noted that city people seldom saw the stars at nights because of the interference of smoke and lights. As a consequence, no sense of awe stimulated the urban imagination. "Can it be entirely accident that the birthplaces of great ideas have been so largely spots whose skies are clear?" it asked.

As the foregoing examples suggest, the Times often demonstrated the virtue of rural and small town life through comparisons with cities. It also attacked them directly, as an example from 2 September 1920 reveals:

> The big city cares nothing for us. It will if it can pull our dollars away and lure our boys and girls into its whirlpool. Why not get over the idea that the bright future of Canada lies in the great cities? It does not. The future which lies in the cities is shopwork, smoked, dirty, and unclean. The true future lies in the country and in the little towns.

Readers of the Times contributed to these verbal assaults. The complaints of a local man visiting Chicago appeared in the paper on 5 January 1922. He especially disdained the great city's sharp class distinctions, its frantic pace, and its congestion and traffic: "There is crowding and confusion. I am witnessing the daily debauch—the indescribable cataclysm which, thank God, our town never sees." The Windy City received a further blast on 6 August 1925 when the Times published a letter from a resident who returned there after living in High River for twenty years. Within six months, he realized his great mistake. He so missed the beauty of the mountains and foothills, the town park with its bits of real wilderness, and the friendly neighbours, that he had to return.

The *Times* often combined its attacks on the cities with its commitment to agrarian political interests. On 5 February 1942 it reprinted an article from another publication entitled "Urban People Do Not Understand," which decried the fact that big cities had "a lot more to say about national policies than they ought to have." The article accused them of destroying rural communities by conspiring with politicians to suppress food prices.

The superiority of rural over urban life also found its parallel in comparing city dailies to country weeklies. Whereas the *Times* once regarded the daily as merely different from the weekly, it now regarded it as distinctly inferior. Its depiction of "the horrible and bloodcurdling events of the day's doing throughout the world is anything but elevating to the younger minds of the country, and instills in them the desires for adventure along unworthy lines," it declared on 12 March 1925. One phrase in an item borrowed from another publication so enamoured the *Times* that it appeared in the paper with only minor variations at least four times between 1924 and 1934: "Turning from the city newspapers to the rural exchange...is like stepping from the slums full of vile odors into an old-fashioned garden sweet with honeysuckle and the scent of perennial flowers."[4]

Many of the attacks on cities appeared as retaliatory responses to urban criticism of the country. After the publication of novelist Lewis Sinclair's *Main Street* in the United States in 1920, which portrayed small town life as narrow-minded, stifling, smug, and mean, social critics and humorists grew increasingly bold in their depiction of rural people as rubes, hicks, and hayseeds. Reporting on the infamous Scopes trial concerning the teaching of evolution in American schools, the journalist H.C. Mencken referred to the rural people of Tennessee as "morons," "hillbillies," "peasants," and "yokels."[5] The *Times* responded directly to urban insults on 27 October 1927:

> There has crept into Canadian parlance the phrase "small town stuff" which is generally spoken in contempt or derision. The words should have no place in the speech of the Dominion, and should certainly never be found in print. It is a meaningless phrase, which in its implications and associations contains a libel of the rural towns and villages of the country. As a matter of plain fact, people in small

towns, as a general rule, can give pointers to many city folk in honesty, integrity and moral rectitude.

The *Times* also defended rural life from the charge that it especially oppressed women. On 18 July 1929, it quoted writer Kathleen R. Strange: "I was never a great advocate of farm life till I came to Alberta," she admitted, but she soon found herself seduced by its big blue skies and fresh prairie breezes. Admittedly, the farm wife faced endless chores, but nonetheless possessed "the quiet satisfaction of knowing that one is doing something really worthwhile helping to produce food for a hungry world." As for the supposed superior social life of the urban woman, she argued that the city often burdened one with "an endless round of social functions, many of them painfully formal and uninteresting."

Moreover, rural women could now enjoy the conveniences of the city without suffering its disadvantages for new technology daily enriched farm life. As the *Times* often noted, gasoline tractors and other new machinery eliminated much gruelling labour in the field, while electricity, running water, and modern furnaces all lightened the burden of the farm wife. "There are no blessings of modern times which have so liberated the average housekeeper as gas and electricity," observed the *Times* on 21 November 1929, "They mark the difference between slavery and freedom." But while the town had been blessed with those new utilities, the countryside had not. In 1927 Calgary Power extended its transmission line into the countryside east of town, but only 24 farmers agreed to pay the $100 hookup fee.[6] Most of the rest continued to generate their own power with small, gasoline-operated units or with windmills, adequate for lighting but not for running appliances. As for indoor plumbing, less than ten percent of the district's farms enjoyed running water by 1931.[7]

Undaunted, the *Times* also pointed out how telephones and radios had eradicated rural isolation and loneliness, even though less than half of the district farms had acquired those amenities by 1931. In addition, motor vehicles provided quicker access to small towns, which, the *Times* assured farm folk, offered social and recreational facilities as good as those in any city. But although the great majority of district farms possessed a motor vehicle by 1931, poor roads, mechanical breakdowns, and icy winters continued to limit their usefulness.

ANY RURAL AREA COULD CLAIM the general virtues paraded in the *Times*, but the paper also argued that the High River district enjoyed advantages that far surpassed those of other small communities. Few places anywhere, it constantly reminded readers, offered such a variety of spectacular landscapes: mountains, foothills, plains, and rivers all graced the land. Whereas the *Times* once depicted the environment as a treasure-house of resources ripe for exploitation, it now praised its aesthetic qualities, the tranquil serenity it brought to its residents, and the pleasure it afforded the hiker, rider, fisherman, and hunter. As the *Times* observed on 21 June 1921, the English language almost failed to supply enough superlatives to describe the beauty: "Not far from us to the westward, the immortal old rock rising high above the valley of the Highwood, and veiled in the softening sheen of a summer sunset, presents a picture so thrillingly enchanting a word, a sentence, nor paragraph utterly fails to give faithful expression of our innermost emotions." The pastoral delight of foothill and plain received their due as well. "The countryside has never been more lovely than at present," the *Times* observed on 13 June 1940, "the blending shades of green on every side are beautiful beyond description...sleek cattle graze, and on every hand, the earth is giving of its fullness."

The town equalled its surroundings: the mountains could be viewed from its vistas, the river meandered through its boundaries, and cottonwood trees swayed in its floodplain. From early settlement, saplings had been transplanted throughout the town, providing it with treelined streets that few prairies towns could match. Relentlessly described as a "pretty little town" after the war, one J.P. Cummings supplied the *Times* with a poetic description on 20 July 1922:

> Lined with the bloom of many species of wild flowers, the road into town is smooth and good to travel upon and affords to the young life of our community an ideal lovers' lane. The people of High River

The children's playground in High River's idyllic park, c. 1918.
Museum of the Highwood 977-065-111.

fully recognize the almost celestial loveliness of their surroundings and each one of them is, in his or her own way, annually adding touches of artistry to his or her own little sphere so that nature...may be to a certain extent, rewarded for all the scenic blessings she has bestowed upon them.

Because it contributed to this idyllic vision, town beautification was one of the few enthusiasms of the booster era to reappear in leaner times. On 10 April 1930 the *Times* announced a new scheme by the Board of Trade to plant more trees and flowers.

Many of High River's bucolic wonders could be found in the expansive town park that had been created by a gift of land from rancher George Lane. The park nestled between the river and the business district under its canopy of giant cottonwoods. Over the years it offered an array of facilities that included outdoor kitchens and picnic tables, a swimming pool fed by the river, a softball diamond, playground equipment, and even an overnight camp ground, all maintained by a paid caretaker. Clubs and organizations could book the park for special events, and it often attracted groups from distant rural areas and even neighbouring towns. The Times praised it endlessly as the envy of every prairie community. "It is one of the most serene and beautiful recreation centers that one could imagine," it bragged on 19 July 1934, "The wealth of clover and fragrant flowers, the increasing number of birds, and the benign shade of the trees make it most restful."

On such occasions the park appeared as a wondrous asset, but it also existed because of the rebellious Highwood River. The park flooded almost every spring, even when the rest of the town did not. Its cottonwoods, so often praised as the envy of all treeless towns, incurred wrath every year in early summer when they clogged the air with white fluff. On 15 June 1939 the Times actually condemned the "obnoxious cottonwood" for generating a "perpetual snowstorm."

In spite of these drawbacks, the park also represented another category of advantages that vaulted High River above other small places: it offered an array of superior amenities and facilities. Thanks to them, a speaker at the Rotary Club insisted that "Our town stands head and shoulders over any other town in this province."[8] The Times frequently singled out particular examples for extended praise. On 13 June 1929 it devoted an entire editorial to the glories of the town's drinking water. It featured virtually all of High River's assets in the gala silver anniversary issue of 4 December 1930. The special issue duly reviewed the water works and sewage systems, the excellent electrical and natural gas service, the concrete sidewalks, the municipal hospital, and the superb schools. Half a dozen churches administered to the devout. As for social life, it listed dozens of clubs and organizations devoted to fraternity, service, recreation, and culture. The district's women need never experience loneliness, the Times wrote, since some 50 organizations existed for them alone. Many others catered to children. Residents could watch or play more than a dozen sports. Superior facilities included polo grounds, golf course, tennis courts, and a covered ice rink. The movie theatre (equipped for sound in 1929) brought the latest marvels of modern entertainment to the town, and for live performances, an excellent town band delighted the residents.

The *Times* once presented such lists as evidence of advancement to city stature, and as necessary incentives to lure new residents and investors. Now they provided evidence of the amenities and comforts available in the small town, and at a reasonable price. On 10 April 1924 the *Times* offered the local golf course as an example: "Ten times our cost per person would be considered little for the privilege of belonging to any city club where the game could be played and right here good playing conditions and pleasant surroundings are to be had for a minimum amount." In 1919 the *Times* began a five-year campaign to acquire a covered ice rink for the town, not because it would attract capital or stimulate employment, but for the joy it would bring the local community. Games played by the Flyers hockey club often received lengthy front page stories that praised the team, not for what it did to advertise the town, but for the entertainment it provided. "From start to finish the house rocked with excitement while the players on the ice staged the grimmest struggle of the season," reported the *Times* on 23 January 1930 of a game against the Drumheller Miners that attracted over 1,500 fans.

As for the sociability of High River, the *Times* ventured the opinion that the district possessed people even more friendly, more caring, and more charitable than those in other small places. "Probably there is no town whose citizens live together more amicably," proclaimed a *Times* editorial on 14 November 1929. The paper loved stories about the compassion of local residents. On 6 May 1926 it wrote about a farmer stuck in hospital with appendicitis, unable to complete his spring seeding. Fifteen neighbours swarmed his farm with seeders and horses and finished the job for him. In the district for less than a year, the sick man and his wife "...have met with nothing but kindness and active sympathy," noted the *Times*, and "they realize their good fortune in locating in a community where the true Christian spirit of olden days still holds good."

The community often extended its goodwill in organized fashion. On 27 December 1934 the *Times* recorded how the town council provided those on relief with Christmas extras such as candy, nuts, and oranges. Meanwhile, the local Sunshine Club provided help for the poor not actually on relief. A local rancher donated beef and others provided toys. Exasperated by its inability to fully describe the charitable qualities of the local residents, on

21 July 1921 the *Times* simply called them "as humanly human as anyone could wish them to be."

As High River learned to celebrate its small town status, it eventually looked back on its ambition to became a great city with amusement. The *Times* even joked about the old booster campaigns, as on 10 November 1949 when it carried reports about a promoter named Dr. Spoofingk who planned to start a post hole factory and hoped to develop steel wool from hydraulic rams. He also intended to sell Rocky Mountain echoes.

BUT HIGH RIVER and the *Times* did not entirely abandon their booster impulses. Indeed, the new focus on rural and small virtues promised to propel economic development in a whole new direction. Tourism depended not on exploiting resources to create a great city, but on preserving both nature and small town ambiance. Formerly associated with elite travel by ship or train to expensive resort hotels, tourism became more democratic and flexible as the middle class expanded, grew more prosperous, and acquired more free time—and more automobiles. The car provided access to new destinations, especially in wilderness areas, and it could transport camping equipment.[9]

High River seemed to first grasp the potential for tourism when the *Times* noted on 26 July 1917 that many organizations from outlying districts and neighbouring towns drove to the civic park to hold group picnics. The *Times* soon touted the other attractions in the area. "The foothill country west of High River has been favoured with everything that nature could provide to make it one of the most desirable tourist resorts in Canada," it argued in an editorial on 8 May 1924. The spectacular scenery and invigorating air invited endless opportunities for hiking, riding, fishing, and hunting, or simply relaxing in contemplation of nature.

High River also promised the tourist an opportunity to observe its fabled ranchlands. In presenting ranching as an attraction, the *Times* elected to emphasize its genteel, elite traditions, both historic and contemporary, rather than a rambunctious wild west. A 1927 pamphlet issued by the *Times* for the benefit of touring English journalists referred to the foothills as the

The arrival of the Prince of Wales, 1919. Glenbow Archives NB-16-35.

"Aristocratic Ranching Country."[10] The legitimacy of such a claim rested on the fact that actual patricians owned ranches in the area: the French count Barle de Foras, the Italian aristocrat George Pocaterra, and the British gentlefolk Captain and Lady Wyndham. These ranchers often hosted visiting gentry. On 14 April 1921 the *Times* recorded visits by the Duke and Duchess of Devonshire, Lord and Lady Cavendish, and Captain Butler. Some of the Canadian ranch owners, like Senator Dan Riley, also exuded aristocratic qualities. The American Frazier Hunt represented a different sort of elite, but he too contributed to the genteel ranch image. The New York writer and editor of *Cosmopolitan Magazine* bought the small Eden Valley Ranch in 1926 as a summer retreat, an event that the *Times* believed would bring "world-wide publicity" to High River and district.[11]

But the most compelling evidence of aristocratic ranching arrived in dramatic fashion when Edward, Prince of Wales and heir to the British throne, decided to buy a ranch in the district. His visit to the Bar U in 1919 so impressed him that he asked his host, George Lane, to inquire about available properties. On behalf of the Prince, Lane secured the nearby Bedingfield Ranch. The young heir gave it a new name, the E.P. Ranch, which stood for Edward, Prince. He planned to use it both as a secluded retreat and as a functional business. He hired a manager and stocked the range with purebred Shorthorn cattle.[12] Edward generated tremendous excitement in the district, and in the pages of the *Times* where stories about his impending visit appeared for weeks prior to his appearance. The town decorated the streets and scheduled a tree planting ceremony to commemorate the occasion. Reporting on his arrival in the 18 September issue, the *Times* generously praised the Prince for a litany of sterling qualities. When it learned about his ranch purchase, it immediately grasped the significance for tourism. "High River will now be on the map," it announced on 9 October and the following week it predicted that "great things are bound to follow in this district."

The ranch would draw many curious tourists to the district, but the greatest numbers could be expected when the Prince was in residence, especially since a train of international reporters always followed in his wake. But Edward forced the *Times* and the community to wait in painful anticipation for four years before he visited again. Speculation about his coming appeared in the *Times* for weeks and when the grand day arrived 1,500 people waited at the train station to greet him. They grieved when he left three weeks later to fulfill other commitments, but the *Times* consoled them on 4 October 1923 with the thought that "we know he would have preferred to live the simple life on his ranch." Still, the *Times* predicted on 11 October that his short visit would bring results: "High River, so much in the public eye on account of the Prince of Wales having his Canadian residence here, will be visited by many Americans next year." Visitors did indeed arrive to see the ranch and the nearby Bar U, and although the E.P. insisted that it was a working enterprise and "in no sense a show place or Dude Ranch," it nonetheless issued a souvenir booklet, catered to touring groups, and even allowed curious individuals to roam about providing they caused no damage, closed all gates, and left no garbage. A Canadian Pacific official reported to his superiors that the E.P. often suffered financial losses partly because of the "extra cost involved in keeping the ranch 'dressed up' as a showplace."[13]

The Prince disappointed the community again and again with the infrequency and brevity of his appearances. His visits in 1924 and 1927 together totalled less than seven days.[14] Nonetheless, the *Times* decided to regard him as a local resident and included much international news about him.

The 28 May 1931 issue reported on a speech he delivered concerning British trade with South America. Excitement soared when the death of the ruling monarch thrust him to the status of King Edward VIII in 1936, but the exhilaration soon died. The community reeled in stunned disbelief when he abdicated the throne later that year to marry the twice-divorced American commoner, Mrs. Wallis Simpson. Although he was demoted to the title of Duke of Windsor, the *Times* felt compelled to defend his honour from the many attacks he now faced. When the controversial couple finally visited the E.P. Ranch in 1941 after Edward's fourteen-year absence, the *Times* praised him unconditionally. "In this practical and candid land," it declared on 25 September, "we still place high valuation on what a man is, than on what his ancestry and titles may be." It then described Edward as a man of "charm, simplicity and great friendliness...direct, natural and considerate of everyone," a man possessing "a warmth of understanding" who most enjoyed "not those of wealth and power, but plain people."

The desire to promote an aristocratic ranch tradition also appeared in smaller ways, including the revival of polo in 1927. Once the dominant sport of the ranch country, the Great War had led to its suspension and to the death of several top players. After the armistice no one revived it, and although riders of various social origins had played polo, the game still conveyed a sense of aristocracy. The *Times* played an active role in its resurrection and continued to devote considerable attention to the sport, especially when the local team won provincial championships.

Tourists could only glimpse at the aristocratic ranches, but they could immerse themselves fully in the western experience by visiting High River's dude ranches. The idea of such retreats originated in the late nineteenth century when hunters who visited the American west began paying ranchers for lodgings. Finding the extra cash attractive, some ranchers began to solicit paying guests.[15] British hunters often stayed at the Bar U in the 1890s, but the first ranch in the High River district specifically designed for the tourist trade originated with Guy Weadick. Originally from Rochester, New York, Weadick worked for Buffalo Bill Cody and other promoters of Wild West shows, mainly as a trick roper. He organized and promoted the first Calgary Stampede in 1912. Weadick met and married a champion cowgirl roper who performed under the exotic stage name of Flores LaDue. In 1920 the couple bought a ranch 35 miles west of High River with the express purpose of creating a resort. They named it The Stampede Ranch, but often referred to it as the T.S. They planned to operate it each summer and spend winters on the American vaudeville circuit performing their roping act.[16] The *Times* immediately praised the new endeavour. "The going and coming of tourists and other benefits of the enterprise cannot but be an advantage to the town," it observed on 4 March 1920.

The second dude ranch in the area emerged from an established enterprise. Born in Italy to an aristocratic family involved in the textile business, George Pocaterra became fascinated with stories about the western frontier while studying the wool business in England. Arriving in High River in 1905, he worked as a cowboy to learn about livestock and then launched the Buffalo Head Ranch to breed horses. By 27 July 1922 he began placing advertisements in the *Times* for a campground at the ranch, and in 1924 the tourist department of Canadian Pacific Railway approached him about operating a dude ranch. According to Pocaterra, the company also talked to Weadick, offering to supply both with tourists. American railways made similar arrangements with dude ranches in the United States during the 1920s.[17] Although Pocaterra sold the Buffalo Head in 1933 when pressing family business called him back to Italy, it continued as a dude ranch under the ownership of R.M. Patterson. During the 1930s, two other ranches accepted guests: the Round T and the Mount Burke.

The dude ranches mostly attracted wealthy guests from big cities in eastern North America who learned about the resorts from Canadian Pacific publicity, from brochures supplied by the ranches themselves, and from word-of-mouth referrals.[18] The Stampede Ranch especially benefited from the publicity its guests could generate since many of them managed and edited eastern newspapers and magazines, and they sometimes wrote articles about the ranch for their publications.[19] The brochures promised guests an exciting experience in the heart of the world's most magnificent scenery. The Round T Ranch guaranteed them a trip "through primeval grandeur to which few white men have penetrated...to the top of the world from which they can look down upon other mountain peaks, silvery waterfalls, deep ravines, dark gorges...and quiet valleys."[20] Scenes of such splendour provided the backdrop for exhilarating experiences like mountain climbing, hiking,

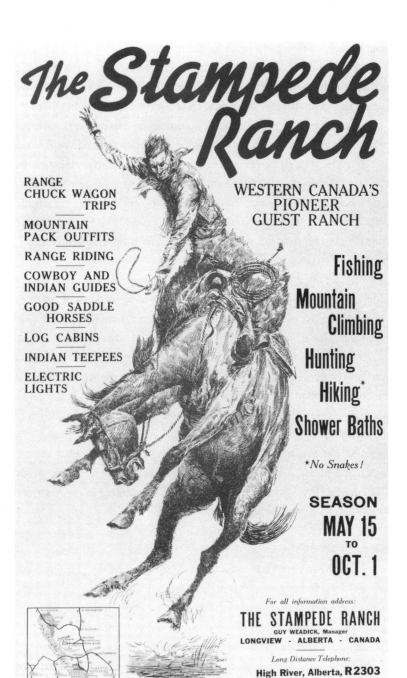

Dude ranch poster. Clark Family Papers.

trout fishing, and big game hunting. The highlight of a visit to a dude ranch was the promise of horseback riding and overnight camping trips. On these adventures, the Stampede Ranch also dispatched real chuckwagons to serve meals. The ranch offered guests their choice of cowboy or Indian guides.[21]

The ranches also provided the opportunity to observe real cowboys performing actual work, and to witness exhibitions of their skill with horse and rope. Guests could also assist in the ranch work and many relished the opportunity to do so. R.M. Patterson, the second owner of the Buffalo Head, remembered that "What pleased the dudes best was to be given something definite to do."[22] When the Round T accepted a contingent of teenage boys from Chicago for five weeks, it promised them hard work as well as adventure.[23]

Guests of the dude ranches could take advantage of as many or as few activities as they wished. Some preferred to loaf about, reading and napping. No doubt familiar with the stuffy formality of many eastern resorts, Weadick emphasized the relaxed social atmosphere: " a REAL place to spend a REAL holiday, where you will not be pestered with uniformed flunkeys [sic]—if you want to be yourself and do not have to 'dress for dinner'—where you can lounge around and be a human being."[24] While guests might wish to rough it on overnight trail rides, the brochures assured them of comforts at the ranch itself. Regardless of whether they elected to stay in cabins or "genuine Indian painted tepees," the Stampede Ranch provided electric lights, and tubs and showers with hot water. High River's dude ranches also advertised "No Snakes," something their competitors in the American southwest could not promise.

The dude ranches remained popular throughout the interwar period. With cattle worth almost nothing in the Great Depression, Patterson relied heavily on the tourist trade since "financially, it carried the place through several very difficult years."[25] Dude ranches remained in operation in the High River district during the 1940s and 1950s, but ironically, the return of prosperity hurt the business. Fewer people vacationed during the war years, and thereafter fashions in elite tourism changed.

While the dude ranches advertised fishing and hunting in season, those activities also emerged as special attractions in their own right. On 25 April

1929 the *Times* quoted a local speaker who proclaimed "the exceptionally fine location of High River, from the standpoint of the sportsman." This fine location meant access to a variety of gaming environments. The mountains and high foothills offered big prey like bears, cougars, wolves, wild sheep and goats, moose, elk, and deer. The prairie offered game birds. Frank Lake and other sloughs attracted plenty of ducks and geese, while the solid ground featured upland birds like the native grouse or prairie chicken, the Hungarian partridge (introduced in 1906), and the ring-neck pheasant (introduced in 1920). The Highwood River and its tributaries ran through this varied terrain and afforded excellent trout fishing.[26]

Hunting and fishing did lead to problems, most notably the depletion of the very game used to lure tourists. Residents of the area began complaining as early as the 1910s when massive agricultural settlement had already destroyed many habitats and introduced many more local hunters. Automobiles and roads increased the accessibility of the district to outside predators, especially from Calgary. Alarm over the depletion of river trout led to the creation of a protective organization in 1921 that evolved into the High River Fish and Game Association. It promoted provincial laws concerning closed seasons, the acquisition of licenses, and limits on the catch. It protected the smaller fish by securing the closure of the Highwood's tributaries for many years. It launched restocking programs for trout and for upland birds.[27] Reviewing these activities on 4 October 1934, the *Times* noted the critical importance of maintaining "the abundance of fish and game" in order to draw tourists. A curious logic propelled local conservation: because of fishing and hunting, stocks grew depleted, which required conservation measures in order to attract tourists who would again deplete the stocks.

The sporting tourists caused other problems. Many careless hunters shot in the direction of farm buildings or accidentally killed domestic animals. They left cattle gates open, broke fences, dumped garbage, trampled crops, and started fires. The *Times* observed on 9 September 1920 that many farmers and ranchers had posted "No Trespassing" and "No Hunting" signs, and an editorial on 6 September 1923 urged all sportsmen to seek permission before wandering onto private property. While the community continued to promote hunting and fishing as a tourist attraction, many residents preferred that they not be publicized. They believed such activity should be reserved for locals, a special reward for those who had chosen an idyllic rural life over an artificial urban existence.

Tourists could not be attracted to all the wonders of the district without providing essential facilities, for the dude ranches accommodated relatively small numbers of wealthy guests. The local hotels continued to advertise in the *Times*, but the paper also encouraged the building of campgrounds, and it applauded the town council on 3 August 1922 for offering free campsites. On 3 July 1930 it praised a private facility that provided cabins, tent grounds, a camp kitchen, electricity, and running water. Much the newspaper's relentless campaign for improved roads in the interwar era focused on tourism. Visitors reached the upper Highwood valley by bouncing over the rough trails opened by lumbering and coal mining companies. The *Times* wanted them graded, gravelled, extended, and posted with road signs indicating destinations and points of interest. The paper criticized senior governments for their refusal to build mountain roads and campgrounds outside of the national parks.[28] When the province decided to build a road to the Kananaskis Lakes from the north instead of through High River and the Highwood pass, the *Times* condemned the project on 16 June 1921 for its failure to take advantage of "unrivaled scenic perfection."

ATTRACTING TOURISTS REQUIRED ADVERTISING. The *Times* urged municipal governments, private organizations, and local businesses to issue tourist pamphlets. This suggestion raised all the same problems of cost and distribution that had plagued the old booster campaign. Many places joined the tourist craze after the Great War, and those in the American West offered the same attractions as High River.[29] All clamoured for attention, but the fiercest competitor lay close at hand. Banff benefited from the mighty publicity arm of the Canadian Pacific Railway, which promoted its own substantial investment in the transporting, lodging, feeding, and guiding of tourists.[30] Banff also featured a greater variety of environmental attractions, including the hot sulphur waters favoured by bathers. The railway provided access to Banff throughout the year, and by the 1930s skiing and winter festivals began to grow in importance. High River's mountain country closed down completely with the first winter snows.

Even though the Times urged travelers to avoid the overrated attractions of Banff in favour of High River, the realization grew that the best hope for capturing tourists was to sidetrack motorists headed towards that famous destination. If roadside signs induced them to stop in town, they could be directed to the tranquil campground in the park or to attractive tourist cabins. Once there, they might be persuaded to explore the Highwood valley and the ranch country before continuing their journeys.[31] If High River extended its fabled small town friendliness and kindness, they might return another time. Such a strategy led the town to align itself with competitors in order to become a stop in a tourist loop. On 1 September 1921, the Times approved a plan by the Calgary Good Roads Association to designate a series of highways and roads from Los Angeles to Lake Louise as the "Banff-Grand Canyon Road," and to identify it with road markers. Two years later, High River agreed to join the Tourist Association of Southeastern British Columbia and Southern Alberta, which collected fees from member towns for including them in its pamphlets and advertising.[32] When two new highways opened, one linking Lake Louise to Jasper and the other connecting eastern British Columbia to Vancouver, a Times editorial on 18 April 1940 predicted that more cars would pass on route to the newly-opened territories, affording opportunities to sidetrack even more motorists.

As it struggled to find ways of alerting tourists to the marvels of High River, the Times discovered a powerful new ally that would publicize the district without costing the community a dime: the movie industry. Using his show business connections, Guy Weadick promoted High River as an ideal location for shooting outdoor adventure films. He invited some Hollywood executives and the famous cowboy actor Hoot Gibson to the Stampede Ranch in 1925, and persuaded them to film *Chip of the Flying U* at the ranch and in High River. The event seemed to presage a shining future, for in 1926 another film crew arrived to shoot an adventure called *The Canadian*. Weadick hatched other schemes. He brought western actor Neil Hart to the Stampede Ranch in 1927 to discuss the creation of a "studio ranch" for the filming of westerns. The next year Weadick became the manager of a Calgary company named British Canadian Pictures that aimed to take advantage of

Hollywood star Hoot Gibson at the High River station, 1925. *Glenbow Archives NA–2711–13.*

recent British government restrictions on the showing of foreign films by providing more "British" fare. The filming of *His Destiny*, a tale of ranching "as it is today," took place at various district locations including the Stampede and E.P. ranches.[33]

Somewhat surprisingly, moviemaking in the district ended abruptly in spite of Weadick's continued exertions, and even his appointment as "technical manager" for a small Hollywood studio in 1937 failed to produce results. No one filmed another movie at High River until 1946 when Britain's Rank studio shot scenes for a film entitled *Harvest*. Soon after, High River, Banff, and Calgary served as locations for a major Hollywood film released in 1948 as *North West Stampede*, the story of a lady rancher who competed in rodeo events.[34] Once more, Hollywood proved herself a fickle mistress, for another long hiatus ensued. In spite of many casual inquires about filming possibilities, decades passed before she returned again. In any event, it seems unlikely that the movies did much for High River tourism aside from providing some short-lived spending during actual filming. If any tourists arrived because the scenery in a movie had captivated them, the fact went unrecorded.

Struggle though it might, High River never attracted the tourist trade it hoped for in spite of the genuine splendour of its hinterland. The Times conceded on 28 August 1930 that most visitors to the district came from Calgary and other parts of southern Alberta, and that most of them stayed only for the day. The owner of a local automobile camp reported to the Times on 14 July 1932 that many of the guests at his establishment also came from Alberta, but the strategy of capturing roving sightseers worked to a limited extent. "Some stay overnight," he reported, "others linger a day or two, and Ontario cars have stayed on for a full week, touring the district." Even though such visitors only appeared during the brief summer season, tourism contributed a little to the diversity and stability of the local economy.

At the same time, tourism also posed a dilemma. A recent history argues that successful tourist centres in the American West entered into a devil's bargain: tourism stimulated the local economy, but it also spoiled the very attractions that drew visitors.[35] High River faced this problem too, for its guests committed many of the same infractions as careless hunters. They caused fires, damaged property, left cattle gates open, and dumped garbage, complaints all reviewed in a Times editorial on 6 August 1931. George Pocaterra, the dude ranch owner who profited directly from tourists, nonetheless criticized them in a letter to the editor on 9 July 1925 for trampling and picking the delicate flowers of the high foothills.

Regardless of the problems, High River and the Times would continue to regard tourism as an important facet of the economic future. But it would undergo an important modification when developments during and after World War II launched the community into a new era.

PART III

1940 to 1966

Overleaf: Mountainous area west of High River. Glenbow Archives NA–3471–54.

8 THE RETURN OF PROSPERITY

ALTHOUGH IT ENGENDERED NEW HORRORS, World War II released the world and the High River district from the grip of the Great Depression. It did not do so immediately since it required several years to eliminate stockpiles of existing goods and to retool for the military market. The government even introduced various measures to discourage wheat cultivation until the great backlog had dissipated. Wheat acreage did not increase again until 1944, but plentiful rainfall proved more important than rising prices, and High River farmers reaped high yields throughout the war. Production difficulties arose when the government rationed tires and fuel, and farmers also scrambled to obtain new implements and machinery parts. They could not afford to replace worn-out equipment during the 1930s, and during the war manufacturers turned to the production of military vehicles. A reform that farmers had fought long and unsuccessfully to realize suddenly arrived as a necessary war measure. In 1944, the Dominion government lifted tariffs on imported agricultural machinery.[1]

Ranchers also struggled to enjoy the full benefits of rebounding markets. Tariffs imposed by the American government had limited sales in the past, but in 1942 the Canadian government banned exports to the United States, fearing beef shortages in Canada and Britain. The ranchers complained, but the government refused to lift the ban until 1948. So while World War II

Airplanes at the High River training school. Glenbow Archives NA-4943-5.

provided welcome relief from the Depression, it did not replicate the agricultural boom that the district experienced in World War I.

The town of High River benefited not only from the agricultural revival, but also from direct military spending. From the outbreak of war, unemployed men found food and shelter in the armed services. By 11 March 1943 the Times could count 428 recruits from High River and district, including 21 women. More significant from an economic perspective, High River became a military centre under the British Commonwealth Air Training Agreement. The Canadian government committed itself to training pilots from Commonwealth nations and ultimately established 105 bases, seventeen of them in Alberta. Although High River already possessed the airport abandoned by the Canada Air Board in 1931, the government initially bypassed it as a site for a training base. Meanwhile, the Number 5 Elementary Flying Training School at Lethbridge discovered that high winds often interfered with its operations. Senator Dan Riley worked politically to ensure the relocation of the school to High River in 1941. Like most Commonwealth training centres, a private company, the Calgary Aero Club, actually ran the school under contract.[2]

The airbase represented an enormous boon to the depression-ravaged town since it involved the construction of over twenty new hangars and other buildings to accommodate as many as 500 students, instructors, and support staff. The base provided quarters for single people, but some 50 families associated with the project required housing in the town.[3] The Times immediately perceived how the construction work, the added population, and an annual payroll over $500,000 would rejuvenate the economy, but it also cautioned local businesses on 24 July 1941 to exercise restraint and not to "gouge" the school. The opportunity to do so did not last long, as the government announced the closing of the base three years later. The Times howled a protest on 26 October 1944, but had resigned itself to the inevitable when it reported the actual closure on 16 November.

Other war-related news in the Times followed the precedents established during World War I. The government again censored all news from the front, but predictably the Times never attempted to compete with the dailies for military information. It even presented its refusal to do so as a positive virtue. "In these days of war and havoc in the larger world," observed an editorial on 28 November 1940, "it seems more important than ever that the weekly paper center on normal progress within its own small sphere." As during World War I, the paper reported on the economic impact of the war locally, including stories on rationing, labour and machinery shortages, and price and wage fixing. It also recorded with pride the activities of local wartime charities and the success of victory bond sales. Once again, the Times delayed rendering an opinion on conscription for overseas duty. When the government finally held a plebiscite to ask Canadians if they would release it from its promise not to impose conscription, the Times supported the "yes," position, but did so confident that its readers overwhelmingly agreed. The Times guessed accurately for 87 percent of those voting in High River district subsequently cast "yes" votes.[4]

AFTER THE WAR, the community and the nation braced for a return to the Great Depression. Hard times had struck after World War I and almost everyone thought that the collapse of wartime demand would again produce a similar result. But only a small slump occurred before the longest era of economic growth in Canadian history ensued. Punctuated only by brief recessions, the boom persisted over the next quarter of a century, and in Alberta it continued through the 1970s. A combination of ingredients fuelled this expansion: increased world trade, the discovery of new resources, technological innovation at an unprecedented rate, huge population increases, and rising standards of living. The boom originated with pent-up demand that developed during the Depression when people could not afford to spend. During the war, they began earning again but found few civilian goods to buy. Everything went into war production, so people bought Victory Bonds instead. After the war, they spent. The onset of the cold war also meant that military spending did not entirely collapse, and considerable money went towards the rebuilding of Europe.

The new economy spurred major changes in wheat farming. A growing global population consumed more bread and in the early 1960s, important new markets opened in China and the Soviet Union. Conversely, rising standards of living in the industrial world meant people ate less bread per capita. Torn between these conflicting trends, wheat prices continued to fluctuate, but on balance they failed to keep pace with inflation. Farmers responded to lower real prices by greatly increasing productivity. A new technological revolution swept through the wheat fields. Tractors, grain trucks, and combine harvesters had evolved into practical machines by the late 1920s, but farmers could not afford them in the 1930s, and during the war manufacturers did not make them. After 1945, farmers bought them in quantity. By 1951 the High River district averaged one truck and 1.3 tractors per farm.[5] Workhorses virtually disappeared, along with all the labour required to care for them. Combines eliminated threshing machines and the need for big harvest crews.[6]

As the size, capability, and quality of farm machinery continued its rapid improvement, farmers could work more and more acres with less labour. The half-section farms that prevailed by World War I gave way to units of one or two or even more sections after World War II. Aging farmers with small operations and no heirs willing to carry on sold out to expanding neighbours. As farms grew larger, the total number of farms declined and the rural population fell. The area covered by the census subdivision of Foothills 31, which surrounded the town of High River, reached its maximum rural population in 1941 with 10,279 people. By 1966 the population had dropped to 6,455.[7]

Farmers also performed more work thanks to efficient and portable gasoline engines and rural electrification. The construction of transmission lines into the countryside made ample power available to farmers by the late 1920s, but few availed themselves of it before the Depression rendered it an expensive luxury. After the war, many farmers formed local co-operatives to acquire power lines. On 25 February 1954 the *Times* reported that the construction of 500 miles of new lines had added 502 local farmers to the electrical grid. By the end of the decade, power lines serviced over 90 percent of the farms in the High River district.[8] Once connected, farmers could abandon the old windmill and gasoline-powered generators that had supplied them with dull lighting. Ample electricity now existed to run power tools and welders; farmers repaired their own machinery and country blacksmiths disappeared. In the (often newly-built) farmhouse, electricity now made it possible to acquire those appliances that been available in town since the late 1920s.

Farm productivity did not increase only because of the substitution of machinery for labour. Yields also improved. Although they still varied with dry and wet cycles, drought no longer caused as much harm as in the past. During the 1930s, the Dominion government's Prairie Farm Rehabilitation Administration began publicizing ways to prevent soil drifting. It advised farmers to stop using ploughs, and to quit cultivating deeply and frequently. It also advocated new implements that cut weed roots with little disturbance to the soil surface, urged farmers not to burn stubble after harvest, and suggested strip farming. The PFRA also encouraged planting the drought-resistant Siberian caragana to create shelterbelts. These measures all helped farmers retain topsoil and moisture in dry years.[9] Yields also improved with the use of chemical fertilizers, insecticides, and herbicides. Scientific research created superior strains of high-yielding grain that better resisted insects and disease, and it discovered better production techniques.[10]

Farmers also lessened their reliance on wheat. Some raised more rye or barley to supply distilleries and breweries, while others raised more flax and rapeseed (both valued for their oil content). Others turned to vegetables, eggs, or dairy products. In the past, farmers had raised such fragile and perishable commodities largely for their own use, for commercial production demanded a large urban market close at hand. The explosive growth of Calgary provided that market, while reliable trucks and greatly improved roads ensured quick and safe delivery. Farmers also raised more livestock. While urbanites ate less bread as their standard of living rose, they compensated by eating more meat. Some farmers in the High River district produced more hogs, sheep, and poultry, but beef cattle towered above them all in importance. Local ranchers had long specialized in this business, but their role changed after World War II as a new symbiotic relationship with farmers developed. Instead of raising cattle to maturity, ranchers focused on breeding and sold calves or yearlings to farmers who fattened them in feed lots with their own hay and grain. Many farmers had been unable to keep much livestock in the past due to water shortages, but the Prairie Farm Rehabilitation Administration assisted in building small dams and dugouts on farms to capture runoff. High River farmers quickly developed expertise in fattening cattle and on 6 December 1956 the *Times* reported that a troop of agricultural educators and scientists were touring feedlots in the district.

As with grain, scientific developments revolutionized stockraising. Artificial insemination, veterinarian medicine, food supplements, and more efficient feeding programs all enhanced production. Some ranchers introduced European breeds like Charolais and crossed them with the smaller British cattle to produce larger calves. Auction sales, held regularly in High River after 1958, provided the means to sell cattle to Calgary meat packing plants. From there, many carcasses moved considerable distances, especially after 1955 when new meat inspection standards helped secure markets in other provinces and in the United States.[11]

Some ranches also continued to breed horses—not the heavy work horses of the past—but light horses for recreational markets in racing, jumping, rodeo, and pleasure riding. Some ranchers still used horses to work with livestock, but beyond the confines of the fenced pasture, cattle now moved by truck. Tractors also invaded the ranches; they cultivated fields and pulled mechanical hay balers and power hay sweeps. Even so, the horse remained a powerful symbol of local ranching tradition, and High River continued to host many horse shows and the meetings of horsemen's associations.[12]

While farmers and ranchers did not receive the massive subsidies awarded to American and European agriculture, they still benefited from a greater array of government programs, including better hail and crop insurance schemes, low-cost loans for improvements, long-term export agreements with other nations, and expanded agricultural research. As farming became more complex and capital intensive, it demanded more financial expertise and more business talent in general. Although some of the larger farms organized themselves into corporations, largely for tax reasons, no "death of the family farm" resulted. Virtually all farms and ranches in the High River district remained family-owned and operated regardless of their legal structure.

Family ownership actually increased after the Burns Corporation decided to sell the biggest ranch of all, the historic Bar U. Financial problems at the ranch did not motivate the sale; indeed, its records clearly illustrate the recovery from the Depression. After a loss in 1937, the Bar U turned a small profit in 1938, and profits grew almost every year until 1948 when it generated a profit of $239,000.[13] The Burns Company decided to sell the ranch because of a strategic decision to invest more capital in meatpacking plants and other ventures. It tried to sell the Bar U throughout the 1940s but its huge size discouraged buyers, so in 1950 it split the property into smaller units and sold them successfully, mostly to local High River cattlemen. The giant had disappeared, but some High River ranches still kept over 5,000 head, while the tiniest kept only 200.[14]

MASSIVE CHANGES in agriculture bestowed mixed blessings on the town of High River. The rural population of its hinterland kept declining, but each farm required more goods and services than in the past. High River became an important centre for the sale, servicing, and repair of automobiles, trucks, and farm machinery, as well as for the provision of bulk petroleum, chemicals, and other farm supplies. No less than 32 such businesses existed

Modern housing in a new subdivision, 1960. *Museum of the Highwood 989–031–595.*

in 1963, including the largest and most successful enterprises in town.[15] High River also grew as a retirement centre for rural people who transferred their farms and ranches to sons, or sold out to expanding operators. Often flush with money, they built new homes in town, usually three-bedroom bungalows in the popular new "ranch" style. These retired farmers were largely responsible for the periodic bursts of new home construction first noted in the *Times* in 1946.[16]

High River also continued to thrive as an administrative centre for medical, educational, and municipal services. It had firmly established itself as the district headquarters for these functions during the interwar years, and they underwent significant expansion in the post-war era. The baby boom created more school children and society expected them to spend more years in school. High River had served as headquarters for the sprawling Foothills School Division since its creation in 1938. The Division extended its geographical reach after the war and by 1959 administered 3,060 students, 130 teachers, nineteen schools, and a huge fleet of buses.[17] The schools in High River did not join the Foothills Division until 1968, but the town remained a favoured destination for the growing number of rural students who wished to complete high school, and reliable buses and improved roads provided the means to attract more of them. In an editorial on 4 October 1945 the *Times* initiated a campaign for a centralized high school that would offer "educational advantages...to the children of the district." The new school opened in 1954.

The postwar years also witnessed the expansion of High River's medical institutions. The Foothills Health Unit spanned 1,800 square miles and served 14,000 people after its creation in 1931. By 1955 it serviced 3,500 square miles and 21,500 people. In 1941, the district hospital could treat 43 patients, but after a major addition in 1959, it accommodated 64.[18] A small private nursing home opened in High River in 1956, but the creation of a rural nursing district by the province led to expectations that a major facility would soon be built. When the town of Vulcan received the nursing home, a *Times* editorial on 15 February 1962 condemned the location, but High River consoled itself with the provincial government's decision in 1960 to build a senior's residence that housed 50 people.[19]

High River had also become the headquarters for the newly formed rural municipality of Highwood in 1944. Further annexations and mergers in 1951 and 1954 created the sprawling Municipal District of Foothills. Like all levels of government after World War II, its functions continually expanded. By 1961, its budget had reached $1.2 million and by 1966 it sported no less than eighteen committees dealing with matters ranging from civil defence to welfare cases and rural zoning.[20]

The post-war expansion of public functions contributed to High River's population and payroll, a phenomenon that occurred in many towns fortunate enough to become administrative capitals for large rural areas. By 1961, public institutions accounted for 22 percent of all employment in Alberta towns with populations between 1,000 and 2,500, a proportion that rose to 28 percent by 1971.[21] The economic value of public institutions did not escape the attention of High River's business community and the town often lobbied for more of them. On 23 September 1954, the *Times* reported the unsuccessful efforts of the council and the Chamber of Commerce to secure a Dominion penitentiary, a facility that most urban neighbourhoods refused to accept. On 8 November 1962 a *Times* editorial also urged the provincial government to establish a veterinary college at High River since "we are at the center of the great Foothills cattle lands." But while some towns benefited from the decentralization of senior government agencies and functions, High River did not.

Two sociologists who examined prairie communities in the 1960s concluded that 50 urban centres in Alberta offered enough services to deserve the designation "farm city," and they included High River in that number.[22] These "farm cities" consolidated their position at the expense of smaller places that increasingly lost economic functions. The prairie village often retained little more than its grain elevators, a service station, and a convenience store. Most of them survived largely as residential and social centres that provided rural neighbourhoods with elementary schools, churches, and meeting halls.[23] Villages within the *Times* reporting area reflected these regional developments. Cayley held 140 people in 1946 but only 133 in 1966. Over the same period, the population of Blackie dropped from 222 to 156. Longview, a village that survived the demise of the Turner Valley oil industry, retained 173 souls in 1966. As unincorporated hamlets, Aldersyde and Brant did not benefit from an official census, but they too survived. By contrast, almost all prairie places with populations exceeding 1,000 in 1946, such as High River, actually grew. Indeed, the number of towns with populations between 1,000 and 2,500 increased in Alberta between 1946 and 1966.[24]

THE FORTUNES of the *Times* itself also improved in the post-war era, and the paper happily left behind the financial and political woes it endured during the Depression. The role of founder Charles Clark declined sharply during the war years and sometime before 1942 he transferred 50 percent of the business to son Charles A. A new agreement that year provided the younger Clark with three-quarters of the profits in consideration of his growing managerial role.[25] Thereafter, Charles senior increasingly confined himself to a little proofreading, mostly of his brother Hugh's column. On 14 January 1949, ten days after he quit working entirely, he died of heart failure at the age of 79 and Charles A. Clark became the sole proprietor of the *Times*.

The Clark family home. Glenbow Archives NA-4397-1.

Although Charles A. had worked steadily at the business since 1929, his influence did not become apparent until after his father's death. While small businesses like weekly newspapers often passed from father to son, such transitions posed a special problem. People inevitably drew comparisons that sometimes unfairly denigrated the younger generation. The senior Clark left giant boots to fill. He not only served as a pillar of his own community, but commanded respect from his peers across Canada. A friendly and gregarious storyteller, everyone seemed to like him. One former associate called him a "prince" of a fellow, and a former employee remembered him as a "great gentleman" and a "superb person."[26] The task of measuring up to his father undoubtedly intimidated Charles A. in his youth and may have accounted for his indifferent effort in high school. The teenager once produced the ultimate embarrassment for an editor's son—a failing grade in an English composition course. The result in no way reflected his true ability, for other newsmen later agreed that he possessed considerable writing talent and demonstrated it when sufficiently motivated.[27]

Not only did Charles A. remain in the shadow of the great man at work, but also at home, for he lived with his parents after returning to High River in 1929. His mother Mary died in 1936 after years of poor health, and rather than leave his father to ramble around in the large house, Charles and Grace moved in following their marriage in 1937. With the birth of their sons in 1939 and 1942, three generations lived under one roof. In some respects, Charles A. never vanquished his father's ghost. Although he usually appeared in the *Times* masthead as "editor," he left much of the actual editing and writing to the capable Hughena McCorquodale, and continued to function as general manager. He dabbled with writing by penning the lyrics to songs, occasionally submitting articles to magazines, and sometimes contributing editorials.[28] But he never trusted his own writing and appeared to lack the confidence necessary to compete against his father's reputation.

None of these problems prevented Charles A. from succeeding in the weekly newspaper world. He became as prominent as his father in the Canadian Weekly Newspapers Association, serving as secretary of the Alberta Division from 1941 to 1949, and as its president in 1950. He also served on the national board of directors from 1943 to 1951 and received a life membership in the national division in 1964 and in the provincial division in 1966.[29] Under his tutelage, the *Times* became an even more prototypical rural weekly. Unlike his father, Charles A. did not come to High River from some other place. Born and raised there, he embraced the community even more passionately, serving in numerous organizations and on many committees. Former employee and subsequent *Times* owner, Bill Holmes, described Charles A. Clark in an eulogy as "a total community man...always seeking to promote the positive aspects of any problem for the betterment of the town and its people."[30]

Post-war prosperity facilitated the resumption of community projects that depression and war had postponed, and campaigning for them had always given the *Times* one of its most pleasurable missions. The paper found much to support and cheer in the two decades after 1945: the paving of streets, the installation of concrete sidewalks; and the opening of many new facilities including a golf course, artificial ice rinks for curling and hockey, rodeo grounds, a race track, and a swimming pool. Yet no project aroused more enthusiasm at the *Times* than the new community centre. An editorial on 18 January 1945 outlined the need for meeting rooms and banquet facilities for the town's many clubs and special events. Organizers christened the project the Highwood Memorial Centre in honour of the community's war dead. The projected cost amounted to $70,000, and financing came from a $35,000 town debenture in addition to the contributions of individuals and organizations throughout the district.[31]

The *Times* doted on the project, reporting on its progress almost weekly and praising it ceaselessly, even when the cost ballooned beyond $122,000. On 3 March 1949 the *Times* declared the Memorial Centre "one of the finest community efforts to be found in all Canada, a magnificent achievement for a settlement of this size." Ten years later, the centre still received accolades. An editorial on 9 October 1958 reviewed the sacrifice of those who provided the funds and the labour for its construction: "a community project in the purest sense of the word," boasted the *Times*, "it represents the heart and soul of a district."

Even more than his father, Charles A. sought to avoid conflict and maintain harmony. The senior Clark had recognized the importance of those principles, but he had a foot in nineteenth-century journalism and a touch of the firebrand sometimes coloured the paper, especially when condemning the community's "outside" enemies. Even those tirades moderated under Charles A. Crime news almost disappeared, and he often lectured the staff on keeping bias out of their stories.[32] When he served as president of the Alberta Division of the Canadian Weekly Newspapers Association, he insisted that the purpose of a weekly was "to build towards a better, homier and friendlier community."[33] Personal circumstances may explain his heightened desire to avoid conflict. He grew up with a Protestant father and a Roman Catholic mother at a time when religious differences still mattered greatly to most people. Charles was a lifelong Conservative who married a confirmed Liberal. Much more reserved than his outgoing father, he also possessed a kind and sensitive disposition. Under his guidance, the *Times* became a bastion for cautious behaviour in general. It frequently issued editorials that urged vehicle safety, fire safety, hunting safety, farm safety, electrical safety, water safety, and any other kind of safety that came to its attention.

Charles's insistence on neutrality and harmony may also have stemmed from growing public knowledge of his political inclinations. They remained subdued for many years while his sister Marnie worked openly for the Conservative Party. Another party activist, Lillian Knupp, started working at the *Times* in 1956.³⁴ Charles became more involved after 1957. "I haven't been too active in politics," he confessed in a letter to his Conservative uncle in Ontario, "but Diefenbaker is a man I'll go out and work for."³⁵ Diefenbaker also inspired his son Joe, who became president of the Progressive Conservative Student Federation in 1961 at age 21. Charles became enamoured of Peter Lougheed as well and introduced him at the Alberta Progressive Conservative leadership convention in 1965.³⁶ Those who worked at the paper disagreed about whether or not any political bias leaked into print.³⁷ But readers did not seem to notice nor care, since most of them also surrendered to Diefenbaker in the great Conservative sweep of 1958. For the first time, the national party became wildly popular in the High River district, and it sent a Progressive Conservative to Ottawa in the next four elections, even though residents continued to vote Social Credit in provincial contests.

Seven years after the death of Charles Clark senior, another prominent figure left the *Times*. Hughena McCorquodale retired in 1956 after almost 30 years service, an occasion that drew 600 people to her farewell party.³⁸ Lillian Knupp began to assume her duties. She started as a bookkeeper but soon undertook some proofreading while "Mrs. Mac" tutored her in the skills of journalism and writing.³⁹ Knupp would maintain a relationship with the *Times* into the 1990s when she still contributed a column. An even younger columnist began writing in 1954. When Joe Clark entered Grade 10, he became the high school correspondent. His "Hi-Lo" column ran for three years and in a breezy style and light-hearted tone, he presented the "highlights" and the "lowdown" on school activities. He also carried out journalistic duties at the school, serving at various times as editor of its newspaper, *The Reflector*, as "publicity director" for student council, and as editor of the 1955–56 year book.⁴⁰ His younger brother, Peter, also pitched in at the *Times*, working in the back shop with the printers. Since Hugh Clark continued to write his "Pertinent Topics" column from Ontario until his death in 1959 at age 92, three generations of Clarks contributed to the paper simultaneously.

Hiring family members and other local people and training them on the job remained a tradition at the *Times*, as it did at many other weekly newspapers. The city dailies had long since succumbed to "professionalism" and employed writers with formal training in journalism. Somewhat surprisingly, the *Times* took a step in that direction in 1962 when it hired Bill Scott, a young man with three years of journalism from Ryerson Technical Institute in Toronto. Lest readers be alarmed by his education, his eastern origins, and his big city ways, the Times reassured them on 5 April: "He's not essentially a city boy and so knows and appreciates the homeiness and hail-fellow qualities of a small town."

From 1945 to 1962 the Times usually supported nine full-time employees, four in the back and four in the front, plus the publisher. Many thought the paper paid poorly, although the back shop came closer to offering urban rates. The only surviving pay book dates from the late 1940s when the three highest paid full-time printers earned $.90 to $1.00 an hour, while the highest paid front shop employee, Hughena McCorquodale, earned only $.63.[41] But the weekly provided other compensations. Peter Pickersgill, a local boy who started at the Times in 1945 and earned $.50 an hour in 1948, moved to the Calgary Herald in 1952 where he remembered receiving "twice the pay for doing half for the work." Nonetheless, he disliked the highly specialized roles assigned to each writer and after five years of boredom accepted a job at the weekly Vulcan Advocate.[42]

The size and structure of the labour force at the Times remained stable because little technological change occurred until the introduction of offset printing in 1961. Offset involved photographing a layout to produce a plastic negative from which a press plate could be made. At that time, offset still produced a greyish newspaper that lacked sharp contrasts, but it offered flexible formatting and it easily reproduced photographs.[43] Clark especially wanted more pictures in the Times. He had developed an early and keen interest in photography and believed it would greatly enhance the newspaper. Most weeklies balked at the cost of switching to offset, but Clark realized the expense could be overcome if several weeklies agreed to pool resources and buy a single press. Since offset plates could be transported easily, a central press made sense. Such arrangements ultimately became commonplace, but when Clark failed to interest his peers, he plunged ahead with the purchase on his own. He assured his son Joe that the cost could be managed since the business "has shown a steady and substantial increase for the past few years."[44]

The profitability that Clark referred to occurred in spite of a major financial amputation. One way to deal with rival weeklies was to own them and the

Times had owned the *Vulcan Advocate* since 1913. In 1947 Charles senior seized an opportunity to extend this strategy by buying the *Okotoks Review*, the paper he had first owned and then sold in order to found the *Times*. No sooner had this transaction occurred than the *Advocate* left the Clark chain. Bob Munro had joined its staff in 1932 and became its editor in 1936. He enlisted in the military in 1941, as did other men at the *Advocate*, with the result that 22-year old Lola Bateman became editor in 1944. Displeased by the rapid turnover, Clark believed that partnership with a co-owner offered more stability. When Munro returned from Europe, he gladly agreed to buy a half interest in the *Advocate*. When Charles senior died in 1949, he left his 50 percent share to his daughter Marnie, and his remaining share of the *Times* to his son. Marnie had no interest in the newspaper business, and Charles A. could not buy her out, so Marnie sold her stake in the *Advocate* to an eager Bob Munro.[45]

Swapping the *Advocate* for the *Review* proved to be a poor, if unavoidable, bargain. Under Munro's ownership, the *Advocate* rivalled and sometimes surpassed the *Times* in circulation, while the *Okotoks Review* never reached a circulation of 500. Meanwhile, the *Times* still contended with a rival to the south, the *Nanton News*, and after 1947 Turner Valley supported its own weekly for nine years. An even bigger threat arrived in the form of the *Rocky View News*, a Calgary weekly that catered to the rural population outside the city. By the 1960s its circulation surpassed that of the *Times* in the Turner Valley-Black Diamond district.[46] At least the *Times* had less to fear from Calgary's free suburban weeklies, an innovation in publishing that proliferated in metropolitan areas in the 1950s. Quite unlike the rural weekly in content and purpose, most were little more than glorified flyers for supermarkets and shopping centres.

In response to its competitors, the *Times* continued to saturate the surrounding rural districts. In 1941 country correspondents reported from fourteen places; by 1962 from about twenty, although not every issue included a report from every outpost. More importantly, the *Times* expanded its country circulation through the kind of agreements with rural government that it had forged with the Municipal District of Dinton in 1927. The municipality had bought subscriptions to the *Times* for all its property owners at reduced rates, and in return, the *Times* printed its notices and minutes. Those subscriptions accounted for part of the anaemic circulation of 1,600 that the *Times* reported on 24 September 1942. When Dinton amalgamated with another municipality in 1943, its agreement with the *Times* extended to the new territory and added more new subscribers. By 11 October 1945 circulation had jumped to about 2,000. A more definitive count of the "net paid circulation" in 1954 pegged it at 1,842, as opposed to the 2,020 copies that left the *Times* office. The creation of the huge Municipal District of Foothills, which surrounded High River, also took place in 1954, and on 21 March 1957 the *Times* announced an agreement whereby all its ratepayers received the paper. As a result, almost every rural home in the High River district received the *Times*. By 1966, the final year of Clark ownership, the net paid circulation reached 2,950.[47]

The subscription list also included people who had moved away, but still took the paper to keep abreast of activities and friends in the old home community. On 6 October 1960 the *Times* announced that it mailed copies across North America and to nine foreign countries. In 1966 no less than 254 subscriptions went to Calgary and 52 to Edmonton.[48] Increased subscription rates did not deter these readers. With both prosperity and inflation rising, the *Times* increased its annual rate from $2.00 to $2.50 in 1946 and to $3.00 in 1951.

The *Times* also enjoyed a surge in advertising after World War II. In the ongoing struggle of the weeklies to win contracts for nationally marketed products, the paper capitulated to the advertising agencies by joining the Audit Bureau of Circulation sometime during the war. Founded in Chicago in 1914, the Bureau verified paid subscription lists, mailing addresses, and other data about newspapers for the benefit of advertisers who doubted the claims of publishers. Although it was costly to join, the *Times* did so because many agencies refused to deal with nonmembers.[49] The amount of brand name advertising in the paper subsequently increased and no less than eighteen brand name advertisements appeared in the 5 October 1950 issue. The *Times* especially welcomed the big, illustrated layouts for cars and trucks; on 7 November 1957 advertisements for De Soto, Chevrolet, Plymouth, Chrysler, Mercury, and Dodge covered several pages. By the 1960s, the *Times* happily paid the agencies their 15 percent commissions since they brought such lucrative advertisements to the paper.[50]

By contrast, the *Times* reached no happy accommodation with senior governments, and it complained chronically about the piles of "unpaid advertising" that arrived in the guise of news items. On 17 February 1949 the *Times* issued an editorial deploring "the mountains of material" it received from public agencies such as the India Information Service of Ottawa. "The only use to which it is put," confessed the *Times*, "is to turn the reverse side for copy paper to write about your new red barn, or the social doings of the district." The Alberta Division of the Canadian Weekly Newspapers Association also denounced unpaid government advertising on behalf of its members, and it vowed to "stamp out this evil."[51]

Local advertisers also remained important after the war, especially farm equipment dealers, auctioneers, clothing shops, and grocery stores. During the 1960s the local IGA food market ran full-page spreads every week. As in the past, many local businesses still insisted on writing their own advertisements, even though they clashed with the slick displays submitted by the national advertisers. On 6 July 1961, for example, a local merchant advertised a "Krazy Daze" sale with no apparent shame.

The growth of advertising resulted in a thicker newspaper. During the Depression it rarely exceeded eight pages and six columns, but in the 1950s it often extended to ten pages and seven columns. The greatest expansion occurred when the introduction of offset technology facilitated the publication of many photos. Although the *Times* reverted to a narrower six-column format, it often reached twenty pages in length during the 1960s. The format of the paper changed to resemble that of a daily by including more columns with by-lines. The *Times* convinced local organizations and experts to provide regular features on youth, homemaking, religion, women's groups, agriculture, education, the provincial legislature, and other themes that appeared and disappeared over the years.

On 18 October 1962 the *Times* even introduced a new "boiler plate" entitled *Rural Alberta*. Published in Calgary and distributed through the province's weeklies, it carried brand name advertising, but did not resemble early twentieth-century readyprint. In place of testimonials promoting miracle drugs, it provided eight pages of light reading on noncontroversial topics. The first issue carried articles on transportation, bees, Lake Wabamun, the Calgary Stampede Queen, and the lack of rats in Alberta. It also offered some features normally missing from rural weeklies, such as horoscopes and crossword puzzles. It even provided coloured photographs (although surviving microfilm cannot confirm the fact). On 21 May 1964 the *Times* replaced *Rural Alberta* with a similar supplement entitled *Alberta Today*, published by the provincial division of the Canadian Weekly Newspapers Association.

With increased advertising, growing circulation, and steady revenue from custom printing, the *Times* provided the Clark family with a comfortable middle class existence, supplemented by Grace's teaching salary and investments in a variety of other assets. The couple remained content to live in the roomy 1909 family house, but in 1963 they treated themselves to the luxury of an around-the-world vacation. Charles assured Joe that sufficient funds still remained to finance the boys' post-secondary education. When Charles sold the *Times* in 1966, the value of the business exceeded $90,000.[52]

COMPARED TO EARLIER PERIODS in its history, tranquillity seemed to prevail in the High River district in the two decades after 1945. No depression ravaged its economy; no major war destroyed its sons. Still, the period was not entirely devoid of troubles and concerns, and the *Times* did not always bask in harmony and contentment. The paper had always pursued a mission, rooted in real community problems and aspirations, and based on the changes in local identity. That purpose did not disappear and the *Times* soon confronted the problems of a prosperous era.

9

FEARING
FOR THE FUTURE

THE PROSPERITY AND DOMESTICITY associated with the post-war era sometimes obscures its fears. In the past, the *Times* had generally ignored the rumbling of distant events until they plunged the local community into war, but nuclear weapons threatened to do so directly at any time. Alarm about instant destruction, the Soviet Union, and the cold war generally began to appear in editorials and in Hugh Clark's "Pertinent Topics" column by the late 1940s. Dominion government programs that encouraged the building of air raid shelters and the formation of plans for emergency evacuations and for stockpiling food, water and medical supplies, heightened such fears and led to the creation of local civil defence organizations, even in small communities like High River. Reports in the *Times* about defence plans and activities peaked between 1960 when the government began promoting the construction of home fallout shelters, and 1962 when the Cuban Missile crisis threatened to ignite global destruction.

These distant events appeared in the *Times* because they directly engaged people and organizations in the local community. So too did the policies and actions of senior governments, corporations, and labour unions that directly affected the self-employed producers of the community. Manifestos supporting agrarian interests still blared from the editorial page, as they always had, but the *Times* continued to focus more attention on local developments that affected the economy. Thanks to wartime activities, the town's population jumped from 1,430 in 1941 to 2,006 in 1946, but after that, growth slowed to a crawl even though High River succeeded as a centre for farm suppliers, public services, and retired rural people. By 1966 the population had only reached 2,339.

Old hopes for new developments based on petroleum quickly died. The Turner Valley fields exhausted their last viable reserves during the war, and after the great Leduc strike of 1947, exploration shifted to other parts of the province. The dream of luring industry also remained as elusive as ever. The town believed that the empty hangars at the abandoned airbase offered excellent facilities for manufacturing, and after considerable lobbying by the mayor, the merchants, and the local member of the provincial legislature, a company called United Trailer opened a factory in 1951. Under contract to the Dominion government to build prefabricated military huts, it employed over 300 people at peak production.[1] Its appearance rekindled local aspirations for more manufacturers, and in 1952 a new Businessmen's Association sponsored an essay-writing competition for students on the topic "What High River Can Offer Industry."[2] But three years after opening, United Trailer abruptly closed and nothing replaced it.

Since senior governments assumed more responsibility for economic growth after the war, they frequently received criticism for the lack of it. On 17 September 1959 a *Times* editorial denounced the Alberta government for failing to encourage the location of industry in small towns. Five years later, the politically engaged Joe Clark wrote his parents with the same complaint, and praised Saskatchewan and Manitoba for devising policies that were friendlier to small centres.[3] Meanwhile, local enthusiasm for securing industry again declined, although the town council considered hiring an "Industrial Development Manager" in 1963 to find a promising enterprise.[4]

The town also continued to blame floods for the lack of development and renewed efforts to tame the river consistently failed. After the completion of a new breakwater dam in 1947, the councillor in charge of the project proclaimed in the *Times* on 5 June that "We positively believe that the town will never again be flooded." The very next year, the Prairie Farm Rehabilitation Administration announced the need for a new water diversion project, and more floods washed over the town in subsequent years.[5] A water problem of a different kind drew some of the blame for stifling growth. High River commissioned the construction of a new sewage system in 1955, but no sooner had it been completed than the town complained that the pipes leaked and the system could not accommodate additional outlets, thus halting the construction of subdivisions. The town sued the contractors for faulty work, and the contractors countersued the town for nonpayment, resulting in years of litigation. The parties finally settled out of court in 1962.[6]

The futility of attracting industry forced the town to revert to its ability to serve the surrounding rural hinterland, but that trade increasingly fragmented after 1945. Farmers patronized High River for agricultural equipment and supplies, but when their families spent money on consumer goods, they looked elsewhere. High River still offered more choice and competition than the two closest newspaper towns of Okotoks and Nanton, neither of which boasted a population of 1,000 in 1966. Instead, Calgary beckoned shoppers. The city had always posed this threat, and passenger trains had always carried day shoppers from High River, but not farm families who had to spend too much time reaching town before they could board the train. In 1955, diesel-driven day liners replaced the old steam locomotives, slashing travel time between High River and Calgary from one hour and 22 minutes, including stops, to 46 minutes direct.[7] In spite of this convenience, people stopped taking the train. The High River station closed in 1965 and passenger service ended entirely in 1968.

Automobiles and roads replaced the train. In the interwar period, merchants feared that motorized transportation would carry more townspeople and farmers to Calgary, but the threat proved more apparent than real given poor roads, undependable vehicles, and winter snows. After the war, rural people became increasingly mobile. By 1951, the number of cars and trucks in High River's rural hinterland exceeded the number of farms. Motor vehicles steadily became faster, more reliable, better adapted to winter conditions, and more comfortable. Roads also improved. With the return of farm prosperity, rural municipalities bought more maintenance and snow removal equipment, and they soon graded and gravelled almost every road allowance in the district. These tributaries carried rural motorists to the main highways where they cruised on smooth asphalt (See Figure 5). The paving of Highway 23, the old Sunshine Trail that flowed through the wheat lands

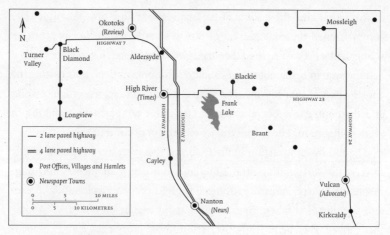

FIGURE 5: *High River Area, 1962.*

east of town and then turned south to Vulcan, commenced in 1958. Highway 23 connected with the Macleod Trail at High River where motorists turned north to Calgary. The MacLeod Trail actually received its first coat of asphalt in 1946, but a more dramatic improvement appeared in 1954 when the provincial government decided to build a new four-lane highway between Fort Macleod and Calgary.

The *Times* had always joined merchants in the past to urge the building of more and better roads that would expand High River's trade area. Now it joined them in cries of outrage when it learned that the freeway would bypass the town by several miles, allowing drivers to roar ahead without so much as a sideways glance, crippling tourism and destroying local business. "Let us not forget that when a main highway misses our towns by even a half mile, certain processes of disintegration and deterioration set in, and the community sinks into secondary importance," the *Times* warned on 28 April 1955.

Hoping to avert the calamity, the merchants, the town council, and the *Times* united to publicize the evils of the new highway. It would appropriate farmland and strip away topsoil to build the roadbed; it would split farms in two and force their owners to make time-consuming detours to reach their own fields; it would cost taxpayers a fortune, yet the government would not adequately compensate farmers for their losses. The freeway would pass

Construction of the High River overpass on the new four-lane highway to Calgary, 1956. Museum of the Highwood 989-031-427.

too far to the east for drivers to fully appreciate the view of the mountains. Instead of circumventing small towns, traffic should bypass cities instead. Funnelling drivers through small towns actually brought benefits, such as preventing accidents by forcing drivers to remain awake and alert, and it would give police a better chance of apprehending motoring criminals.[8]

Throughout 1955 and into 1956, the *Times* maintained its campaign against the highway, and High River joined six other towns in protesting the route. They accomplished nothing against an array of opposing forces that included trucking firms, the Alberta Chamber of Commerce, and the provincial government. Even Ivan Casey, High River's own representative at the legislature, defended the freeway. All of them agreed that the swelling torrent of traffic that now included monstrous diesel trucks should not be squeezed into bottle necks where it did not wish to stop. Freeways permitted faster movement, relieved congestion on urban streets, entailed lower construction costs, caused fewer accidents, and facilitated civil defence measures in the event of nuclear attack.[9] To all these considerations, the *Times* declared on 10 February 1955 that "it is a heartless age in which everything must be sacrificed to some material progress."

When the new Highway 2 opened, it bypassed High River as originally planned. Ivan Casey lost his seat in the 1955 provincial election to mayor Ross Ellis, who received a joint nomination from the Liberal and Conservative parties. On 7 July the *Times* attributed Casey's defeat largely to his defence of the freeway bypass.

After the highway opened, drivers from High River could reach downtown Calgary in 40 minutes without breaking any speed limits. In 1960, the Chinook Shopping Centre opened on the southern edge of the city. It featured a comfortable indoor mall lined with specialty shops, a department store, and a modern supermarket. The High River resident could reach this Mecca of consumerism within half an hour, and almost every rural household within the town's traditional trade area could reach it in an hour or less. By the 1960s, Calgary had clearly emerged as their favourite source of consumer products. A detailed survey of shopping habits in the High River district revealed that residents even bought everyday items in the city. As reported in the *Times* on 28 March 1968, people within six miles of High River spent less than two-thirds of their grocery money in the town, and even town residents bought more than ten percent of their groceries elsewhere.

BUT A VILLAIN MORE DEADLY than Calgary lurked in the countryside itself. Even if High River recaptured all the trade within driving distance of the town, rural depopulation threatened to annihilate it. According to provincial government surveys, High River's trade area held steady at 1,400 square miles between 1952 and 1969, while the trade area population dropped from nearly 10,000 to 7,000 before recovering slightly.[10] The statistics only hinted at the severity of the crisis, for the town and the *Times* knew that much of the rural population consisted of children. Products of the post-war baby boom, most of them would flee the area after high school as mechanization and expansion continually created bigger and fewer farms. The provincial District Agriculturalist stationed in High River predicted that only fifteen percent of the boys living on farms in 1961 would ever become farmers.[11] And without farmers to service, the town could not provide its own children with economic opportunities. They, too, would escape to the city. This danger loomed larger in the post-war era than it did during the depression when a lack of work elsewhere kept many youth in the district. Now the cities beckoned with infinite possibilities.

The *Times* foresaw this gloomy future as early as 17 October 1946 and thereafter it frequently ran stories on rural depopulation. On 15 October 1959 the paper presented the chilling forecast of Professor William Baker of the University of Saskatchewan that two-thirds of the 1,500 communities in his province would disappear within 30 years. The *Times* developed a "nurseries of the nation" theme that argued that small towns and rural areas poured immense resources into raising and educating youth for the subsequent benefit of the urban economy. A 1950 informational brochure on High River also spotted a trend that would accelerate: "Every year there are those rural students with an aptitude for other skills who continue their studies in universities, seeking wider fields of endeavour."[12] High River's desire to build a consolidated high school even threatened to further that end. More than once, the *Times* argued that rural areas should be compensated by the provincial government for the huge costs incurred in making their "free" contribution to urban society.[13]

The topic of rural depopulation represented one component of a growing focus on children and youth in the *Times* that bordered on obsession by the 1960s. The 21 April 1966 issue featured fifteen articles directly related to youth and their activities. After the appearance of Joe Clark's "Hi-Lo" column in 1955, reports from the high school became a standard feature in the *Times*. The paper also provided a weekly column for the local Teen Town club, founded in 1943. While the *Times* ordinarily declined to pay for nationally-syndicated columns, it began to carry the breezy feature on youthful exploits entitled "Sugar and Spice," by Ontario school teacher Bill Smiley. Irregular reports also appeared on Brownies and Girl Guides, Cubs and Boy Scouts, Canadian Girls in Training (CGIT), church youth groups, and every sport involving children and teenagers. On 18 September 1958 the *Times* offered one of its earliest reports on local rock-and-roll dances. By then, an annual Teen Queen contest began to receive extensive coverage, and after the introduction of offset printing also included many photos. "It is not likely any other area in the province surpasses the interest we hold in our children and thus in our future," boasted the *Times* in an editorial on 21 June 1962.

Personal reasons no doubt fuelled this interest, for the Clark boys, Joe and Peter, grew up during the 1950s, and their mother Grace resumed teaching at the high school. Charles's sister, Marnie Soby, helped run the Teen Town club.[14] Their involvement with youth mirrored a national fixation as the post-war baby boom created a huge new demographic group. Its sheer size accounted for the growth of educational institutions and youth organizations, and it exerted a major economic impact that even caught the attention of High River advertisers. Earl's drive-in theatre catered to teenagers with double features like *Bucket of Blood* and *Attack of the Giant Leeches*, whose lurid advertisements glared from the pages of the *Times* on 17 May 1962. Advertisements for the trampoline park "Bounceland" appeared on 7 June. Even the Royal Lumber Yards discovered a way to cash in on the youth market. Its advertisement on 28 September 1961 stressed the importance of a quiet place to study and urged Dad to "Build Her a Room of Her Own."

While a positive tone usually characterized its coverage of children and youth, the *Times* shared North America's anxiety over the perceived growth of juvenile delinquency. The paper reacted strongly against reckless behaviour and acts of vandalism in the community. Speeding and auto racing, throwing bottles from cars, drunkenness, shooting at streetlights, tormenting animals, smashing cemetery headstones, and pelting eggs at cars all received severe condemnation.[15] In searching for solutions to youthful misconduct, an editorial on 11 June 1964 offered parents strong advice: "LESSON ONE IS TO KEEP THEM FROM LOAFING AROUND THE STREETS LONG AFTER DARK."

While the *Times* fretted about local troublemakers, it consoled itself with the thought that conditions could only be worse in the cities. "When one reads of the atrocious crimes, [and] the acts of wantonness and cruelty committed by teen age gangs in the cities," it wrote on 1 September 1955, "bye and large, this town and this district must take great pride in the general caliber of the young people." As in the past, the *Times* found it more satisfying to blame malevolent outsiders. When a local boy was beaten, the *Times* reported on 18 November 1954 that "A trio of unsavory teen-agers from Calgary oozed down into High River and tried out their terrorizing tactics here." Although fears of juvenile delinquency seemed like a fresh concern, in reality they simply represented a modern version of the indictments the *Times* had once levelled at the behaviour of young bachelors during the frontier era.

Although the focus on youth encompassed many different themes and concerns, most of them ultimately returned to the spectre of rural depopulation. For that reason, the *Times* paid particular attention to local 4-H clubs. The name referred to Head, Heart, Health, and Hands. Founded in the United States, the organization entered Alberta in 1917 and devoted itself to inculcating agricultural skills and interests in children and young teens. Many specialized 4-H clubs appeared throughout the High River district. Some concentrated on raising particular crops or livestock, or on gardening, cooking, or sewing, and all of them encouraged public speaking and citizenship. The clubs received ardent praise in the *Times* for attempting to commit children to agriculture, even as it realized that circumstances would drive most of them from the land.[16]

THE FEAR OF RURAL DEPOPULATION extended to other topics besides youth and helps to explain local animosity toward Hutterites. The Anabaptist religious sect first entered Alberta via the United States in 1918. A strictly rural people, the Hutterites formed colonies of 100 to 150 people. They owned all agricultural assets communally and lived in centralized villages. Although they accepted modern agricultural technology and methods, they clung to many traditional beliefs and customs, including their German dialect and their distinctive manner of dress. They stubbornly resisted cultural assimilation and sought to preserve religious purity by minimizing contact with non-Hutterites.[17]

Given their extraordinarily high birth rates, their settlements soon became overcrowded and the Hutterites bought more land to launch daughter colonies. The number of colonies in Alberta climbed from eleven in 1918 to 42 by 1942.[18] A willingness to endure a low standard of living provided the savings to finance these expansions. Hutterites first appeared in the High River area in 1937 when they purchased two ranches of about 4,500 acres each to start colonies in the Cayley district. Animosity towards them initially arose from their iron resistance to cultural assimilation, their strict isolation, and the alien "communism" of their economic and social life. During World War II they earned more scorn for remaining both pacifists and German-speaking. The rural press often condemned them during the war, and it received the blessing of the Alberta Division of the Canadian Weekly

Newspapers Association for helping to "suppress disloyal and subversive elements within our boundaries."[19]

But the war also did much to blunt old nativist views. It led to the repudiation of Nazi racial theories, and a host of post-war influences encouraged greater tolerance of cultural, ethnic, and racial minorities. Oblivious to the overt nativism that coloured the *Times* in the early twentieth-century, an editorial on 6 September 1951 ventured the opinion that "this vicinity is more-thannormally free of bigotry, racial, or religious intolerance, or the various forms of fanaticism and prejudice which can split communities." On 19 September 1957, the *Times* applauded a Leduc, Alberta school board for supporting the eligibility of a young black woman as a teacher, stating that in Canada "there is no place for racial or religious antagonisms." The *Times* again urged racial tolerance in an editorial on 8 November 1962, but the disappearance of anti-Chinese tirades from the paper marked the most notable change in attitude. The new tolerance mirrored changes in the community itself. Chinese restaurants now proudly advertised "Chinese" food. Marjorie Wong successfully attracted Caucasian children to her dance classes and their performances drew large crowds.[20] A Chinese girl appeared as a contestant in the Teen Queen competition reported in the *Times* on 17 March 1966—an unthinkable occurrence a generation earlier.

Bigotry did not disappear after World War II, but it no longer paraded as respectable opinion. Post-war anger towards Hutterites stemmed less from old-fashioned prejudice than from fear that the growth of colonies would destroy communities in the district. Hutterites were surprisingly self-sufficient in providing for most of their simple needs, and although they required farm machinery and supplies, they often bypassed small town merchants and negotiated directly with city dealers and wholesalers. To preserve the purity of their life and faith, they refused to participate in any organization or activity in the local community. Their self-imposed isolation also extended to education. Compelled by law to enrol children in school, the Hutterites insisted on segregated classes at the colonies themselves, and they withdrew children from the educational system as soon as the regulations permitted. A *Times* editorial on 16 May 1946 complained that "They are the very negation of community spirit." Rural communities also believed that Hutterites used the religious status of colonies to evade taxes, thereby freeing money to outbid other farmers for land.

The provincial government responded to these concerns, introducing a wartime ban on Hutterite land purchases in 1942 and replacing it with the Communal Property Act of 1947 that restricted and controlled their expansion. The Times heartily approved of these measures. "We continue to view the increase of their holdings with concern and alarm," it stated on 20 February 1958; if unchecked "towns and communities would disintegrate from disuse and lack of support, and services would disappear."

This fear intensified in 1960 when Hutterites proposed to establish a third colony in the district. More than 500 protesters crowded a hearing of the provincial Communal Property Control Board that was held in High River, and presented it with a petition from 21 organizations. The petition predicted the destruction of local businesses and social institutions, plunging real estate values, and rising property taxes for non-Hutterites.[21] A Times editorial on 8 December 1960 strongly supported the protest. Hearings held the following year resulted in a virtual replay of these protests and concerns.[22] Yet another attempt to establish a colony near the village of Brant in 1964 brought another round of massive local protest led by High River mayor Ross Ellis.[23] Local farmers willing to sell out to Hutterites for handsome prices faced scorn and contempt. The residents feared the immediate impact of more colonies in the district, and many of them agreed with a letter to the Times on 2 April 1964 prophesying that Hutterites would use their high birth rates and purchasing power to ultimately buy all the farmland in Alberta.

Although the Communal Property Control Board denied the Hutterites permission to establish a colony at Brant, they circumvented the ruling. Six Hutterites purchased land as individuals and then proceeded to form a communal colony informally. The Hutterites also launched a lawsuit against the provincial government. After appeals, the Supreme Court of Canada found in favour of the province on the grounds that the ruling involved land planning rather than religious persecution. The Hutterites who purchased the land individually were fined $100 each, but the colony remained. As resentment smouldered in the High River, Brant, and Vulcan districts, the Social Credit government that had authored the Communal Property Act fell from

Deterioration in downtown High River, 1960s. *Museum of the Highwood 975-043-012.*

power in 1971. The new Progressive Conservative administration concerned itself more with petroleum and urban issues, and it repealed the act as contrary to human rights.[24] Hutterites could now expand without restriction.

Most students of the dispute believe that rural Albertans exaggerated the impact of Hutterite expansion. One preliminary study suggested that Hutterites did spend money in local towns, although not as much per capita as other rural residents.[25] Given their minute representation in the population, the idea that they would overwhelm rural Alberta seemed absurd; by the early 1970s they owned less than 1.5 percent of the farmland in the province.[26] By then declining birth rates, fast-rising land prices, and the Hutterites' own desire for higher living standards all limited their ability to sustain the expansion of the past. One scholar suggested that local communities targeted Hutterites as "scapegoats" for the rural decline caused largely by technology and the urban shopping habits of non-Hutterites.[27] Nonetheless, the intensity of feeling in the High River district clearly indicated the depth of its fears about the future.

IN THE FACE OF HUTTERITE EXPANSION, rural depopulation, urban shopping, and a lack of industry, town merchants grew reluctant to expand or invest in improvements. Between 1952 and 1969, the number of businesses in the town held steady between 150 and 160.[28] While some large new enterprises served the agricultural sector, the retail shops deteriorated and looked shabby by the 1960s. They contrasted sharply with the newly-built houses in town, and by 1966 residential properties provided almost three-quarters of all municipal taxes.[29]

An outside agency offered a solution. In 1951 the province created planning commissions to guide future expansion in the metropolitan areas of Edmonton and Calgary. The boundary of the Calgary Regional Planning Commission extended south to include the Municipal District of Foothills and the town of High River. It did not interfere with existing local governments, but advised them on land use and approved plans for new subdivisions. In 1961 a commission speaker told High River merchants that they must rebuild their dowdy stores regardless of the expense if they hoped to combat the steady loss of business. The commission even urged the town to build its own shopping centre outside the existing business core. In 1965 it again presented a development plan that called for all sorts of improvements, including downtown renewal, new recreational facilities, and new subdivisions for commerce, industry, and housing.[30] Alas, the commission did not explain how to finance these elaborate projects.

The merchants themselves fell back on familiar, less costly tactics. The *Times* co-operated with them in condemning peddlers and out-of-town shopping, and in sponsoring buy-at-home campaigns, employing all the hoary arguments that had first appeared half a century earlier. Even these efforts grew increasingly half-hearted as a fatalistic pall engulfed the merchants. Resignation soon bred apathy. The *Times* pondered reasons why boards-of-trade had appeared and disappeared in High River over the years, and attempted to explain why no current enthusiasm existed for one. On 13 March 1952, the paper speculated that "most residents are pretty well content with the town as it is." Ten years later, W.O. Mitchell rendered a similar opinion: "some feel that the town does not *want* to grow....one explanation is that it has too many financially secure retired people resisting change and any improvement that might mean a rise in taxes."[31]

The reluctance to change that W.O. Mitchell observed can be illustrated by attitudes towards a new stop sign placed at a High River intersection. At one time such a development might have been hailed as evidence of growing traffic and hence a measure of progress, but now residents resented it. One man who had been ticketed for ignoring the sign grumbled to the *Times* on 24 August 1961: "I've been crossing here for 40 years, never stopped."

DURING THE INTERWAR YEARS, the High River district had confronted hard times and dashed hopes with the comforting thought that virtue resided in rural and small town life. This attitude did not vanish in the post-war era. Hughena McCorquodale remained with the *Times* until 1956 and she continued to shape and defend that viewpoint. Charles A. Clark shared her passion. In a 1981 interview, he admitted that he was no city man and he expressed his love for small towns, countryside, and wilderness; and his fondness of such outdoor pursuits as hunting, fishing, and photography. As he once told a gathering of weekly publishers, "We who have chosen to live in a small town have chosen that life in preference to the rush and hardness of a city."[32]

Another writer dedicated to the small community appeared in High River. Born and raised in Weyburn, Saskatchewan, W.O. Mitchell arrived in 1945 and two years later won critical claim for *Who Has Seen the Wind*, a novel about a small town boy who confronts the mystery of life and death. Mitchell soon fell in love with his adopted town. Like many locals, he enjoyed the mountain scenery, the open spaces, the wooded floodplain of the river, and the convenient access to fishing. He enjoyed living in a place where he could afford a house with a yard large enough for gardening and other projects, and where people engaged in friendly banter as they conducted their business. Most importantly, High River provided grist for his fiction.[33] Mitchell created an imaginary foothills town named "Shelby" that provided the setting for his novels *The Kite* (1962) and *Roses are Difficult Here* (1990). Although Mitchell undertook extended sojourns to Toronto and other cities, he retained his High River home and returned there repeatedly.

Mitchell lived across the street from Hughena McCorquodale. Since both wrote about small communities, they encouraged each other in their work and soon became fast friends. Mitchell particularly admired Corky's satirical attacks on the pseudo sophistication of the city slicker. In "The Sex Life of Old Mount Rundle," which appeared in the *Times* on 19 June 1947, she lampooned a Hollywood movie producer who described High River's ranch country as "sexy." "Not that Albertans are against sex, such as it is," she wrote. "They've seen manifestations of it here and there, and are ready to admit that quite a number of noteworthy personalities and developments in the world have had origin in sex."[34]

Bigger challenges from the city soon arrived. A series of articles in the *Calgary Herald* attacked small towns for a litany of familiar sins: conformity, narrow vision and interests, lack of culture, nosiness, gossip, superficial friendliness, and neighbourliness based largely on borrowing items. The *Times* struck back with an editorial on 6 January 1949 that simultaneously denied the allegations and claimed that cities suffered from the same maladies. A similar confrontation erupted in 1951 when sociologist Jean Burnet published *Next-Year Country: A Study of Rural Social Organization in Alberta*. Based on a case study of the Hanna district, Burnet's book appeared in a series designed to explain how the disease of Social Credit had infected the province. The book did not present an entirely unsympathetic portrait of country life, but it contained elements similar to the allegations in the *Calgary Herald* articles and a *Times* editorial on 20 December 1951 savagely attacked Burnet. It pronounced her unfit to study rural life and declared her research superficial, based on a short field trip to Hanna where she undoubtedly talked to all the wrong people.

Burnet's book and the *Times* editorial inspired Mitchell's novel *Roses are Difficult Here*. Although not published until 1990, Mitchell drafted the basic elements of the story in the 1950s as part of a larger, unpublished manuscript entitled "The Alien."[35] Dedicated to Hughena McCorquodale, the novel concerns Matt Stanley, editor of the weekly *Shelby Chinook*. Matt had long abandoned his literary ambitions and now wrote bland accounts of social gatherings and editorials about the first signs of spring. His dreary routine is disrupted when a lady sociologist arrives from the east intent on studying the dynamics of small town life. Matt assists with her research and the townspeople embrace her with warmth and friendliness, only to recoil in horror when her book accuses them of narrow prejudices, cultural backwardness, and petty self-interest. The sociologist's accusations inspire Matt to discover the legitimate calling of the country editor when he pens a passionate defence of the community and its people.

But while the *Times* still found utility in defending rural and small town life, the image of the High River district underwent a significant metamorphosis in the post-war years. It began to see itself as a particular kind of small community: an old-fashioned western town with a colourful frontier past. The *Times* played a major role in presenting and shaping the new identity.

10 THE OLD, WILD WEST

AS HIGH RIVER and the *Times* gradually replaced an identity rooted in rural and small town virtue in favour of one based on the Wild West, they began to reconsider the nature of the district's ranching tradition. Two visions had always presented themselves: aristocratic gentility and frontier rowdiness. In his novel, *Roses Are Difficult Here*, W.O. Mitchell presents these contrasting visions. When the visiting sociologist asks the aging Senator about the area's history, he tells her about polo, fancy balls, and ladies with calling cards; the Senator's crusty foreman tells her about whiskey traders and cowboys, and about ladies without any need for calling cards.[1] Throughout the interwar years, High River and the *Times* had emphasized the aristocratic elements of ranching history, but after World War II, they no longer did so. The leading symbol of the aristocratic ideal, the abdicated king, now the Duke of Windsor, had never spent much time at his E.P. Ranch, and local residents no longer entertained hope that he would do so in the future. His last visit was in 1950. The E.P. had long been a money loser, and after failing to discover oil on the property, the Duke sold it to a local rancher in 1962.[2] By then, the wild and woolly west had completely overwhelmed genteel ranching in local imagery.

A raw and violent frontier had long been ingrained in American popular culture. Tales of Indians and wilderness adventures appeared in the eighteenth century, and they continued to proliferate as Americans poured over the Appalachian Mountains and across the Mississippi to points farther west. The popular image of cowboys propagated by dime novels and the Wild West shows of Buffalo Bill Cody appeared at the same time as the big ranches in the late nineteenth century. Virtually from their origins, Hollywood films featured a wild west, but they reached the pinnacle of their popularity from the 1940s to the early 1960s, when many of the most famous and popular westerns appeared. During the 1950s, television brought the western to the small screen where it soon entrenched itself as the dominant dramatic genre. The singing cowboy also appeared on screen and on radio, fuelling the growth of western music. Advertisers adopted western logos and icons, and an array of cowboy merchandise appeared: comic books, toys, and clothing. The golden age of the Wild West as popular culture had arrived.[3]

High River was not immune to these influences for its local theatre also showed the films of John Ford and the towering presence of John Wayne, its radios and record players blared the sounds of Gene Autry and Hank Williams, and after 1954 its newly-purchased television sets presented Hopalong Cassidy and other western heroes. The stoic Marlborough Man inhabited its magazine stands, and its stores sold Roy Rogers lunch buckets, toy six-shooters, and cowboy boots. High River readily embraced such a powerful engine of popular culture since it could claim a legitimate Wild West legacy of its own.

Since its founding, the *Times* had presented stories of the area's frontier past, but after 1945 they appeared more often and grew more fanciful. A particularly dramatic example of this new enthusiasm appeared on 25 April 1946 when the *Times* published a lengthy account of the "Lost Lemon Mine." The story concerned a fabulous gold strike high in the foothills that had been abandoned by the original prospectors and now awaited rediscovery. Several accounts existed about the origin of the story. In the most common one, Senator Dan Riley first heard the tale from High River old-timer Lafayette French. French claimed to have financed the original prospectors and to have taken many subsequent trips in the search of the lost treasure. He often asked Riley for money to finance new expeditions, and Riley sometimes humoured him with a donation.[4]

The story was embellished over the years. In the version published by the *Times*, two adventurers named Blackjack and Lemon ventured deep into the hills in search of gold. They discovered a vein of immense value but argued violently about how to proceed with their claim. That night Lemon grabbed an axe and split the head of his sleeping companion. Unbeknown to him, two Stoney Indians had followed the pair and witnessed the foul deed. They rushed to Chief Bearspaw who swore them to secrecy, fearing that whites would swarm the foothills if news of the gold leaked out. Lemon fled the area, but overwrought with guilt, he confessed his sin to a priest. The priest dispatched a half-breed mountain man to the crime scene where he buried Blackjack and covered his grave with rocks. The Indians subsequently scattered the rock pile and removed all evidence that the site had ever been visited. The following spring, Lemon led a search party into the hills, but teetering on the brink of insanity, he failed to relocate the site.

Lafayette French became obsessed with finding the mine since he claimed to possess a map drawn by Lemon. Hearing that the Stoneys knew the exact location, French tried to bribe members of the tribe into telling him the secret, but whenever someone agreed to help, he succumbed to madness or suffered a bizarre death. Chief Bearspaw had employed powerful medicine to protect the secret and soon the bravest Stoney shuddered in fear at the very mention of the lost mine. Over the ensuing decades, more adventurers attempted to find its location. They all failed, many victimized by supernatural events.

Over the years many sleuths attempted to separate fact from fiction in the legend of the Lost Lemon Mine, but truth or falsehood mattered little. The real significance of the legend was that it verified High River's claim as an authentic western town with a colourful past. On 12 and 19 February 1931 the *Times* had reported that some foolish souls passed through town in search of the gold. But when the paper recalled the incident on 16 November 1961, the trickle of treasure seekers suddenly became a "gold rush" of some 500 men.[5]

While nothing the *Times* published afterwards could match the Lost Lemon Mine for its utility as a frontier legend, it continued to print tales about the infamous local whiskey post, Fort Spitzee and the adventures of local Indians, traders, cowboys, and Mounties. A lengthy story on 11 February 1954 told how Howell Harris founded Fort Spitzee. On route from Montana, 200 Indians confronted Harris and his seven companions. When their chief spit in Harris's face, Harris knocked him over with a savage blow. Just as the

Indians threatened to slaughter the whites, none other than Gabriel Dumont—the fabled Metis chieftain who would later fight in the North-west Rebellion—rode into view and ordered the Indians away.

The Times did not act alone in promoting this new Wild West heritage of the High River district; many others in the community actively participated. Indeed, the Times often relied on the contributions of local writers who also published elsewhere, especially Guy Weadick, Senator Riley, Roy Fowler, Don King, and others who sometimes provided the paper with transcripts of talks they gave at local gatherings. In 1951, George D. Stanley published A Round-up of Fun in the Foothills. One of the first medical doctors in High River, Stanley arrived in 1901 and subsequently served terms as a provincial legislator and town councillor before moving to Calgary. The foreword to his book promised tales about the "wild and woolly west" during the early days of the "cowtown," and its pages delivered hard drinking, wild pranks, high-stakes poker, remittance men, gunplay, and much else. Stanley admitted that he presented his yarns "without any intention to provide a story of systematic continuity or logical sequence," and added that "it is not the writer's desire to attach any serious significance to these incidents from a strictly historical point of view."[6] In spite of these disclaimers, the Times praised the book on 10 January 1952 as "a real contribution to Alberta's history."

For an extensive collection of tales about the district, nothing surpassed the offerings in Leaves from the Medicine Tree, published in 1960. In many respects it served as a prototype for hundreds of community-based histories that would be written across western Canada in the 1960s and 1970s. It originated as a Jubilee project in 1955 to help celebrate Alberta's fiftieth anniversary as a province. The High River Pioneer and Old-Timers Association established a committee to plan a history of the area before 1900. The cut-off date conveniently eliminated the era of agricultural settlement and town development, which offered little more than a tame and civilized history, and instead focused the book entirely on the era that promised to yield more excitement.

The committee decided that the history should largely be told through biographical sketches of the early frontiersmen. The book would be a collaboration of the entire community, and residents throughout the district would send in stories and pictures. The committee advised contributors to carefully check the accuracy of important facts, but also encouraged them to include legends and tall tales. Given this conflicting advice, no clear distinction between fact and fancy ever emerged. Contributors consulted few documents for any aspect of the history and nearly all of it relied on oral tradition. Committee members settled disputes over facts and interpretations by arguing amongst themselves.[7]

The *Times* reported on the progress of the project from its inception, offering boundless praise and encouragement to its contributors and editors. As the book reached completion, the *Times* announced that nearly all of the 1,000 copies from the initial printing had been pre-sold, as well as 600 banquet tickets for the book launch at the Memorial Centre.[8] *Leaves* did not disappoint its audience: it bristled with tales of whiskey traders, wolfers, Indians, cowboys, and Mounties; and with the sort of antics that had populated Dr. Stanley's history. The extensive biographical section featured wild men like Lafayette French of the Lost Lemon Mine fame who once saved the famous Blackfoot chief, Crowfoot, from an assassin; Shorty Nier, a man so filthy that "his shirt collar looked like the mouth of a prairie dog hole;" Charlie Parks, a man who once performed in Buffalo Bill Cody's Wild West show but "was fired for shooting an Indian in the arse;" and Charlie Bowlegs, who could "ride pretty near everything with hair on it."[9]

Bad men appeared too, like the murderous Big Jim McDonagh; the shifty-eyed Slippery Bill, who busted out of a Texas jail and escaped to Alberta; and Walter Kesee, a man of "no morals" who had something to do with the mysterious disappearance of Slippery Bill. *Leaves* happily reported that the notorious American outlaw, Harry Longabough, better known as the Sundance Kid, had worked for the Bar U Ranch. Unfortunately, he had behaved himself while in the district.[10] *Leaves* also tried to correct some historical misconceptions, such as the legend of Liver-eating Johnson. He supposedly earned his name for his habit of consuming the livers of Indians he had killed. In actuality, he had only pretended to eat an Indian's liver in order to horrify his partner.[11] Aside from these outright "desperadoes," most of the rough characters in *Leaves* were good-hearted, adventure-loving fellows. Fiercely proud and independent, they lived by their word and judged others by what they could do rather than who they were.

The medicine tree.
Glenbow Archives NA–2711–12.

If fact and fantasy blended together in histories like Leaves, other writers preferred purely fictional forms. Catherine Bond Dick published her cow country poems in Trails I've Ridden in 1946, and Kerry Wood's Cowboy Yarns for Young Folk appeared in 1952. Don King published two novels about Indians and whiskey traders, Sukanabi and Spitzee Anota. Frances Fraser, the daughter of an Indian agent, wrote a collection of Blackfoot legends entitled The Bear Who Stole the Chinook.[12] Other forms of artist expression appeared. On 15 September 1960 the Times praised Lily Harper of High River for her paintings of Indians, early ranchers, and pioneers, many of which were subsequently acquired by the Glenbow Foundation in Calgary. Bert Smith emerged as the artist most often praised for his contributions to western heritage. Exhibitions of his rangeland photography and his paintings were held in Alberta and Montana, and he published cowboy colouring books for children.[13] Local musicians contributed less to High River's western tradition, but a cowboy band known as the Pekisko Kids provided music at local events in the 1940s and 1950s.

High River and the *Times* also searched for a symbol or icon that might represent the district's western past and in 1959 they found one. Five miles west of town stood the "medicine tree," an aging cottonwood, or rather two cottonwoods linked by a common branch. According to legend, the Blackfoot and Stoney Indians believed that this botanical oddity possessed magical powers, including the ability to lure buffalo and heal the sick, and they often left gifts at its base to nurture its spirit. The *Times* first wrote about the tree on 18 October 1906 and occasionally thereafter, but it did not become a cherished symbol until a fierce wind blew it down in 1958. Almost immediately, the town council, the Rotary club, and other interested parties hatched a scheme to rescue the fallen giant and resurrect it in the town park. The *Times* printed Catherine Dick's poem "The Medicine Tree," and issued an editorial urging High River to adopt the tree's likeness as a logo that might appear on official stationery and on souvenirs for the tourist trade. Shortly thereafter, a local saddle shop began making tooled leather coasters depicting the tree, and an organization calling itself the Medicine Tree Pow Wow Committee asked the town council to design a coat of arms that bore its likeness. The Committee also hoped to launch a Medicine Tree Museum.[14]

Meanwhile, the Medicine Tree Arch Committee cut a section from the fallen cottonwood and hauled it to the town park, where it contributed to the park's new role as an historic site. In 1950 Guy Weadick suggested that the town name it "George Lane Memorial Park," to honour both ranching history and the man who originally donated most of the land. The Committee invited Lieutenant-Governor Percy Page to unveil an historical plaque about the tree at a ceremony held in conjunction with a massive picnic that served a 1,000 pounds of barbecued beef. The committee reminded everyone to "dress western" for the occasion.[15] That same year, the name "Medicine Tree Manor" graced the newly-built seniors' residence, and the eagerly anticipated local history appeared with the title *Leaves from the Medicine Tree: A History of the Area Influenced by the Tree, and Biographies of Pioneers and Old Timers Who Came Under Its Spell Prior to 1900*. For decades thereafter, the tree continued to provide many local institutions with a logo or name.

Local businesses also contributed to High River's image. Some, like the Ranchero Restaurant, incorporated western themes in their names. The Citizen's Lumber Company depicted an Indian in ceremonial headdress in its advertisements in spite of the dubious connection between plains Indians and lumber. The weekly spread for the High River Creamery pictured a toddler in cowboy garb and the *Times* added an illustration of a mounted cowboy to its own stationery.[16] High River businesses most often identified with the old west during special events like rodeos. At such times, virtually everyone seemed compelled to feature the silhouette of a bucking bronco or similar icon in advertisements. Mistakes sometimes occurred. The June 1955 issues of the *Times* featured a logo with a cattle skull and wagon wheel stuck in shifting sand—an image associated with the American southwest. Western decorations also appeared on storefronts during rodeo week. In 1949 the window display of cafe owner Quon Chong featured an Indian maiden, teepee, and a campfire with flapjacks in the pan.[17] During the 1960s, High River merchants combined three days of price-slashing sales with a variety of entertainment and dubbed the event Pow Wow Shopping Days. Other shopping festivals were held under the banner of Rodeo Roundup.[18]

Two businesses towered above the rest in promoting High River's western heritage: Bradley's and Eamor's. By the end of World War II, Bradley's had become the oldest surviving business in town. Established in 1900 by John Bradley, but more closely identified with brother Levi who took control in 1902, it began by making harness and collars for workhorses, but in the late 1920s it gradually converted to boot and saddle-making. After World War II, it continued to manufacture and supply riding gear, but increasingly sold western clothing: Stetson hats, fancy belts, chaps, cowboy shirts, Indian moccasins and beadwork. Renovations to the store in 1950 produced a "rustic" effect and a special department for riding and rodeo equipment was dubbed "The Corral."

In contrast to most High River retailing, the business rapidly expanded. Bradley opened branch stores in Fort Macleod and Lethbridge, and a mail order catalogue appeared that supplied 25 percent of all sales by 1952. By then Bradley's claimed to offer the largest inventory of western fashions in Canada, selling extensively to ranchers throughout the west, as well as to tourists and "drugstore" cowboys. Levi's son Lou, who began working at

Felmer Eamor demonstrates the art of fancy saddle making, 1956.
Museum of the Highwood 001–004–318.

the store in 1946 and took control in 1954, also served terms on committees for rodeo and other western events. The Times often celebrated Bradley's contribution to High River's western heritage. It rewarded the long-standing and loyal advertiser with special features and lengthy historical accounts on its 50th and 60th anniversaries.[19]

The Times accorded no less honour to Eamor's Saddlery. The business began in 1941 when Felmer Eamor bought out his former employer Claude Mills, another early saddle maker. Although Eamor made everyday saddles for cowboys and pleasure riders, he distinguished himself with fancy, custom-made show saddles. Like Bradley's, Eamor's issued mail order catalogues. They promised customers "old-time hand wrought workmanship [by] artists of the old school" who proudly resisted "this modern age of assembly line production."[20] Eamor also ensured that his shop looked the part. On 21 August 1952 the Times reported of a remodelling effort that "the exterior is going definitely western…[with] imitation log in natural rustic shade." Eamor also linked his name to local western events and in 1954 he succeeded Lou Bradley as president of the High River Rodeo Association.

Even more than Bradley's, Eamor's fame spread to the outside world. The *Montreal Standard* carried a story on the business in 1951, as did the American magazine *Western Horseman* in 1957 when Eamor was inducted into the "Hall of Fame of Saddlemakers." Among the store's customers were such international celebrities as the singing McGuire Sisters and Prince Rainier of Monaco. Eamor's had long claimed the title of the largest custom saddle builders in Canada, and when the new shop opened in 1963, its 29 employees could produce 50 saddles a week.[21]

THE HIGH RIVER DISTRICT also affirmed its identity by staging various western events, especially rodeo. Controversy surrounds the origins of rodeo: some hold that the sport emerged from impromptu competitions among cowboys in the course of performing their duties, while others suggest that it owed more to the showmanship of the Wild West shows.[22] Depending on how the word is defined, several places in Mexico and the American west lay claim to the distinction of staging the first rodeo sometime during the nineteenth century. There are also competing claims for the first rodeo in Canada. Single event contests such as bronco busting certainly appeared in southern Alberta in the nineteenth century, and the High River district held its fair share of these competitions. High River also contributed to the most famous rodeo of all when George Lane became one of the "Big Four" investors who underwrote the first Calgary Stampede in 1912, although it did not become an annual event until 1923. High River's fair sometimes included rodeo events and the town staged stampedes in 1928 and 1929, but High River attached no special significance to these events.[23] On 5 July 1906 the *Times* even ventured the opinion that calf-roping contests were cruel.

High River did not seriously engage rodeo until 1945 when the Agricultural Society decided to incorporate it into its annual sports day. It considered the decision carefully, for the construction of a grandstand, corrals, and racetrack entailed considerable expense. The willingness to spend money for such purposes indicated the dual function of High River's growing identification with a wild west. It provided residents with a satisfying identity that enjoyed considerable renown in the wider world, and it also promised to lure tourists. Previous efforts to attract visitors had emphasized two sorts of attractions: viewing natural wonders and participating in outdoor activities. These enticements had yielded limited results, and rodeo now added entertainment as a third component to High River's attractions.

As the *Times* explained on 17 July 1947, rodeo provided High River with a natural tourist attraction since it originated from the historical experience and current activities of actual ranches, and it would stimulate the desire of tourists to sample other attractions of the district. The *Times* frequently noted the interrelationship of entertainment, outdoor activity, and sightseeing, and presented its case in a particularly forceful editorial on 24 August 1961:

> This is a town as rich in history as any in Western Canada. It was founded by whiskey traders, whom the Mounties marched west to disperse. Before the whiskey men, it was a site of Indian encampment and ceremony. After the Mounties, it became a bustling ranching centre. It is a town surrounded by natural beauty... To the east stretch the farming plains. To the west are foothills and the rugged Rocky Mountains. Fishing streams and camp spots abound in the west country....Wandering tourists are almost invariably attracted by history and beauty. If they come to look or rest, they also buy.

Tourism's new component neatly dovetailed with another reality. High River could transform its deteriorating business district into an asset. The rodeo soon advertised itself as "A Western Show in an Old Western Town," and even successful businesses like Bradley's and Eamor's endeavoured to look weather-beaten and rustic. At the same time, tourism provided a potential escape from economic stagnation. "Calgary shouldn't be the only one to get a major slice of the money pie," the *Times* argued on 10 May 1962, "High River will benefit...if a little thought is given and little work done and a little promotion is made." The *Times* often listed the advantages of tourism over other endeavours. On 8 March 1951, it suggested that "The tourist industry is the happiest industry in which we could be engaged," since it relied on endlessly renewable resources and allowed local residents to work with people intent on enjoyment.

The utility of rodeo as a tourist attraction forced the *Times* to change its opinion of the activity. Whereas it had once condemned calf-roping as a sport, a 31 July 1947 editorial fiercely defended rodeo against accusations of animal cruelty emanating from eastern Canada and Britain. The major rodeo of the season quickly developed into an elaborate two-day affair that by the 1950s had become known as Frontier Days. It always began with a big parade that set the proper tone. Besides presenting costumed Indians and cowboys, it recreated scenes from the old west. On 14 July 1955 the *Times* described the Alberta Hotel float that staged a poker game in a rough saloon. Another float "recaptured those colorful days...acting out the wild free life, even to an outlaw dangling by his neck."

Frontier Days also sponsored a queen contest, dances, carnival, horse fair, horse racing, novelty acts, and raffles for prizes. The rodeo itself presented calf-roping, bareback and saddle bronco riding, steer decorating, and bull riding. It also offered that special Canadian contribution to rodeo, chuckwagon races. High River promoted the event as its own invention, arguing that it originated during a cattle roundup in the district in 1892 when four chuckwagons (the horse-drawn wagons that carried the camp cooks and their supplies) decided to race to a new campsite.[24] Souvenir booklets outlined all these activities in spirited fashion. The 1948 program promised a "rollickin' rangeland rumpus."[25] Sprinkled with words like "durnest" and "howdy," these booklets freely plagiarized the language of western movies.

Although rodeo became an indispensable event for any place claiming a Wild West tradition, it did not distinguish High River from countless other towns in the North American west and it competed directly for tourists against the famous Calgary Stampede. High River responded that its rodeo was more authentic. The Mayor's greeting in the 1951 souvenir program offered plenty of assurance on that account: "Here, horseflesh and rodeo events are part and parcel of community and country life. Here you see no 'drug store cowboys.' They are the real item, and the show they produce are the result of everyday practice on ranch lands in the slopes of the foothills."[26] The *Times* reiterated the theme in an editorial on 26 June 1958:

> High River only needs to change its dress and habits modestly for these Frontier Days. Riding, roping and the development of good livestock

remain an integral part of our lives[, and...] most of the folks you see wandering around in jeans and high-heeled riding boots are authentic.

On 28 June 1956 the *Times* admitted that Frontier Days could not hope to rival Calgary's "supreme show in magnitude, glamour and clamor," but insisted that its smaller rodeo offered a "reality that a larger spectacle may lack." Fans sat closer to the action and could better appreciate the skills of the cowboys. From the High River rodeo grounds spectators could view the countryside that provided a natural setting for the events they witnessed. All in all, the High River rodeo was "much closer to the real west," than the Calgary Stampede.

Although the *Times* presented rodeo as a natural extension of everyday activities in the district, it had already become a quasi-professional sport by the time High River introduced it, and the town merely became another stop for the Foothills Circuit Rodeo Association. Most of the contestants came from outside the district, even as High River itself contributed its share of cowboys to the circuit. High River took great pride in their accomplishments at big shows like the Calgary Stampede, especially the heroics of Ron Glass who began winning chuckwagon championships in the 1940s, launching a family dynasty in the sport that would prevail into the twenty-first century.

The question of authenticity remained troubling in other ways, for if real cowboys could be defined as those who rode horses to work with cattle, then they had vanished with the closing of the open range and the end of the great roundups. When *Calgary Herald* reporter H.V. Kelly published *The Range Men* in 1912, he claimed that the true practitioners had long disappeared, the victim of "present economic conditions and half-education along socialistic lines."[27] The *Times* sometimes admitted that the working cowboy had vanished. On 19 January 1928 it observed that ranch hands spent almost all their time on foot: fixing fences, diverting water, weeding gardens, milking cows, collecting hay. In a long article on the history of the cowboy in the 18 August 1955 special Alberta Golden Jubilee edition, the *Times* noted that the modern cowboy now spent most of his time riding tractors. He rode horses not to conduct any legitimate ranch work, but for the sole purpose of honing his rodeo skills.

Boys compete in the colt scramble before a packed grandstand at the Little Britches rodeo, 1965. Museum of the Highwood 999–016–044.

In spite of dubious claims to "authenticity," most of the small ranching centres claimed to possess it, and High River cast about for some novel approach to rodeo that would distinguish the town from its rivals. In 1962 it experimented with an all-girl rodeo, the first ever held in Canada. Although the popular culture of the Wild West closely identified itself with masculinity, it always reserved a place for the frontier heroine and cowgirl, from the fictional Calamity Jane to real-life trick shooters like Annie Oakley and singing cowgirls like Dale Evans. High River boasted its own skilled cowgirl, Guy Weadick's wife "Flores LaDue," the vaudeville roping champion. Women had competed in early rodeos, including the first Calgary Stampede, and all-girl rodeos had already been held in the United States. The High River show attracted contestants from as far as Texas, and featured competitions considered less dangerous than traditional events: cow riding, calf roping, a cutting horse competition, goat tying, barrel racing, and horse racing.[28] Unfortunately for High River, women's rodeo had already started a steep decline by 1962, and henceforth the participation of women in rodeos would be increasingly confined to barrel racing, specialty acts, and queen contests.[29]

A much more successful novelty show started in 1959 when High River presented a children's rodeo known as "Little Britches." Featuring boys and girls 16 years of age and under, it was another idea imported from the United States where the first one had first been staged in 1952. With special attractions like wild colt scrambles and pony wagon races, Little Britches became the annual event that ultimately gave High River its fame within the rodeo world. Held on Victoria Day weekend in May before the regular rodeo season began, it soon featured the same variety of festive activities as Frontier Days and often rivalled it in popularity.[30]

Aside from High River's major rodeos, the *Times* also reported on smaller competitions held at private ranches. Numerous clubs appeared in the district devoted to single events or special activities such as quarter-horse racing or cutting competitions whereby horse and rider demonstrated their ability to separate a targeted animal from a cattle herd. Gymkhana clubs also appeared and sponsored various kinds of riding competitions. Tourists who appeared between major rodeo events could witness any of these events.

Indians occupied a prominent place in the legends of High River's frontier past, and their presence in the flesh became mandatory at western events. None lived particularly close; the nearest Blackfoot reserve lay 40 miles distant, and the nearest Stoney reserve even further until the creation of a satellite reserve 30 miles up the Highwood in 1948. Even so, they often responded to invitations (and promises of food and money) to attend parades, appearing as early as High River's Victoria Day celebration in 1909, and much more frequently after 1945. Of course, the welcome extended only to ceremonial Indians who appeared on horseback in museum quality costumes, displayed traditional handicrafts, and performed traditional dances.[31] Decidedly less welcome were the visits to town by out-of-costume Indians on ordinary days, especially those who appeared drunk, begged for food and money, camped on the golf course, and rooted through the nuisance grounds.

No less than Indians, Caucasians also needed to appear in costume. Cowboys in the era of the big ranches did not dress distinctively. As late as the 1906 roundup, a reporter noted that "as to dress, it is entirely as you please. No special cowboy costume is affected, not even the cowboy hat."[32] High-heeled boots, spurs, chaps, neck handkerchiefs, and wide brim hats

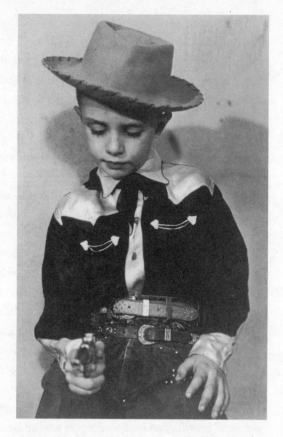

Joe Clark, c. 1945: the future Prime Minister demonstrates High River's affinity for western fashion.
Glenbow Archives PA–3520–546.

did have some use on the range, but dude versions of these items emerged as early as the 1880s. By the 1910s such accessories appeared in silent films. Although the blue jeans of Levi Strauss and the headgear of John Stetson made important contributions to western fashion, highly stylized costumes appeared after 1945. Nudie Cohen of North Hollywood designed sequined and yoked outfits for singing cowboys, who also sported fancy tooled boots and decorative saddles.[33]

As western wear assumed the mantle of fashion rather than function, it became an important ingredient in High River's self-image. Lou Bradley recalled that no one wore riding boots in town before World War II, but many did so thereafter, as well as jeans and cowboy hats.[34] Bradley exploited this trend and began to carry an extensive line of western garb in his own store. His huge inventory suggests that many people besides actual cattlemen began wearing cowboy clothes. Bill Scott, the new *Times* employee from Ontario, laid out a week's pay for a pair of fancy cowboy boots soon after his arrival in High River in 1962.[35] Children certainly affected the look and many small boys rarely appeared without cowboy duds, holsters, and toy six shooters. Women participated too, and on 26 April 1962 the *Times* claimed that High River hosted Canada's first ever cowgirl fashion show.[36] But if some people adopted the western persona in their daily attire, it seems clear from photos that most people in the area did not, and men's stores like Golightly's or Pickersgill's advertised the sort of white collar wear common to the urban office, while Maude's Fashions advertised the metropolitan origins of its women's clothing. But nearly everyone bought western clothes to wear to special events, and on such occasions the *Times* often reminded everyone to "dress western."

Costumed Indians and cowboys were imagined representations of High River's past for none of its legendary characters remained alive and resident in the district after World War II, save one. A profile of 80-year old William S. Henry appeared in the 1948 rodeo program. Billy Henry arrived in the area in 1885 and earned his reputation as a real frontiersman by taking steers to the Klondike in 1898 to feed hungry gold miners. Henry's stature as a living legend grew ever larger as he conveniently managed to stay alive. The *Times* routinely told his story on notable birthdays and for his 100th in 1967 the town planned a "Billy Henry Day." W.O. Mitchell took a keen interest in Henry, who probably provided the inspiration for Daddy Sherry, the 111-year old fictional character in Mitchell's novel *The Kite*.[37]

AS IN THE INTERWAR PERIOD, tourism challenged High River to advertise in the wider world without incurring high costs. The promotional efforts of the *Times* reached many parts of North America at no expense, thanks to the subscriptions of former residents. It also published, or printed on behalf of others, guidebooks with such titles as *This is High River: The Cowtown Capital of the Foothills*. Once again, High River found it cheaper to join other communities in southern Alberta in a common promotional campaign. They designated an area to be called "The Roamin' Empire" and prepared 25,000 travel guides.[38] Roadside signs also offered a cheap method of persuading tourists on route to Calgary and Banff to stop for a few days, or even a few hours. The Times frequently promoted the erection of historical markers and on 28 January 1960 it cheered the appearance of a plaque about Spitzee Post. On 10 May 1962 the paper eagerly anticipated sidetracking the stream of motorists that would pass by the town on route to the Seattle World's Fair or to the new highway through British Columbia's Roger's Pass.

High River always welcomed the chance to persuade others to advertise the district for nothing. Whenever touring journalists ventured near, the Times arranged for them to visit foothills ranches and to witness "western events." It reported with gratification on 21 October 1948 that a Chicago newspaper had carried an account of the rodeo under the heading "Cow Town Holiday." In 1962, touring Dutch journalists who attended the all-girl rodeo promised to send stories "around the world."[39] On 25 February 1965 the Times announced that the Little Britches would receive the international attention that the "first class tourist attraction" deserved when the British government publication, Commonwealth Today, asked for pictures to publish in an upcoming issue. On one occasion, the Times itself staged an event for the benefit of the national press. In 1949 it hosted the annual convention of the Canadian Weekly Newspapers Association in Jasper, Alberta. The Times arranged for a chuckwagon complete with four outriders to serve a western pit barbecue. Guest speaker Guy Weadick fed them western folklore, and a singing cowboy provided the entertainment.[40]

Before World War II, High River hoped that the movie industry would stimulate tourism in the district, but after the release of North West Stampede in 1948, Hollywood filmmakers produced nothing more than rumours and casual inquiries. The Times celebrated a more modest production by the National Film Board of Canada in 1961. The Saddlemaker told the story of a fourteen-year old girl who longed to win a prized saddle from the famous Eamor shop. The old medium of radio and the new one of television also provided some publicity, particularly the Canadian Broadcasting Corporation. Its mandate to focus on Canadian themes brought it to High River on several occasions. A two-day visit in 1949 to prepare a national radio show for "John Fisher Reports" resulted in a favourable "western image," for the town, and the *Times* printed the transcripts of the show on 17 and 24 November. In 1957 CBC Television conducted a camera tour of Bradley's western shop and saddle-making department for its "Country Calendar" program. In 1960 the CBC again returned to High River to televise the Little Britches rodeo.[41]

High River ranches also received considerable media attention after 1945, especially Jim Wyatt's Wyalta Ranch that bred the beautifully spotted Appaloosa horses. Its fame grew when Hollywood cowboy Slim Pickens purchased one of its horses to ride in his western movies. "Speckles Three Dot" later became a regular on the American television show "The Outlaw." The Canadian Television Network produced an entire show about the ranch and its famous horses.[42]

While the *Times* welcomed favourable publicity, it lashed out at any slight to High River or its western persona. On 14 November 1963 it blasted the Canadian government for issuing a tourist booklet listing several Alberta towns that held rodeos, "but High River, the home of stampede, the heart of the west, home of the finest horsemen and horsewomen east or west of the Rockies doesn't even rate a misspelled line." In a 14 April 1960 editorial the *Times* condemned the unflattering parodies and stereotypes of the cowboy that sometimes appeared in the metropolitan media, especially his portrayal as an "aggressive bundle of bombast beneath a ten-gallon hat, or an awkward, illiterate, and ludicrous rube." Denouncing such images as "both false and unfortunate," the *Times* suggested that an accurate portrayal would stress the cowboy's individualism, determination, patience, sense of justice, good character, and love of adventure.

Although the *Times* collaborated with local organizations and businesses to promote the Wild West image, not everyone approved. The *Times* itself employed the most indignant critic, Lillian Knupp, whose own family roots in the High River area extended to the 1880s. In a 1987 interview she vented her anger:

> I object to them [the promoters] using the phony to build an image for their town. I don't think that an American tourist comes up here...to see a cheap imitation of a Hollywood vision of the west. They don't want to see slabs on the front of our buildings, they don't

want to see the old-timers walking around in calico dresses wearing dust caps. They want to come up here to see our country as it exists, not some imitation, not some glorification of the Sundance Kid.... [They] don't want to see us put on a phony imitation of what they have at home.[43]

More importantly, Knupp herself did want to see a phoney imitation, perhaps because she regarded it as an insult to her own family's long history in the community. Knupp become High River's best and most conscientious local historian, and in several books did what she could to "correct" historical misconceptions about the district.[44]

In spite of all efforts, tourism failed to deliver significant revenue to the district, even though rodeo often attracted more visitors than High River could handle. The grandstand soon expanded to 4,000 seats, and on 8 July 1948 the *Times* claimed that 8,000 people packed the town for the first day of the competition. Frontier Days reported similar attendance throughout the 1950s and the Little Britches also drew large crowds. On 21 May 1964 the *Times* reported that "an estimated 8,000 to 9,000 persons from points far and near filled the grandstand seats, overflowed the grounds, and in some cases even into the infield." High River residents helped accommodate these crowds by taking guests into their homes, but the major rodeos flooded the town with spenders for only a few days each year.

High River hoped that the rodeos would persuade tourists to linger in the district or return to it in order to sample other delights. Ideally, it hoped to cultivate patrons like W.D. Elliot of Blenheim, Ontario. He returned almost every year between 1927 and 1957 to fish and hunt.[45] But most visitors consisted of stray tourists bound for other destinations or day visitors from nearby points in southern Alberta. In 1953 the Chamber of Commerce tried to calculate the value of tourism by asking merchants to record purchases by out-of-district visitors. The survey claimed that the average tourist spent $8.00 per visit for a total of $10,000 for the year, but the estimate did not include service stations or lodgings.[46] Some businesses benefited more than others, particularly the restaurants and western shops. Bradley's guest book recorded visitors from virtually every state and province in North America.

Visitors also sustained a modest collection of businesses devoted exclusively to tourism. Dude ranching began to decline in popularity, but in 1947 a cabin camp opened that also provided spaces for house trailers complete with electrical hookups. In 1955 a more elaborate tourist camp featured a motel, restaurant, service station, and trailer spaces with connections to water, sewer, and electricity. In 1960 the town built a new campsite on 4.5 acres within the spacious town park. In addition to local hotels, as many as four campgrounds operated simultaneously in and around the town.[47] Nonetheless, these ventures profited only during the brief summer and the autumn hunting season. Farming and ranching, and the servicing of those activities, continued to drive the local economy. In the final analysis, the energetic promotion of the old Wild West did more to provide the district with an identity than with a source of income.

11 A PARADE
OF INDIVIDUALS

THROUGH SIX DECADES of traumatic change, the Times helped fashion three distinct visions of the High River district. During the settlement boom, it presented the community as a modern, progressive place destined for metropolitan grandeur. When that dream died, the Times consoled residents by emphasizing the virtue of rural and small town life. When rural depopulation threatened the community, it portrayed High River as an old-fashioned ranching district with a wild and colourful past.

Throughout these changes in local identity, some reports in the Times remained constant and timeless, as these three examples indicate:

Mrs. Mercer, who has spent the last two weeks with her aunt, Mrs. Rolls, left on Monday morning for her home at Alix.

J.H. Golightly is enjoying holidays at the coast during August.

Mrs. Martha Westergreen is a patient in the High River hospital. Our thoughts are with her and hope she will soon be able to return home.

These items appeared on 7 December 1905, 5 August 1937, and 21 November 1963 respectively, but similar entries could be plucked from any issue in any era.

The columns of the town and country correspondents consisted of little more than brief personal notes, but almost every story presented an opportunity to include the names of local individuals. One energetic reader of the Times reported to the editor on 11 August 1932 that some 600 names had appeared in a recent issue, generated by 250 reports relating to places, organizations, and events. A quick glance at virtually any issue of the Times illustrates its propensity for listing names. The 47 people who donated money towards the purchase of baseball uniforms all received mention on 11 August 1921, and the fourteen donors inadvertently left out had their names published in the next issue. On 17 August 1961 the Times listed all 178 graduates of local swimming classes. Local fairs provided the opportunity to list prize winners in dozens of categories, but on 29 August 1918 the Times may have set a record for itself in publishing names related to a single story when it identified all 481 individuals who donated money to the wartime Red Triangle Fund. "If it were possible," the Times insisted on 15 September 1960, "an editor would like to have Everyone's name in the paper Every Week." Many country editors checked subscription lists to ensure that each reader appeared in the paper at least once or twice a year and a 1956 study even suggested that a weekly's success depended on such coverage. For that reason editors often admonished their country correspondents for repeating the same names in their weekly columns.[1]

A new way to include individuals in the paper presented itself after 1960 when the introduction of offset printing facilitated the publication of photographs. Instead of concentrating on the fabulous scenery that it often boasted about, the Times photographed people. Twelve pictures appeared in the paper on 14 March 1963, of which eleven portrayed district residents, and ten of those provided captions that identified each person.

Whenever possible, the Times ventured beyond the mere listing of names to include a brief commentary on each individual in a story. An account of a masquerade dance on 7 February 1918 described the costumes worn by more than 40 individuals. A report on a women's baseball game between High River and Claresholm on 19 August 1926 paid tribute to every participant:

> Miss Clara Elocate pitched the entire game for High River and showed fine control, speed and remarkable coolness in the critical moments.

> Miss Smith performed nobly behind the plate despite a slight nervousness that will vanish with more experience. Lila Thompson our "old reliable" excelled at first base.

The story continued in a similar fashion and singled out each player for praise, but the *Times* discovered many ways to confer celebrity. "Last Friday evening J.R. Hinshaw brought in...a huge turnip which weighed fifteen pounds," announced the paper on 13 September 1906. George Cummingham astonished onlookers with a giant mushroom, which received favourable notice on 16 September 1954. Such stories simultaneously satisfied an inexhaustible appetite for freaks of nature and afforded recognition to the individuals lucky enough to have grown or discovered them. A person did not need to do anything more significant than catch the sniffles in order to earn a comment in the rural weekly. "We are pleased to report Mrs. K. Andrews, who had a severe attack of cold, is in a fair way to recovery," the *Times* announced on 23 December 1909.

The *Times* even connected local names to the limited national and international stories that found their way into the paper. "War news" that appeared on 27 April 1916 concerned the paper's own employee:

> Pte. Tommy Logan, writing from France, states that one day he was reclining in the trenches, taking life easy for a short spell, when a voice shouted as if in authority, "Private Logan, what do you take this place for—a rest camp?" Tom sprang to attention, and was amazed to see his old college chum, Pte. Harry Richards, instead of his superior officer. Needless to say they were glad to see each other, and High River was the topic of conversation.

Local residents could be linked to world events in any number of imaginative ways, as a story on 23 April 1942 demonstrates:

> Tom Fetherston was in quite a dither on Monday. It was his birthday, and as usual should have been a great cause for rejoicing. But what upset him was the realization that he had to share birthday honors with Hitler. The thought was beyond endurance. So Tom is unofficially

postponing his birthday for one week to clear himself of this contamination.

In addition to brief snippets, almost every issue of the *Times* singled out some individuals for extended commentary. Personal achievements provided a ready opportunity, especially when they occurred in the "outside world" and brought distinction to the district. Local farmers and ranchers earned a story whenever their livestock won major prizes. Odette de Foras, the daughter of a local rancher who excelled as an opera singer in London and New York, received accolades in the *Times*, but so did nine-year old Eugene Murphy when he achieved honours in an international music exam.[2] The paper also bestowed praise for relatively mundane accomplishments. When Zeb Leigh received a life membership in the Canadian Plumbing and Mechanical Contractors Association, the *Times* honoured him on 1 October 1964 with an account of his early training as a plumber and his long years in the business in High River.

Residents who traveled to far away places received considerable attention. A two-column story on India that appeared on 14 July 1921 largely recorded the experiences and perceptions of a High River missionary and his wife. Not surprisingly, such stories revealed more about the travelers than the places visited. When H.W. Blaylock returned from an extended trip, he declared in the 25 October 1906 issue that Japan was an interesting place so long as a person did not mind being wheeled about in a "baby carriage [by] half-clad men," and "taking off his boots about fifty times a day."

But common events like births, deaths, weddings, anniversaries, birthdays, retirements, and relocations also presented opportunities to single out individuals for special notice. Except for famous people, the metropolitan dailies reduced such stories to curt announcements stacked in columns like so many classified advertisements. By contrast, the weeklies paid them considerable attention.[3] The wedding story of Norma Spangler and Jesse Percifield that appeared in the *Times* on 17 January 1952 provided biographical information on the bride and groom, a summary of the remarks made by the minister and by those offering toasts, and long descriptions of the clothing worn by the entire wedding party. The story presented similar details about the decorations, the dinner, the dance, the honeymoon plans, and the bride's traveling clothes. A list of the out-of-district guests also appeared. Obituaries provided the occasion to assure families that their dearly departed led noteworthy lives. A front-page story on 3 May 1928 announcing the death of a local resident provided a full column of text, which read, in part:

> Mrs. Gillis was almost ninety-three years of age, and although failing physically for some time, she retained her keenness of intellect and interest in external events to the last. She was a woman of strong and beautiful character, beloved by all. Her life was filled with kindly deeds, with service and with brightness.

Numerous examples demonstrate that the *Times* did not restrict extended stories on individuals to people of prominence. Certainly, notable residents like George Lane, Senator Dan Riley, or Guy Weadick often appeared in print. And stories of entertaining by the wealthier and more socially active residents sometimes resembled the society pages of the metropolitan daily. When Mrs. T.W. Robertson invited twenty ladies to a bridge party at her home, the *Times* provided a lengthy account of the affair on 30 July 1908, including a description of the decorations: "the color scheme of the room being effectively and charmingly carried out by the bouquets of yellow daisies on the tables, clusters of the same flowers being inter-twinned with ribbon in a deeper shade of the same color and bunches of wheat tied with yellow ribbon to the chandelier." Such stories validated the social position of those who could afford to entertain lavishly, to host guests for lengthy periods, or to travel on extended and expensive vacations.

But by no means did the *Times* ignore those in less prestigious circumstances. On 8 September 1949 a long article honoured Harry Pollard who served 36 years as a school janitor and 42 years as the Anglican Church organist. Similarly, on 28 August 1941 the *Times* carried a ten-paragraph story on local postal worker, Bob Telfer, who had logged 12,400 miles hauling mail between the train station and the post office. Fifteen years later when postal authorities decided to move mail in and out of town by truck, Bob lost his job. The *Times* paid him tribute on 27 January 1955: "he has been a faithful servant of the public in all kinds of weather, at all hours of day and night. In earlier years there were four mail trains daily which meant a much more demanding job than the present generation realize." Additional stories about Teller's mail-carting days appeared on 21 and 28 April.

The *Times* easily gathered information about local people because they willingly offered it to the paper's reporters and correspondents. But the *Times* also routinely asked readers to submit stories about themselves to the paper directly. It specifically asked for information related to births, marriages, deaths, arrivals and removals, losses, robberies, accidents, illness, crops, land deals, social gatherings, out-of-district visits, and out-of-district visitors.[4] Those who provided the information also became its chief audience. Individuals derived their identity from many sources, but having it confirmed in hard print provided considerable gratification. Most urban people were denied that pleasure; their names did not appear in the daily press unless they occupied positions of importance or committed a noteworthy act (whether noble or criminal). A *Times* editorial observed on 30 July 1931 that, "The editor of the metropolitan daily sees the whole picture of the world's doings pass before him. But he has neither the leisure or the opportunity to dig down into the intimate lives of his own people." Even when the daily provided "human interest" stories, only a tiny percentage of its readers knew the profiled individual. By contrast, 81 percent of the weekly readers surveyed for the 1960 study of the *Lacombe Globe* said that their name, or that of a family member, had appeared in the paper in the past year.[5] And every reader of a weekly knew many, or even most, of the names that appeared in each issue.

News about family, friends, neighbours, and acquaintances comforted readers almost as much as stories about themselves. It confirmed the existence of an intimate society in a real community and provided assurance of one's membership in it. "What may seem trivial to outsiders is of great importance and interest to the local readers and to readers who have moved away from their home town," noted a Canadian Weekly Newspapers Association publication.[6] In 1948 that organization co-operated with the National Film Board of Canada to produce *The Home Town Paper*, a documentary that explored a British Columbia weekly, the *Vernon News*. When it interviewed a local angler about his catch, the narrator informed viewers that "this is the very stuff of the home town paper, the local intimate thing."

A poem by Effie Crawford entitled "The Newsy Weekly Paper from the Old Home Town" which the *Times* printed in whole or part on several occasions, also identified news about "the folks we know" as the heart and soul of the rural press.⁷

The thirst for information about local individuals also explains why subscribers routinely read the classified advertisements. An astute reader could combine a commercial notice with other information to draw a fuller picture of an individual's activities or circumstances. "Piano in good condition, $200," resonated with meaning for the knowledgeable reader. Even if no name appeared in the classified ad, a sleuth could often determine who placed it by noting the phone number provided. People in small communities came to know dozens of four digit numbers that remained unchanged for decades.⁸ As the film *The Home Town Paper* explained, "advertising in the weekly press, where the paper is read from front to back, falls very much into the category of news." The weekly thus appeared as a big puzzle that challenged the reader to connect every item in it with someone they knew personally. This peculiarity helps explain why weeklies rarely offered the sort of entertainment features found in the dailies; the entire paper provided entertainment.

The plethora of personal items in the *Times* might suggest that small communities deserved their reputation as hotbeds of gossip. But if gossip is defined as unsubstantiated rumour of a derogatory nature, then the weekly did not indulge in gossip. Virtually no disparaging comment about any local individual ever appeared in the paper. On 18 October 1923 the *Times* specifically warned its correspondents against providing any information that might embarrass anyone, such as "insider" comments or items about "courting." The policy was consistent with the weekly's desire to avoid conflict and controversy within the community, and to offend neither reader nor advertiser. Yet the *Times* did not always avoid embarrassing news. In its first decades of existence it routinely published all the final grades of school pupils, including those who failed, and it sometimes named local people who had been fined or convicted in court. During the 1930s it published the names of all who applied for relief, those who received it, the amounts granted, and the goods authorized for purchase.⁹ But under Charles A. Clark, fewer unpleasant facts appeared. He once wrote to his son Peter that he had always tried to convince other weekly editors about the importance of "manners, principles; appearance and courtesy."[10]

To a considerable extent, the *Times* avoided derisive comments and unsubstantiated rumour because most individuals supplied the information about themselves directly. Instead of appearing in print, gossip in small communities circulated verbally, as W.O. Mitchell accurately observed in *Roses are Difficult Here*. When the editor of his fictional weekly assists the visiting sociologist with her study of the community, virtually everyone hears that they are having an affair, except the editor himself. By contrast, written gossip only appeared in urban publications where it focused on celebrities rather than ordinary people.

Those who criticized the weeklies complained about more than a propensity for gossip or trivia. They believed that by ignoring divisive local issues and avoiding criticism and controversy, the weeklies had abdicated journalistic responsibility. They painted unrealistic, perhaps even fraudulent, portraits of communities and their residents.[11] Such indictments of the weekly press mirrored indictments of the small community itself. When sociologists began systematically studying it during and after the 1930s, they found no end of social divisions based on class, occupation, religion, ethnicity, race, behaviour, morality, longevity in the community, and other characteristics, and they often reported seething resentments among such groups.[12] These studies provided the scholarly "evidence" for the attacks that metropolitan journalists and novelists starting launching against rural and small life in the 1920s.

The *Times* often denounced such critics and denied the existence of any significant social divisions or conflicts. In defending the small community, the *Times* also defended its own portrayal of it. Even when the paper hinted at troubles (generally unspecified), it made no apology for ignoring or minimizing them. It confessed to treating all stories with "a kindly touch that is widely different from the unfeeling publicity of the city press." While the dailies wallowed in human depravation, the *Times* proudly chose to present "cheerful little stories [from] the happier side of life."[13]

Local critics of both the community and the *Times* certainly existed, although their views were rarely documented and preserved. Grace Clark once received a letter from a former student who expressed herself candidly.

The girl's father, a wife-beater, had abandoned the family, leaving mother and three children in poverty. She hated school because she had to wear "hand-me-downs," and she never "fit in" socially. "I was looked down upon [by] the town of High River," she complained. She dropped out of school and worked as a waitress for four years. She finally returned to her education, but continued to wait tables at night. Her bitterness never dissipated and she ended the letter with a vow that "someday I'm going to tell the town of High River to kiss my rear end."[14] This young lady perhaps represented the 1960s version of the "knockers and kickers" that the *Times* often denounced during the booster era. The specific complaints of such people never appeared in the paper, although a rare letter to the editor on 5 October 1916 denounced High River as an unsociable place, especially for single people. Country editors also knew that some people in their communities always mocked the weeklies; and some always asked that their names be kept out of the paper.[15]

In spite of the existence of such people, it is clear that the great majority of residents supported the vision of the community that the *Times* presented. The survival and success of the newspaper, and the adulation and awards it received from its peers, testify that the *Times* knew how to best satisfy its audience. Its most articulate residents often spoke out in defence of the community, and by extension, in defence of the *Times*. W.O. Mitchell never denied or ignored the dark side of small town society in his novels, yet he expressed an authentic love for his adopted home: "High River is special for me, and I cannot tell what sets this town of mine apart from the others in my affection, any more that I could analyze the stresses in a spider's web."[16] Charles A. Clark did not present a positive view of High River simply because his job as publisher required it. After his death, Grace told an interviewer that Charles actually believed that the only conceivable place in the world to live was High River.[17] "It was inherently a generous place," remembered Joe Clark, "a place where people would quite genuinely sacrifice some of their interests to help their neighbour. I can't think of many people with whom I grew up who are exceptions to that rule."[18]

Readers sometimes expressed in writing what they most cherished about the newspaper's representation of the community. Tributes most often came from former residents, or those temporarily removed from the district because of school or military duty—people who had occasion to write letters about such matters. "Only those away from home know the enjoyment that comes from opening the homepaper," wrote Varno Westersund in a letter to the editor that appeared on 5 March 1942 explaining what the Times meant to a boy in the service: "I devour every line, even read the classifieds and each and every ad. In fact, I have got down to putting the paper on a ration basis, so that each night a section can be read to dispel the aches one feels so far from home." The following year, Sergeant Westersund felt compelled to amplify his views in a letter published on 1 July 1943: "The pages of that little paper crystallize what we are fighting for, the homey editorials, the item that Mr. and Mrs. John Doe celebrated a silver anniversary, that next Saturday is auction day, that the church is holding a supper, that Mr. Smith has some good seed oats for sale."

In 1945 former High River resident Ellison Capers of Poughkeepsie, New York wrote a personal letter to Charles Clark not intended for publication in the Times. Capers expressed his joy upon receiving the paper and noted three items in a recent issue that particularly impressed him: an editorial by Hughena McCorquodale ("...we still think she is the best editorial writer in the world"); an article about flooding in the park, which reminded him of the softball games played there on hot summer nights; and an account of the safe return of a local boy from the war. "It all makes me very homesick," wrote the nostalgic subscriber.[19] Capers identified stories that represented the three broad categories of the newspaper's appeal: one that reflected the image and aspirations of the community as a whole, one that focused on its organizations and activities, and one that identified the place of the individual in local society.

Through each era of change in the High River district, the Times reflected and recorded local activities, attitudes and aspirations, articulated them in print and defended, justified, and validated them for the community as a whole, for its many institutions, and for its individual residents. In doing so, it performed functions quite unlike those of the metropolitan daily. One of the reasons why scholars have neglected the weekly is that none of the great issues that engulf journalism seem relevant to the rural press: freedom of speech, bias and objectivity, the confidentiality of sources, ethics in collecting information, the protection of privacy, and the independence of the press. Indeed, a more appropriate comparison for the weekly within the realm of communications is not with the daily press, but with the institutional newsletter, especially those issued by organizations small enough for many of the members to know each other personally. Whether issued by a business, a school, a church, or a sports club, the newsletter does not exist to inform, educate, or entertain, but rather to reflect and articulate the goals and aspirations of the institution. It avoids internal controversies and conflicts, and emphasizes "the happier side of life." It clogs its pages with names that bind individuals to the institution and to each other. And it is read in its entirely and with pleasure by those who already know what it is likely to say.

PART IV

AFTER 1966

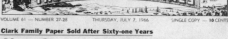

Front page announcing the sale of the Times, 7 July 1966. Clark Family Papers.

Overleaf: Boys compete in the colt scramble before a packed grandstand at the Little Britches rodeo, 1965. Museum of the Highwood 999-016-044.

12 | POSTSCRIPT
HIGH RIVER AND THE *TIMES* AFTER 1966

IN 1966 CHARLES A. CLARK decided to sell the *Times*. The fortieth anniversary issue of 6 December 1945 had predicted that the business would remain under Clark management for another 40 years thanks to the births of Joe and Peter Clark. The boys worked at the paper during childhood and even developed complementary skills: Joe began writing while Peter learned about printing. For a time, Joe seemed destined for a career in journalism. Using his high school column as a springboard, he wrote for the student newspaper at the University of Alberta, *The Gateway*, and became its editor. In summer, he also penned some articles for the *Calgary Herald* and *Edmonton Journal*. At age 21 he still considered becoming a journalist, but a more compelling interest in public affairs ultimately carried him into politics.[1] Peter decided on a career in law.

In 1964 Charles A. wrote to a friend: "I don't think either Joe or Peter will be interested [in the business] and there seems little reason why a fellow should knock himself out trying to build for succession duties."[2] Charles also complained of heart problems. Later that year he wrote to the boys:

> Seems, as the years go on, that the management and finances of the office cut deeper into time available. No longer can you do the work you would like to do—it becomes work that must be done, regardless of how distasteful it may be. And recently I don't get the work

done as fast as I once did and can't spend the night hours. Those are some of the reasons, Joe, why I don't do enough writing or even photography any more....too damn many spelling errors creep into the Times (It's another thing I'll have to do—proofread).³

Charles became less active in the daily operation of the business, and two years later sold the Times to his back shop manager, Don Tanner, an experienced printer who joined the staff in 1960. Back shop employee Tommy Logan, who first started at the Times in 1913, also decided to retire in 1966. Charles devoted himself to a host of community projects and organizations during his retirement. He died on 10 May 1982 at the age of 71. His wife Grace lived until 1997.

It would be too tidy to pronounce the sale of the Times as the end of an era. Nonetheless, a gradual shift in the destiny of the High River district became evident by the late 1960s. Rural depopulation did not empty the countryside as the Times had feared, and High River continued to function as an important service centre for ranchers and farmers. Indeed, the 1970s proved to be a decade of great prosperity for rural Alberta. High River also retained its importance as an administrative centre for education, health and government, but other developments soon overwhelmed these traditional functions. Calgary's explosive growth continued unabated. Most of its new population settled in sprawling suburbs, especially on the south side of the city where construction intruded into the Municipal District of Foothills as early as 1955. By 1959 applications for new subdivisions in the rural municipality had become commonplace and land annexations by Calgary brought the borders of the city within 26 miles of High River by 1964.⁴ The infringing city raised the value of farmland beyond anything warranted by agricultural activity, which pleased many landowners, but some worried about the urban invasion. A speaker at the High River Rotary club warned his audience that when city people encroached on the countryside, they suddenly demanded the abolition of feedlots and other agrarian activities.⁵

The four-lane highway that had so raised the ire of High River and the Times also made it feasible to live in the town and commute to Calgary. The Times claimed that this phenomenon first began in 1958, and on 23 April

1959 it reported that five people who worked in downtown Calgary had organized a car pool. Commuting became much more common during the 1970s. Throughout North America, many people desired to escape the city that they associated with congestion, crime and pollution, and the suburbs that they condemned for sterility and boredom. "Back to the land" enthusiasts bought small acreages in rural areas, which soon reversed the trend of rural depopulation near metropolitan areas. Others moved to small towns within commuting distance of their work, hoping to take advantage of lower real estate costs and the imagined benefits of small town social life. Ironically, they moved into new High River subdivisions quite indistinguishable in layout and architecture from the Calgary suburbs they had fled.

Robert Stead had predicted such a future for High River in the 30 May 1912 issue of the *Times*. He discussed the futility of boosterism in small prairie towns and claimed that few of them would sustain their frontier growth rates. Still, he believed High River would grow because of its proximity to Calgary. Some day, he claimed, city people would move there to take advantage of its scenic charms and reasonable land costs.

The commuters did not completely overwhelm the old town. A population of 2,339 in 1966 slowly but steadily climbed to 9,345 by 2001. Towns closer to Calgary experienced more vigorous growth, including Okotoks. It had always been much smaller than High River, but surpassed it as a commuter town with a larger population in 1986.

High River finally addressed the long-standing problem of a deteriorating downtown. As fears of depopulation abated, merchants became more interested in new investment, especially when others promised to pay for major redevelopment costs. Inspired by the Alberta Urban Renewal Advisory Committee, the town learned that senior government agencies could be tapped for funds. Under the auspices of the Research and Planning Staff of the Calgary Regional Planning Commission, a bold and ambitious plan emerged to demolish buildings in three downtown blocks and to replace them with a shopping centre, a pedestrian mall, low cost public housing, off-street parking, and other improvements. The project would be financed by a partnership involving three levels of government and various private interests that included the Canadian Pacific Railway. The partnership would buy and redevelop the properties, and then sell them back to individual owners. Under this proposal the town government would pay less than twenty percent of the costs.[6]

On 28 March 1968 the *Times* argued that High River needed the project to maintain and expand its trade, to generate more tax revenue, and to stimulate the economy generally. Charles A. Clark, now free from the work of the newspaper, devoted his time to the High River Community Development Association, which provided local input for the project. The ambitious plan never fully materialized. The senior levels of government pulled their support and only the first phase of the project, representing about one-third of the total work, reached completion.[7] Nonetheless, on 18 October 1973 the *Times* reported on the grand opening of the new Pioneer Square and the controversial windmill sculpture that graced it.

Not only did the growth of High River proceed in an unanticipated fashion after 1966, but it did not bring as many benefits as predicted. Additional people stimulated the local economy, but it also attracted new businesses that seized trade from the old merchants. Moreover, a tremendous volume of consumer shopping still took place in Calgary. Growth also created tension between those still in engaged in the life of the old agricultural service centre and the new commuters, a collection of strangers who often seemed detached from the community and its traditional interests.

Another economic development delivered further surprises. High River realized a long-standing ambition when it finally captured a major industry. An attempt by the provincial government to launch a magnesium factory in the town ended in failure, but in 1989 the Cargill corporation opened a monstrous beef-packing plant near the town that employed 1,600 shift workers by 1996 and could process 3,600 cattle per day.[8] Cities throughout North America began to banish such industries from their borders, determined to eliminate corrals of bawling cattle and the stench of manure and slaughter. The big meatpackers happily migrated to rural areas that offered cheaper land, lower taxes, and fewer critical residents.

Although High River acquired the industrial base that it had always craved, it did not contribute to the town in the manner anticipated. The *Times* had always argued that industry would provide jobs for High River residents, but Canadian workers now balked at toiling in slaughterhouses. Most of

Cargill's employees consisted of recent Asian immigrants who preferred to live in Calgary where they maintained ties to their ethnic communities. They commuted to High River by bus.[9] Each day on the highway they passed carloads of High River residents commuting to white-collar jobs in Calgary.

High River's long-standing interest in tourism remained intact and it continued to market itself as an old Wild West town. Chuckwagon races and the Little Britches rodeo still sustained that image. The old stone railway station became a provincial historic site in 1983 and then home to the Museum of the Highwood. The federal government contributed to High River's western heritage by creating an historic site at the ranch headquarters of the old Bar U in 1995. During the 1990s, the town commissioned the painting of seventeen giant murals on the sides of downtown buildings. Most of them portrayed scenes from the district's frontier era.[10]

Few people questioned the legitimacy of High River's Wild West past. By the late twentieth century, small towns everywhere began creating far more artificial images for themselves. St. Paul, Alberta built a landing pad for alien spacecraft in 1967. High River's old rival, Vulcan, lurched further in that unlikely direction. It took advantage of the curious fact that the town's name matched that of the home planet of an alien being in the cult television program "Star Trek." The town vigorously promoted itself as a destination for fans of the program by building a model spaceship, sponsoring "Star Trek" conventions, and selling related souvenirs. Other Alberta towns succumbed to gigantism. Vegreville built a giant model of an Easter egg; Glendon, a giant pyrogy; Vilna, giant mushrooms; Andrew, a giant duck; Smoky Lake, a giant pumpkin; and Mundare, a giant sausage.[11] Each town claimed some historical connection to its monstrosity and each hoped that tourists would visit, but perhaps these stunts represented a desperate cry for recognition and identity.

The role of the *Times* also changed in the new era that unfolded after 1966. For many years, little seemed different as the paper continued to exhibit all the characteristics typical of the rural weekly press. But a glance through recent issues of the *Times*, or at the companion *Regional*, published by the *Times*, and five other weeklies, reveals that many familiar traits have disappeared or become muted, while more characteristics of the urban daily have appeared. Notably absent are extensive social notes on the activities of individuals in the town and various rural districts. That focus made increasingly less sense as the town acquired more commuters and thereby increased the pool of strangers who would not all come to know each other personally.

More subtle changes also appeared. The community and the Times had traditionally worked together to promote economic growth and to create local identities. Increasingly, these campaigns became the engineered products of paid bureaucrats, analysts, and consultants.[12] Instead of acting as a participant in these community affairs, the Times increasingly restricted itself to reporting on them.

Technological and organizational changes accompanied this transformation. The Times relied more on computers for writing and formatting. It quit printing its own copy and joined a central offset press in Calgary in 1979, pursuing a course that Charles A. Clark had tried to initiate in the early 1960s. Even so, the paper remained locally owned and edited for many years. Don Tanner sold the Times to his son Glen and to Bill Holmes, a High River native who first performed odd jobs at the Times as a child. Glen Tanner subsequently sold his interest to George Meyer, but Holmes remained a partner until 1995. By then the huge corporate chains that had long ago swallowed up Canada's dailies finally turned their attention to the rural weeklies of southern Alberta. Westmount Publishing bought the Times and other rural papers in 1995. A quick series of corporate take-overs soon placed the Times under the ownership of Quebecor World, the largest printing company on earth.[13] Managers and editors at the Times became employees instead of owners, and the distinction between the newspaper and the community it served grew sharper.

In spite of these changes, the Times and its employees remained proud of their newspaper's long history and its contribution to local heritage, a role it continued to honour on the front page of every issue with the words "Founded in 1905 by Charles Clark."

NOTES

ABBREVIATIONS

AWN   Alberta Weekly Newspapers Association Papers, Glenbow Archives, Calgary
BU   Bar U Ranch Collection, Parks Canada, Calgary
CFP   Clark Family Papers, privately held, Peter Clark, Calgary. (Most now deposited in Glenbow Archives, Calgary.)
GA   Glenbow Archives, Calgary
HRT   High River Times
MH   Museum of the Highwood, High River, Alberta

INTRODUCTION

1. Paul Rutherford, *The Making of the Canadian Media* (Toronto: McGraw Hill-Ryerson, 1978), 2–6; W.H. Kesterton, *A History of Journalism in Canada* (Toronto: McClelland and Stewart, 1967), 1–9; Anthony Smith, *The Newspaper: An International History* (London: Thames and Hudson, 1979), 47, 75–76.
2. Kesterton, *History of Journalism*, 10–23; Rutherford, *Canadian Media*, 12.
3. Paul Rutherford, *A Victorian Authority: The Daily Press in Late Nineteenth-century Canada* (Toronto: University of Toronto Press, 1982), 36–37,

190–94; F.S. Siebert, "The Libertarian Theory of the Press," in Siebert and others, eds., *Four Theories of the Press* (Urbana: University of Illinois Press, 1963), 39–71; Rutherford, *Canadian Media*, 24–31; Kesterton, *History of Journalism*, 56–57.
4. Rutherford, *Victorian Authority*, 213.
5. H.E. Stephenson and Carlton McNaught, *The Story of Advertising in Canada: A Chronicle of Fifty Years* (Toronto: Ryerson, 1940), 265. For the general decline of political influence see Minko Sotiron, *From Politics to Profit: The Commercialization of Canadian Daily Newspapers, 1890–1920* (Montreal and Kingston: McGill-Queen's University Press, 1997).
6. Rutherford, *Canadian Media*, 7.
7. Leonard D'Albertanson, ed., *The Printed Word, 1904–1955: The Story of Alberta Division, Canadian Weekly Newspapers Association* (Wainwright, Alta.: Alberta Division, Canadian Weekly Newspapers Association, 1955), 36; Executive Meeting Minutes, 15 Sept. 1951, AWN, box 1 file 1, GA.
8. HRT, 18 Sept. 1930. Scarcely a year passed prior to 1966 that the *Times* did not receive an award or honourable mention in some category, either provincially or nationally.
9. HRT, 14 May 1936.
10. J. George Johnston, *The Weeklies: Biggest Circulation in Town* (Bolton, Ont.: Canadian Weekly Newspapers Association, 1972), 25.
11. See, for example, HRT, 14 Nov. 1907, 3 Mar. 1921.
12. Certificate of Honourable Carrier Record with *The Calgary Herald*, Sept. 1953 to May 1956, CFP.
13. Charles A. Clark, taped interview with T.W. Kirkham, 1981, GA; Johnston, *The Weeklies*, 248.
14. Canadian Weekly Newspapers Association and the Alberta Division of the Canadian Weekly Newspapers Association, "A Readership Study of a Canadian Weekly Newspaper," unpub. ms., 1960, 18, AWN, box 15 file 145, GA. The weeklies anticipated some of these findings in Alberta Weekly Newspapers Association, *Meet Mr. Alberta* (by author, 1953?); HRT reported similar findings in the United States on 3 Apr. 1947, 27 Feb. 1958.
15. Kesterton, *History of Journalism*, 153–54.
16. See, for example, Alexander B. Brook, *The Hard Way: The Odyssey of a Weekly Newspaper Editor* (New York: Bridge Works, 1993), which focuses on a crusading weekly that behaved much more like a daily; or Robert Hill, *Voice*

of the Vanishing Minority: Robert Sellar and the Huntingdon Gleaner (Montreal and Kingston: McGill-Queen's University Press, 1998) which examines opinion in a country weekly about the decline of English-speaking farmers in rural Quebec. Journal articles often focus on even narrower themes; see, for example, Jean Folkerts and Stephen Lacy, "Weekly Editors in 1900: A Quantitative Study of Demographic Characteristics," in Journalism Quarterly 63 no. 1 (Spring 1987): 429–33.

17. Robert Fulford, "The Press in the Community," in D.B.L. Hamlin, ed., The Press and the Public (Toronto: University of Toronto Press, 1962), 23–34. Press influence is discussed in Melvin L. DeFleur and Sandra J. Ball-Rokeach, Theories of Mass Communication, 5th ed. (New York: Longman, 1989).

18. Mary Vipond, The Mass Media in Canada (Toronto: James Lorimer, 1989), 101–4; Denis McQuail, Towards a Sociology of Mass Communications (London: Collier-Macmillan, 1969), 44–49, 96.

19. Alex S. Edelstein and J. Blaine Schulz, "The Leadership Role of the Weekly Newspapers as Seen by Community Leaders: A Sociological Perspective," in Lewis A. Dexter, ed., People, Society and Mass Communications (London: Free Press of Glencoe, 1964), 231.

20. D'Albertanson, Printed Word, 33, 61, 66; Johnston, The Weeklies, 234–50.

21. Mary Clark attended local Roman Catholic services and functions. In 1906 Charles became a charter member of the local Masonic lodge (which only Protestants could join), but he was not baptized in the local Anglican church until after his wife's death in 1936. See "Certificate of Baptism: Diocese of Calgary," 18 Mar. 1937, CFP. Historical sketches of sixteen High River churches appear in Lillian Knupp, Life and Legends: A History of the Town of High River (Calgary: Sandstone Publishing, 1982), 49–61.

22. Quoted in Johnston, The Weeklies, 45–46.

23. Quoted in Bill Holmes, "Up a Windmill," HRT, 13 May 1982.

24. Johnston, The Weeklies, 27; D'Albertanson, Printed Word, 36.

25. Lillian Knupp, taped interview with Kimberly Speers, 1 July 1998. Privately held by Kimberly Speers.

26. Charles A. Clark, taped interview.

27. Donna Livingstone, "Joe Clark's West," Glenbow Magazine 13 no. 2 (Summer 1993), 5.

28. Johnston, The Weeklies, 39.

1 HIGH RIVER BEFORE THE *TIMES*

1. The Blackfoot word "sspiksil" means "tall wood;" the word "sspssi" means "high." See Donald G. Frantz and Norma Jean Russell, *Blackfoot Dictionary of Stems, Roots, and Affixes*, 2nd. ed. (Toronto: University of Toronto Press, 1995), 227, 228; Hugh A. Dempsey, "Blackfeet Place-Names," *Alberta Historical Review* 4 no. 3 (Summer 1956): 30.
2. Margaret Kennedy, "Final Report: Research Excavations at EdPl-12; A Whiskey Trade Era Structure, High River ASA Permits 85–80 and 86–27," unpub. ms. prepared for Archaeological Society of Alberta, Dec. 1986, MH; Margaret A. Kennedy, *The Whiskey Trade of the Northwestern Plains* (New York: Peter Lang, 1997), 74–77.
3. Paul F. Sharp, *Whoop-Up Country: The Canadian-American West, 1865–1885* (Norman: University of Oklahoma Press, 1973; first published 1955), 51–53; William R. Hunt, *Whiskey Peddler: Johnny Healey, North Frontier Trader* (Missoula, Mont.: Mountain Press, 1993), 57–60.
4. High River Pioneers and Old Timers Association, *Leaves From the Medicine Tree: A History of the Area Influenced by the Tree, and Biographies of Pioneers and Old Timers Who Came Under Its Spell Prior to 1900* (High River, Alta.: by author, 1960), 29; Philip Weinard, "Early High River and the Whiskey Traders," *Alberta Historical Review* 4 no. 3 (Summer 1956): 14–16.
5. Julia "Lula" Short, "Grandma's Childhood: Pioneer Life in Southern Alberta," unpub. ms., n.d., 12–14, Short/Knupp Family Papers, GA; Julia "Lula" Short Diaries, 1884–87, Lillian Knupp Papers, MH; HRT, "25th Anniversary Issue of *Times*," 4 Dec. 1930; Roy L. Fowler, "Chronology of Farming in the Okotoks-High River Area (1879–1930)," *Alberta Historical Review* 2 no. 2 (April 1954): 21–22, 24.
6. Sheilagh S. Jameson, "Era of the Big Ranches," *Alberta Historical Review* 18 no. 1 (Winter 1970): 2; High River, *Leaves*, 21.
7. A.B. McCullough, "Gordon, Ironside and Fares," unpub. ms., 1994, 3, BU. The best introduction to Alberta ranching is David H. Breen, *The Canadian Prairie West and the Ranching Frontier, 1874–1924* (Toronto: University of Toronto Press, 1983). See also Simon Evans, "Spatial Aspects of the Cattle Kingdom: The First Decade, 1882–1892," in Anthony W. Rasporich and Henry C. Klassen, eds., *Frontier Calgary: Town, City, and Region, 1875–1914* (Calgary: McClelland and Stewart West, 1975), 41–56; and Sheilagh S. Jameson, "The Ranching Industry of Western Canada: Its Initial Epoch, 1873–1910," *Prairie Forum* 11 no. 2 (Fall 1986): 229–42.

8. For ranch land policy see Breen, *Ranching Frontier*, 23–69.
9. A.B. McCullough, "Frederick Stimson and the North West Cattle Company," unpub. ms., 1994, BU; Simon M. Evans, "Land Acquisition: The Bar U Ranch," unpub. ms., n.d., BU; A.B. McCullough, "Eastern Capital, Government Purchases and the Development of Canadian Ranching," *Prairie Forum* 22 no. 2 (Fall 1997): 213–35.
10. Patrick A. Dunae, *Gentlemen Emigrants: From the British Public Schools to the Canadian Frontier* (Vancouver: Douglas and McIntyre, 1981); Patrick A. Dunae, ed., *Ranchers' Legacy: Alberta Essays by Lewis G. Thomas* (Edmonton: University of Alberta Press, 1986); Sheilagh Jameson, "The Social Elite of the Ranch Community and Calgary," in Rasporich, *Frontier Calgary*, 57–70; David H. Breen, "The Turner Thesis and the Canadian West: A Closer Look at the Ranching Frontier," in Lewis H. Thomas, ed., *Essays on Western History* (Edmonton: University of Alberta Press, 1976), 147–58.
11. High River, *Leaves*, passim; Frederick W. Ings, "Tales from the Midway Ranch," unpub. ms., 1936, 76–9, GA; *Calgary Herald*, 7 Sept. 1892; *Macleod Gazette*, 15 Sept. 1892; Tony Rees, "Polo and Paddlewheels: How the Ross Brothers Spent Their Remittance," *Alberta History* 49 no. 1 (Winter 2001): 6.
12. High River, *Leaves*, 92.
13. Simon M. Evans, "American Cattlemen on the Canadian Range, 1874 to 1914," *Prairie Forum* 4 no. 1 (Spring 1979): 121–36; Warren M. Elofson, *Cowboys, Gentlemen and Cattle Thieves: Ranching on the Western Frontier* (Montreal and Kingston: McGill-Queen's University Press, 2000); See also many essays in Simon Evans, Sarah Carter, Bill Yeo, eds., *Cowboys, Ranchers and the Cattle Business: Cross-Border Perspectives on Ranching History* (Calgary and Boulder: University of Calgary Press and University Press of Colorado, 2000).
14. Simon M. Evans, "Some Observations on the Labour Force of the Canadian Ranching Frontier during its Golden Age, 1882–1901," unpub. ms., n.d., BU; McCullough, "Frederick Stimson," 52.
15. Terry G. Jordan-Bychkow, "Does the Border Matter? Cattle Ranching and the 49th Parallel"; Joy Oetelaar, "George Lane: From Cowboy to Cattle King"; Simon M. Evans, "Tenderfoot to Rider: Learning 'Cowboying' on the Canadian Ranching Frontier During the 1880s"; all in Evans, *Cross-Border Perspectives*, 1–10, 43–59, 61–80.
16. Ings, "Midway Ranch," 84–5; A.B. McCullough, "The Ranching Industry in Canada," unpub. ms., 1994, 589–90, BU; Simon M. Evans, "Labour Force and Wages: 'CC' Ranch," unpub. ms., n.d., 4, BU.

17. Weinard, "Early High River," 16.
18. Hugh Dempsey, *The Golden Age of the Canadian Cowboy: An Illustrated History* (Saskatoon and Calgary: Fifth House, 1995), 33.
19. Among many accounts see High River, *Leaves*, 369–70; Grant MacEwan, *John Ware's Cow Country* (Edmonton: Institute of Applied Art, 1960).
20. See especially, High River, *Leaves, passim*; Short, "Grandma's Childhood," 24.
21. John F. Varty, "Polo and British Settlement in Alberta," *Alberta History* 43 no. 3 (Summer 1995): 9; Tony Rees, *Polo, the Galloping Game: An Illustrated History of Polo in the Canadian West* (Cochrane, Alta.: Western Heritage Centre Society, 2000).
22. Terry G. Jordan, *North American Cattle-Ranching Frontiers: Origins, Diffusion, and Differentiation* (Albuquerque: University of New Mexico Press, 1993).
23. McCullough, "Frederick Stimson," 49.
24. Reprinted in Susan Jackel, ed., *A Flannel Shirt and Liberty: British Emigrant Gentlewomen in the Canadian West, 1880–1914* (Vancouver: University of British Columbia Press, 1982), 95–110. See also T.B. Higginson, "Moria O'Neill in Alberta," *Alberta Historical Review* 5 no. 2 (Spring 1957): 22–24; Sheilagh Jameson, "Women in the Southern Alberta Ranch Community, 1881–1914," in H.C. Klassen, ed., *The Canadian West: Social Change and Economic Development* (Calgary: University of Calgary and Comprint Publishing, 1977), 63–78.
25. Ings, "Midway Ranch," 97.
26. Short, "Grandma's Childhood," 25.
27. Phil Weinard to Kenneth Coppock, 1 Sept. no year, Ralph C. and Kenneth R. Coppock Papers, GA.
28. North West Mounted Police File, BU.
29. David H. Breen, "Plain Talk from Plain Western Men," *Alberta Historical Review* 18 no. 3 (Summer 1970): 8–13; David H. Breen, "The Canadian Prairie West and the 'Harmonious' Settlement Interpretation," *Alberta History* 47 no. 1 (January 1973): 63–75; McCullough, "Frederick Stimson," 43–45.
30. Breen, *Ranching Frontier*, provides the best account of changes in ranching regulations.
31. HRT, 12 Sept. 1907.
32. McCullough, "Frederick Stimson," 32–34, 69–70; Evans, "Land Acquisition," 7–10; McCullough, "Gordon, Ironside," 3–6, 9.

33. Simon M. Evans, *Prince Charming Goes West: The Story of the E.P. Ranch* (Calgary: University of Calgary Press, 1993), 126, 174.
34. HRT, 24 Oct. 1912, 19 June 1913; Simon M. Evans, "George Lane: Purebred Horse Breeder," unpub. ms., 1994, BU.
35. See Warren M. Elofson, "Adapting to the Frontier Environment: Mixed and Dryland Farming near Pincher Creek, 1895–1914," *Prairie Forum* 19 no. 1 (Spring 1994): 32–37.
36. Calculated from *Census of Canada*, 1901, 1911.
37. Paul Voisey, *Vulcan: The Making of a Prairie Community* (Toronto: University of Toronto Press, 1988), 18.
38. HRT, 6 Dec. 1906.
39. Voisey, *Vulcan*, 129, 132.
40. HRT, "Homeseekers' Number," 16 May 1912.
41. Excellent descriptions of the foothills environment appear in Simon M. Evans, "Bar U NHS: Inventory of Resources," unpub. ms., n.d., 3–4, 6, BU; Evans, *Prince Charming*, 21, 40–41.
42. Alberta Department of Economic Affairs, Industrial Development Branch, *Survey of High River* (Edmonton: by author, 1959), 2–3; Alberta Department of Business and Tourism, Regional Services Branch, *High River Community Survey* (Edmonton: by author, 1974), 1; Canada Land Inventory, "Soil Capability for Agriculture, Map 082I."

2 THE PRESS COMES TO BOOMTOWN

1. Lewis G. Thomas, "The Rancher and the City: Calgary and the Cattlemen, 1883–1914," in Dunae, *Ranchers' Legacy*," 39–60; Maxwell Foran, *Calgary: An Illustrated History* (Toronto and Ottawa: J. Lorimer and National Museum of Man, 1978), 11–66.
2. For High River's early history see HRT, "25th Anniversary Issue of *Times*," 4 Dec. 1930; Knupp, *Life and Legends*, 1–39; High River, *Leaves*, passim; Simon M. Evans, "Evolution of a Transport Network in the Pekisko Region: Routes to the Bar U," unpub. ms., n.d., 1–3, BU; transcript of excerpts from Edith Short McIntosh Diary, 28 April 1892, May 1892, Short/Knupp Family Papers, GA.
3. HRT, 2 May 1913.

4. HRT, 19 Sept. 1907, 8 Oct. 1908, 16 May 1912; George Colpitts, *History of the Highwood River* (High River, Alta.: Highwood River Restoration and Conservation Association, 1991), 51; Bert Sheppard, *Spitzee Days* (Calgary: by author, 1971?), 71–94.
5. HRT, 7 Mar. 1907; *Census of Canada*, 1901, 1911.
6. HRT, 15 Nov. 1906, 25 Apr. 1907.
7. HRT, 25 Aug. 1955.
8. Hugh A. Dempsey, ed., *The Best of Bob Edwards* (Edmonton: Hurtig, 1975), 7; see also Grant MacEwan, *Eye Opener Bob: The Story of Bob Edwards* (Edmonton: Institute of Applied Art, 1957).
9. HRT, "Alberta Golden Jubilee Edition," 18 Aug. 1955.
10. HRT, "25th Anniversary Issue of Times," 4 Dec. 1930; various documents relating to South Africa, CFP.
11. HRT, "25th Anniversary Issue of Times," 4 Dec. 1930.
12. HRT, 22 Mar. 1906.
13. Boiler plate is discussed in Johnston, *The Weeklies*, 124, 342; D'Albertanson, *Printed Word*, 34; Gloria Strathern, *Alberta Newspapers, 1880–1982: An Historical Directory* (Edmonton: University of Alberta Press, 1988), xv; Donald G. Wetherall and Irene R.A. Kmet, *Town Life: Main Street and the Evolution of Small Town Alberta, 1880–1947* (Edmonton: University of Alberta Press and Alberta Community Development, 1995), 67; Charles A. Clark, taped interview.
14. Short, "Grandma's Childhood," 21; see also Ings, "Midway Ranch," 46; W.B. Yeo, "Pekisko: Heart of a Rural Community," unpub. ms., 1998, 16, BU.
15. Photocopy of letter, Post Office Inspector's Office to Postmaster General, 27 Mar. 1889, Post Office File, BU; Yeo, "Pekisko," 4–5.
16. Thomas B. Braden, "When the Herald Came to Calgary," *Alberta Historical Review* 9 no. 3 (Summer 1961), 2.
17. High River Club Letters Book, High River Club Papers, 1906–10, GA; Letter Book Correspondence, High River Club, 1908–10, Hunt and Watt Ltd. Papers, GA.
18. HRT, 18 Feb. 1915.
19. HRT, 8 and 15 Mar. 1906.
20. Clarence Karr, "Robert Stead's Search for an Agrarian Ideal," *Prairie Forum* 14 no. 1 (Spring 1989): 37–57; George Melnyk, *The Literary History of Alberta, Volume One: From Writing-on-Stone to World War Two* (Edmonton: University of Alberta Press, 1998), 90–91, 93–94.

21. HRT, 20 and 27 June 1912.
22. Howard Palmer, *Patterns of Prejudice: Nativism in Alberta* (Toronto: McClelland and Stewart, 1982).
23. HRT, 26 Sept. 1907; D'Albertanson, *Printed Word*, 34; see also Rutherford, *Victorian Authority*, 163–70.
24. HRT, 16 Apr., 18 June 1908.
25. Palmer, *Patterns of Prejudice*, passim; see also Peter W. Ward, *White Canada Forever: Popular Attitudes and Public Policy Towards Orientals in British Columbia* (Montreal and Kingston: McGill-Queen's University Press, 1978).
26. HRT, 1 June 1911.
27. HRT, 29 June, 24 Aug., 21 Sept. 1911.

3 BOOSTING THE EMERGING METROPOLIS

1. Alan F.J. Artibise, "Boosterism and the Development of Prairie Cities, 1871–1913," and Paul Voisey, "Boosting the Small Prairie Town, 1904–1931: An Example from Southern Alberta," both in Alan F.J. Artibise, eds., *Town and City: Aspects of Western Canadian Urban Development* (Regina: Canadian Plains Research Center and University of Regina, 1981), 147–76, 210–235; Wetherall, *Town Life*, 79–113.
2. Wetherall, *Town Life*, 67–72; Rutherford, *Victorian Authority*, 195. For the American west see Elizabeth Keen, "The Frontier Press," *Studies in Literature of the West* 20 (1956): 75–100.
3. John C. Hudson, *Plains Country Towns* (Minneapolis: University of Minnesota Press, 1985), 1–16, 54–69.
4. HRT, 17 May 1906, 14 Mar. 1907.
5. HRT, 2 July 1908.
6. W. Roland Murray, *The Murray-Hurlbert Homesteads* (Los Angles: by author, 1981), 6, GA.
7. HRT, 12 Nov. 1908.
8. HRT, 27 Oct. 1949.
9. The staging of special events to lure farmers to towns is discussed in Wetherall, *Town Life*, 143–45, 259–67.
10. HRT, 12 Nov. 1908.
11. HRT, 12 Sept. 1907, 30 Sept. 1909, 19 May 1910.
12. Murray, *Murray-Hurlbert*, 43.
13. Wetherall, *Town Life*, 129–30.

14. HRT, 4 Aug., 8 Dec. 1910, 23 May 1912, 9 Nov. 1916.
15. For other towns semi-professional baseball often served the same purpose; see Voisey, "Boosting," 55.
16. HRT, 30 Aug. 1906.
17. HRT, 30 July 1908.
18. Subscription Book, 1905–09, Charles A. Clark Papers, GA.
19. HRT, 2 July 1908.
20. Reprinted in HRT, 30 May 1912.
21. HRT, 14 June 1906.
22. HRT, 22 Mar. 1906, 9 Jan. 1908.
23. HRT, 15 Nov. 1906.
24. HRT, 9 Jan., 20 Feb., 28 Aug. 1913; Walter van Nus, "The Fate of City Beautiful Thought in Canada, 1893–1930," *Canadian Historical Association Historical Papers* (1975): 191–210. The Alberta Town Planning Act of 1913 encouraged beautification schemes; see Peter J. Smith, "The Principle of Utility and the Origins of Planning Legislation in Alberta, 1912–1975," in Alan F.J. Artibise and Gilbert A. Stelter, eds., *The Usable Urban Past: Planning and Politics in the Modern Canadian City* (Toronto and Ottawa: Macmillan and Institute of Canadian Studies, Carleton University, 1979), 211.
25. Minutes of the High River Civic League, 1914–1917, CFP; for limited results in other towns see Wetherall, *Town Life*, 164–68, 278–85.
26. Rutherford, *Victorian Authority*, 163–81; Wetherall, *Town Life*, 221–39.
27. HRT, 13 June 1907, 16 Jan. 1908, 10 Oct. 1912.
28. Sheppard, *Spitzee Days*, 112–4; Charles A. Clark, taped interview.
29. HRT, 23 May 1918; Donald G. Wetherall with Irene Kmet, *Useful Pleasures: The Shaping of Leisure in Alberta, 1896–1945* (Regina: Alberta Culture and Multiculturalism and Canadian Plains Research Centre, 1990), 354.
30. John H. Thompson, "'The Beginning of Our Regeneration:' The Great War and Western Canadian Reform Movements," *Canadian Historical Association Reports* (1972): 227–45.
31. Clark voted against prohibition in the provincial referendum of 1920 as recorded in Poll #155, High River West, 1920, Poll Books, Politics File, MH.
32. Paul Voisey, "The 'Votes for Women' Movement," in Hugh Dempsey, ed., *The Best from Alberta History* (Saskatoon: Western Producer Prairie Books, 1981), 166–83; Thompson, "Regeneration."

4 BOOSTERISM AND THE NEWSPAPER BUSINESS

1. Johnston, The Weeklies, 126. D'Albertanson, Printed Word, 106 suggests $500 cash and $1,000 owing on equipment.
2. In 1918 wages represented 73 percent of all expenses at the weekly Vulcan Advocate; see Statements of Revenue and Expenses, Inventory: Vulcan Plant, 20 Mar. 1919, CFP.
3. Johnston, The Weeklies, 5–9.
4. HRT, 23 Feb. 1911.
5. Johnston, The Weeklies, 81–8. The Times paid them small sums by the 1920s and after 1945 payment per line of copy became standard at most weeklies; Charles A. Clark, taped interview; William "Bill" Holmes interviewed by Paul Voisey; R.C.R. "Bob" Munro interviewed by Paul Voisey.
6. Subscription Book.
7. Johnston, The Weeklies, 116–17.
8. HRT, 24 Mar., 28 Apr. 1910.
9. HRT, "Alberta Golden Jubilee Edition," 18 Aug. 1955. On 6 Dec. 1945 the Times claimed that it required six workers to hand set type. For general descriptions of printing procedures at most weeklies see Johnston, The Weeklies, 111–12; D'Albertanson, Printed Word, 10–15, 106.
10. In 1918 subscriptions to the weekly Vulcan Advocate accounted for only seven percent of all revenues; see Statement of Revenue and Expenses.
11. HRT, 16 Sept. 1909. The frequency of this practice is noted in Johnston, The Weeklies, 159.
12. HRT, 7 Nov. 1912.
13. Subscription Book.
14. HRT, 19 Apr. 1906, 10 Dec. 1908.
15. See, for example, HRT, 24 and 31 Oct. 1907, 3 Dec. 1908.
16. Kesterton, History of Journalism, 144, 150; Vipond, Mass Media, 16; HRT, 1 Aug. 1929.
17. Stephenson, Story of Advertising, 38, 49–54.
18. Stephenson, Story of Advertising, 18–35; for American precedents see Daniel Pope, The Making of Modern Advertising (New York: Basic Books, 1983).
19. Stephenson, Story of Advertising, 339; Johnston, The Weeklies, 177–78.
20. R.D. "Don" Tanner, interview by Paul Voisey; Peter Pickersgill interviewed by Paul Voisey; Munro interview.
21. Johnston, The Weeklies, 257–61; much correspondence in AWN, especially box 1 file 5.

22. HRT Account Book, 1905–08, 90, Charles A. Clark Papers.
23. Johnston, *The Weeklies*, 166.
24. In 1918, job printing accounted for 33 percent of the revenues of the weekly *Vulcan Advocate*; see Statement of Revenue and Expenses. The importance of print jobs was verified by Charles A. Clark, taped interview; Knupp, taped interview; Munro interview; Doug Caston, taped interview with Joe Clark, 1971?, CFP.
25. HRT, 26 Aug. 1909.
26. HRT, 15 Oct. 1908.
27. HRT, 20 Jan. 1949.
28. Johnston, *The Weeklies*, 137–40.
29. D'Albertanson, *Printed Word*, 34; Col. G.C. Porter, "The Old-Timer Talks: News-Gathering Real Chore in Old Days," *Winnipeg Tribune* clipping, 30 Oct. 1943, CFP.
30. HRT, 5 Sept. 1907.
31. HRT, 28 Mar. 1907, 18 Jan. 1912.
32. HRT, 10 May 1906.
33. HRT, "25th Anniversary Issue of Times," 4 Dec. 1930; Mayor F.L. Watt on municipal history in HRT, 4 Feb. 1937.
34. Eric J. Hanson, *Local Government in Alberta* (Toronto: McClelland and Stewart, 1956), 32; HRT, 16 Oct. 1913.
35. HRT, 16 Feb., 11 May 1911.
36. Max Foran, "The CPR and the Urban West, 1881–1930," in Hugh A. Dempsey, ed., *The CPR West: The Iron Road and the Making of a Nation* (Vancouver: Douglas and McIntyre, 1984), pp. 89–106; Foran, *Calgary*, 25, 28, 45, 48, 74.
37. HRT, 10 June 1909; 11 Aug., 1 Sept. 1910.
38. HRT, 13 Oct. 1910, 13 Feb. 1913; Voisey, *Vulcan*, 55–7.
39. Charles Clark did appear as proprietor in the new paper itself; see *Vulcan Advocate*, 6 Aug. 1913.
40. Hector J. MacLeod, "Things I Remember," unpub. ms., n.d., Hector J. MacLeod Papers, GA.
41. Letters to the editor, HRT, 21 May 1908, 3 Mar. 1910.
42. Robert Stead, "Observations," HRT, 11 April 1912.
43. *Census of Canada*, 1911.
44. R.G. Dun and Co., *The Mercantile Agency Reference Book*, 1908, 1912.

45. Oliver Knight, "The *Owyhee Avalanche*: The Frontier Newspaper as a Catalyst in Social Change," *Pacific Northwest Quarterly* 58 no. 2 (April 1967): 74; Wetherall, *Town Life*, xiii–xvii, 28–29.
46. William L. Bowers, "Country Life Reform, 1900–20: A Neglected Aspect of Progressive Era History," *Agricultural History* 45 no. 3 (July 1971): 211–22; Voisey, *Vulcan*, 21–23.

5   THE COMMUNITY IN TROUBLED TIMES

1. Wetherall, *Town Life*, 48–49; Voisey, "Boosting," 167–70.
2. John H. Thompson, "'Permanently Wasteful but Immediately Profitable:' Prairie Agriculture and the Great War," *Canadian Historical Association Historical Papers* (1976): 193–206.
3. Max Foran, "Mixed Blessings: The Second 'Golden Age' of the Alberta Cattle Industry, 1914–1920," *Alberta History* 46 no. 3 (Summer 1998): 10–19; McCullough, "Ranching Industry," 588–89.
4. HRT, 22 Apr. 1920, 17 Apr. 1924.
5. David C. Jones, *Empire of Dust: Settling and Abandoning the Prairie Dry Belt* (Edmonton: University of Alberta Press, 1987).
6. Evans, "George Lane," 24; for ranching problems generally see Foran, "Mixed Blessings," 14.
7. Simon M. Evans, "The Burns Era at the Bar U Ranch," unpub. ms., 1997, 15, BU; HRT, 10 Nov. 1927.
8. High River Agricultural Society Minutes, 1925–36, GA; HRT, 6 and 27 Mar. 1930.
9. HRT, 22 Aug. 1918, 29 Jan. 1920, 17 Mar. 1921, 9 Feb. 1928, 19 Nov. 1936, 20 Apr. 1944.
10. HRT, 5 June 1930.
11. HRT, 29 Dec. 1927, 5 Apr. 1928; various documents, 1928, Ford Coals Limited-Ford Highwood Collieries Limited Papers, GA.
12. Evans, "Burns Era," 40–43.
13. HRT, 3 Dec. 1936, 19 Aug. 1937.
14. HRT, 4 Feb. 1937; see also correspondence, file 5, Hunt and Watt Papers.
15. HRT, 10 Apr. 1930; see also 16 Aug. 1934.
16. HRT, 28 Oct. 1926.
17. HRT, 28 Jan. 1932.

18. HRT, 6 Mar. 1924; The acquisition of a liquor store was announced on 21 June 1934.
19. Various correspondence, May 1938, Hunt and Watt Papers, file 5.
20. HRT, "Harvest and Oil Issue," 6 Oct. 1938; Sheep River Historical Society, *In the Light of the Flares: History of Turner Valley Oilfields* (Turner Valley, Alta.: by author, 1979), 17–18.
21. Charles A. Clark, taped interview; HRT, 5 May 1938.
22. HRT, 16 and 23 Jan. 1930, 29 Mar. 1934.
23. HRT, 3 May 1906, 24 Oct. 1907.
24. The flooding of the Highwood has been the subject of many studies including E.K. Yaremko and G.V. Gehmlich, *Historical Aspects of Highwood River Diversion to Little Bow River Basin at High River* (Edmonton: Northwest Hydraulic Consultants Ltd. for Alberta Environment, Tech-Services Division, rev. ed., 1992); Northwest Hydraulic Consultants, *Highwood River Flood Plain Study for the Town of High River and Department of the Environment* (Edmonton: by author, 1994); A.G. Underhill, *Highwood River Study* (Calgary: Water Resources Division, Dept. of Agriculture, Province of Alberta, 1964); Colpitts, *Highwood River*, 72–92.
25. Reviewed in HRT, 4 Feb. 1937.
26. Underhill, *Highwood River*.
27. HRT, *High River and District at a Glance* (High River: by author, 1927); HRT, 13 Jan. 1921, 4 Dec. 1930.
28. Mayor F.L. Watt to R.B. Bennett, 13 July 1934, Hunt and Watt Papers, file 5.
29. Calculated from statistics for Census Division 4, Alberta, in *Census of Canada*, 1931.
30. HRT, 27 Oct. 1927.
31. The slow progress of automobile transportation is studied in Rod Bantjes, "Improved Earth: Travel on the Canadian Prairies, 1920–50," *Journal of Transport History* 3rd series 13 no. 2 (Sept. 1992): 115–40.
32. HRT, 12 May 1927.
33. Norman T. Moline, *Mobility and the Small Town, 1900–1930: Transportation Change in Oregon, Illinois* (Chicago: University of Chicago Department of Geography, Research Paper no. 132, 1971); Hudson, *Plains Country*, 128–29.
34. HRT, "25th Anniversary Issue of Times," 4 Dec. 1930.
35. High River Hospital and Nursing Home, "In the Spirit of Good Medicine:" *A Story of Health Care in the High River Hospital District* (High River: Sandstone, 1990), 8–10; Knupp, *Life and Legends*, 112–15.
36. High River, *Good Medicine*, 21–23, 27, 101; HRT, 18 Nov. 1920, 4 Dec. 1930.

37. HRT, *This is High River, Alberta: The Cowtown Capital of the Foothills* (High River: by author, 1950), 6; HRT, 6 Oct. 1938, 18 Aug. 1955.
38. Knupp, *Life and Legends*, 39–42.
39. HRT, 6 and 13 Feb. 1936, 17 June 1937; Thomas Curtis Sugden, "The Consolidated School Movement in Alberta" (M.Ed. Thesis, University of Alberta, 1964); Robert F. Wolf, "The Attack on the Problems of Education in Alberta by the Social Credit Government from 1935 to 1945" (M.Ed. Thesis, University of Calgary, 1979), 20–48.
40. HRT, 30 Nov. 1944; HRT, *This is High River*, 3; various records, Foothills School Division No. 38 Papers, GA; Tales and Trails History Book Society, *Tales and Trails: A History of Longview and Surrounding Area* (Longview, Alta.: by author, 1973), 154.
41. Historical sketches of rural local governments in the area appear in HRT, "25th Anniversary Issue of Times," 4 Dec. 1930; Walter Walchuk, *Alberta's Local Governments: People in Community Seeking Goodness* (Edmonton: Municipal Administrative Services Division, Alberta Municipal Affairs, 1987), 29–62.
42. HRT, 4 Feb. 1943, 6 Jan. 1944.

6 THE *TIMES* IN TROUBLED TIMES

1. HRT, 10 Dec. 1908, 13 Jan. 1921, 4 Dec. 1930.
2. HRT, 24 Feb. 1927, 11 Dec. 1941; Strathern, *Alberta Newspapers*, xv. The relative advantages and disadvantages of such arrangements for the weeklies was the subject of considerable debate; see correspondence and clippings, AWN, box 6 file 54.
3. Strathern, *Alberta Newspapers*, 18, 24, 59, 229; HRT, 30 Dec. 1909, 27 Nov. 1913, 28 June and 19 July 1917.
4. Inventory: Vulcan Plant, 20 Mar. 1919, CFP.
5. Munro interview.
6. Inventory: Vulcan Plant, 20 Mar. 1919.
7. D'Albertanson, *Printed Word*, 98–9; Johnston, *The Weeklies*, 113, 124; Pickersgill interview. A good description of backshop operations at a weekly in the interwar era is offered by Randall B. Kester, "Recollections of a Printer's Devil," *Oregon Historical Quarterly* 99 no. 1 (Spring 1998): 62–78.

8. Dun, *Mercantile Agency*, 1919–1932. For some unknown reason, Clark and his wife Mary incorporated the *Times* in 1919, but disbanded the company in 1925, selling its assets back to Charles and Mary for $15,000; see Minutes of *High River Times* Limited, 15 and 31 Jan. 1919, 23 Sept. and 10 Oct. 1925, CFP.
9. There is a large collection of material related to the trip in CFP.
10. HRT, 25 Aug. 1927. The cost of the building is based on a contractor's estimate; Percy Taylor to HRT, 14 May 1927, CFP.
11. HRT, 27 Oct. 1927; Toronto Type Foundry Co. to Charles Clark, 9 Nov. 1927, CFP.
12. HRT, 3 Nov. 1927.
13. Dun, *Mercantile Agency*, 1937.
14. HRT, 1 Sept. 1932, 21 Sept. 1933; entry, "Extracts From the Diary of Roy L. Fowler, High River, 1932 to 1941 Inclusive," 31 Oct. 1932, GA; Grace Clark, taped interview with Margaret Crosby, 18 June 1987, Oral History Project, MH.
15. Johnston, *The Weeklies*, 159, 177–78.
16. D'Albertanson, *Printed Word*, 47–48.
17. For the growth of advertising aimed at women see Stephenson, *Story of Advertising*, 218–33.
18. Copy of letter, Charles Clark to W.R. Howson, 11 Feb. 1933, CFP.
19. HRT, 14 July, 29 Sept. 1932.
20. Johnston, *The Weeklies*, 9–11.
21. Johnston, *The Weeklies*, vi, viii; D'Albertanson, *Printed Word*, 25–36; Charles A. Clark, taped interview.
22. Considerable material relating to these activities appears in AWN.
23. HRT, 9 Apr. 1931; Johnston, *The Weeklies*, 306, 313, 332; D'Albertanson, *Printed Word*, 52.
24. HRT, 4 Dec. 1932, 5 Dec. 1935, 5 Dec. 1940, 25 Mar. 1943.
25. Charles A. Clark, taped interview; Grace Clark, taped interview.
26. High River, *Good Medicine*, 5, 25; Tanner interview.
27. Grace Clark, taped interview; HRT, 26 Aug. 1937.
28. Biographical sketch, HRT, 28 June 1956.
29. Lillian Knupp, "W.O. 'Bill' Mitchell," transcript of speech, 4 June 1982, MH.
30. Dick Liddell, taped interview with Kimberly Speers, Aug. 1999, privately-held by Kimberly Speers; Knupp, taped interview; Charles A. Clark, taped interview; Pickersgill interview; W.O. Mitchell, "Bob Edwards

'Successor,'" *Calgary Herald* clipping, n.d., W.O. Mitchell Papers, file 19.43.13, University of Calgary Library; Hughena McCorquodale files, Mitchell Papers, file 19.8.19.
31. Johnston, *The Weeklies*, 91–104; see also Marjory Lang, *Women Who Made the News: Female Journalists in Canada, 1880–1945* (Montreal and Kingston: McGill-Queen's University Press, 1999).
32. Historical information on the column appears in HRT, 15 May 1958.
33. HRT, 26 Apr. 1934; Charles A. Clark, taped interview.
34. David R. Elliott and Iris Miller, *Bible Bill: A Biography of William Aberhart* (Edmonton: Reidmore Books, 1987), 148.
35. Elliott, *Bible Bill*, 182.
36. Elliott, *Bible Bill*, 232; Strathern, *Alberta Newspapers*, 32; HRT, 16 Jan. 1936.
37. HRT, 22 Oct. 1936.
38. Robert C. Hill, "Social Credit and the Press: The Early Years" (M.A. Thesis, University of Alberta, 1977), 41–51; Joseph A. Boudreau, ed., *Alberta, Aberhart, and Social Credit: Canadian History Through the Press Series* (Toronto: Holt, Rinehart and Winston, 1975), *passim*; Elliott, *Bible Bill*, 263–4.
39. Hill, "Social Credit," 103–4.
40. HRT, 15 Oct. 1936; Johnston, *The Weeklies*, 265–7; D'Albertanson, *Printed Word*, 43–44.
41. Gostick argued that the Accurate News and Information Act would actually "free" the press from the tyranny of the money interests; see G. Stuart Adam, "The Sovereignty of the Publicity System: A Case Study of the Alberta Press Act," in Adam, ed., *Journalism, Communication and the Law* (Scarborough: Prentice-Hall, 1976), 165–66.
42. It was considered an appendage of the Social Credit Act that was declared *ultra vires*; Hill, "Social Credit," 113; Adam, "Sovereignty," 167–69; J.R. Mallory, *Social Credit and the Federal Power in Canada* (Toronto: University of Toronto Press, 1954), 87.
43. *Edmonton Journal*, 2 and 3 May 1938; HRT, 12 May 1938.
44. HRT, 23 Sept. 1937; Elliott, *Bible Bill*, 273; Alvin Finkel, *The Social Credit Phenomenon in Alberta* (Toronto: University of Toronto Press, 1989), 70; Lynne Bowen, "Roads and Recall," *The Beaver* 80 no. 4 (Aug./Sept. 2000): 16–21.
45. HRT, 18 Mar. 1937, 14 July 1938.
46. HRT, 29 July 1937, 13 Jan. 1938.
47. Charles A. Clark to Daniel E.C. Campbell, 21 Aug. 1945, AWN, box 1 file 5.
48. Charles A. Clark, taped interview.

49. Charles A. Clark, taped interview; also quoted in Michael Nolan, *Joe Clark: The Emerging Leader* (Toronto: Fitzhenry and Whiteside, 1978), 24.
50. George R. Gordon to Attorney General of Alberta, 30 Jan. 1940, High River Correspondence, Municipality Correspondence Files, Alberta Dept. of Municipal Affairs Papers, 78.133 file 437c, Provincial Archives of Alberta.
51. Charles A. Clark, taped interview.
52. Joe Clark, taped interview with Kimberly Speers, 12 Jan. 1998, privately held by Kimberly Speers.
53. John A. Irving, *The Social Credit Movement in Alberta* (Toronto: University of Toronto Press, 1959), 321. Although Aberhart failed to curry favour in the press, he nonetheless continued to rule the airwaves, using radio to great political advantage.

7   RURAL AND SMALL TOWN VIRTUE

1. The best analyses appear in two classic works: Henry Nash Smith, *Virgin Land: The American West as Symbol and Myth* (Cambridge: Harvard University Press, 1950) and Richard Hofstadter, *The Age of Reform, From Bryan to F.D.R.* (New York: Knopf, 1955). For Western Canada see David C. Jones, "'There is Some Power About the Land'—The Western Agrarian Press and Country Life Ideology," *Journal of Canadian Studies* 17 no. 3 (Fall 1982): 96–108.
2. Voisey, *Vulcan*, 21–23; Bowers, "Country Life"; Clifford B. Anderson, "The Metamorphosis of American Agrarian Idealism in the 1920s and 1930s," *Agricultural History* 35 no. 4 (Oct. 1961): 182–88.
3. HRT, 14 Apr. 1927, 21 Apr. 1932.
4. HRT, 20 Mar. 1924, 19 Aug. 1926, 10 May 1928, 1 Feb. 1934.
5. Ray Ginger, *Six Days or Forever?: Tennessee vs. John Thomas Scopes* (New York: Oxford University Press, 1974; first published 1958), 129. See also James H. Shideler, "Flappers and Philosophers, and Farmers: Rural-Urban Tensions of the Twenties," *Agricultural History* 47 no. 4 (Oct. 1973): 283–99. Defensive responses to urban attacks are discussed in Richard R. Lingeman, *Small Town America: A Narrative History, 1620–The Present* (New York: G.P. Putnam's Sons, 1980), 364–95.
6. Histories of electrical power in the district appeared in HRT, 15 and 22 May 1952, 26 Apr. 1962.

7. Statistics on farm facilities in the district were calculated from data for Census Division 4, Alberta, *Census of Canada*, 1931. The erratic spread of telephones, automobiles, radio, and electrical appliances in rural areas during the interwar years is discussed in Katherine Jellison, "Women and Technology on the Great Plains, 1910–1940," *Great Plains Quarterly* 8 no. 3 (Summer 1988): 145–57; Angela E. Davis, "'Valiant Servants:' Women and Technology on the Canadian Prairies, 1910–1940," *Manitoba History* 25 (Spring 1993): 33–42; Robert M. Pike, "A Chequered Progress: Farmers and the Telephone in Canada, 1905–1951," *Journal of Canadian Studies* 33 no. 3 (Fall 1998): 5–30.
8. HRT, 19 Nov. 1936.
9. Wetherall, *Useful Pleasures*, 191–202.
10. HRT, *High River and District*.
11. HRT, 8 Apr., 29 July 1926.
12. HRT, 18 Sept. 1919; Evans, *Prince Charming*, 23, 61.
13. *H.R.H. Prince of Wales "E.P. Ranch" Souvenir* (High River: n.d.); also HRT, 1 Sept. 1927, 14 June 1934; S.G. Porter to Sir Edward Beatty, 11 Nov. 1936, Canadian Pacific Railway Land Settlement and Development Papers, Box 30 file 357, GA.
14. Evans, *Prince Charming*, 90–114.
15. Lawrence R. Borne, "Dude Ranches and the Development of the West," *Journal of the West* 17 no. 3 (July 1978): 83–93.
16. Donna Livingstone, *The Cowboy Spirit: Guy Weadick and the Calgary Stampede* (Vancouver: Greystone Books, 1996), 1–55, 77–87; Guy Weadick, "Origin of the Calgary Stampede," *Alberta Historical Review* 14 no. 4 (Autumn 1966): 20–1; HRT, 1 June 1922, 28 Aug. 1927.
17. Norma Piper Pocaterra, "Son of the Mountains: The Story of George W. Pocaterra, Pioneer Alberta Rancher, Explorer, and Friend of the Stoney Indians," unpub. ms., 1970, 1–28, GA; George Pocaterra, taped address to Calgary Kiwanis Club, 16 Nov. 1965, GA; Lawrence R. Borne, *Dude Ranching: a Complete History* (Albuquerque: University of New Mexico Press, 1983), 163–64.
18. Buffalo Head Ranch Register of Guests, George and Norma Piper Pocaterra Papers, 1848–1978, box 11 file 170, GA; Don Blake, taped interview with Tom Kirkham, 22 Oct. 1980, GA; HRT, 24 July 1924.
19. These guests and their writings are noted in HRT, 16 Aug. 1923, 5 Apr. and 10 May 1928.

20. *Round T Ranch* (1937?), Ranching Files, MH; see also *Buffalo Head Ranch* (n.d.), Pocaterra Papers, box 15 file 198; *The Stampede Ranch* (n.d.), Guy Weadick Papers, GA.
21. *Stampede Ranch*; for similar attractions at American dude ranches see Lawrence R. Borne, "Dude Ranching in the Rockies," *Montana, Magazine of Western History* 38 no. 3 (Summer 1988): 14–27.
22. R.M. Patterson, *The Buffalo Head* (Victoria: Horsdal and Schubart, 1994; first published 1961), 154–55.
23. *Round T Ranch*.
24. *Stampede Ranch*.
25. *Buffalo Head*, 154.
26. The most extensive list of hunting opportunities appears in HRT, *This is High River*, 10–13.
27. George W. Colpitts, "Fish and Game Associations in Southern Alberta, 1907–1928," *Alberta History* 42 no. 4 (Autumn 1994): 19–22; see also Archie Hogg Papers, GA; High River Fish and Game Association Papers, GA.
28. HRT, 11 Dec. 1924, 26 May 1927, 17 July 1941; also Evans, "Transport Network," 4; Colpitts, *Highwood River*, 102.
29. Hal K. Rothman, "Selling the Meaning of Place: Entrepreneurship, Tourism, and Community Transformation in the Twentieth-Century American West," *Pacific Historical Review* 65 no. 4 (Nov. 1996): 525–57; Lloyd E. Hudman, "Tourism and the American West," *Journal of the West* 33 no. 3 (July 1994): 67–76.
30. E.J. Hart, *The Selling of Canada: The CPR and the Beginnings of Canadian Tourism* (Banff: Altitude Publishing, 1983).
31. HRT, 10 May 1923.
32. HRT, 18 Oct. 1923, 22 May 1924.
33. HRT, 7 May, 2 July 1925; 9 Sept. 1926, 12 May 1927; 22 Mar., 7 June, 16 Aug. 1928; Colpitts, *Highwood River*, 107–9.
34. HRT, 15 Apr. 1937; 25 July, 29 Aug. 1946; 3 and 17 July 1947, 6 May 1948.
35. Hal K. Rothman, *Devil's Bargains: Tourism in the Twentieth-Century American West* (Lawrence: University Press of Kansas, 1998).

8 THE RETURN OF PROSPERITY

1. Ian MacPherson and John Herd Thompson, "An Orderly Reconstruction: Prairie Agriculture in World War Two," *Canadian Papers in Rural History* 4 (1984): 11–32.
2. Patricia A. Myers, "Watching the War Fly By: The British Commonwealth Air Training Plan in Alberta," Ken Tingley, ed., *For King and Country: Alberta in the Second World War* (Edmonton: Provincial Museum of Alberta, 1995), 243–54; D.C. Jones, *A History of No. 5 E.F.T.S. (R.C.A.F.): High River and Lethbridge, Alberta* (High River: 1945), Program Files, MH; 5 E.F.T.S. Souvenir Program, Third Anniversary, Sept. 4, 1944 (High River: 1944), CFP.
3. HRT, 9 Jan., 8 May 1941.
4. HRT, 2 and 30 Apr. 1942.
5. Calculated from statistics for Census Division 4, Alberta, *Census of Canada*, 1951.
6. Major changes in post-war agriculture are traced in Diana M. Lapp, *The Structure of Alberta Farms, 1941–1974* (Edmonton: Alberta Land Use Forum, Technical Report No. 11, 1974); R.G. Ironside, "Rural Alberta: Elements of Change," in B.M. Barr and P.J. Smith, eds., *Environment and Economy: Essays on the Human Geography of Alberta* (Edmonton: Pica Pica Press, 1984), 95–110; Bruce Proudfoot, "Agriculture," in P.J. Smith, ed., *Studies in Canadian Geography: The Prairie Provinces* (Toronto: University of Toronto Press, 1972), 51–64; R.A. Stutt, "Changes in Land Use and Farm Organization in the Prairie Area of Saskatchewan During the Period 1951 to 1966," *Canadian Farm Economics* 5 no. 6 (Feb. 1971): 11–19.
7. In 1971 the *Census of Canada* recalculated historical population statistics to conform to new municipal boundaries. See also Michael L. Szabo, "Depopulation of Farms in Relation to the Economic Conditions of Agriculture on the Canadian Prairies," *Geographical Bulletin* 7 no. 3–4 (1965): 187–202.
8. Calculated from statistics for Foothills 31, Census Division 6, Alberta, *Census of Canada*, 1961; see also lengthy stories on rural electrification in HRT, 15 and 22 May 1952.
9. James Gray, *Men Against the Desert* (Saskatoon: Western Producer, 1967).
10. J.S. Dunlop, "Changes in the Canadian Wheat Belt, 1931–69," *Geography* 55 part 2 no. 247 (Spring 1970): 156–68 is largely concerned with increased yields.

11. Major changes in cattle raising are traced in Knud Elgaard, *Cattle Ranching in Southern Alberta* (Regina: Economics Branch, Canada Department of Agriculture, 1968); Wade D. Clark, "Big Business on the Big Ranch: The Making of the Modern Cattle Industry in Alberta in the Post-World War Two Era, 1950–1976" (Honours Thesis, History, University of Calgary, 1995).
12. Wade, "Big Ranch," 33–34; HRT, *This is High River*, 26–27.
13. Evans, "Burns Era," 54.
14. Evans, "Burns Era," 91–92; HRT, *This is High River*, 26–27; HRT, 22 June 1950.
15. Alberta Weekly Newspapers Association, *Data: Alberta Weekly Newspapers* (by author, Oct. 1963), 19, box 10 file 96, AWN.
16. HRT, 11 Apr., 1 Aug. 1946; 20 Oct. 1955; Alberta Department of Economic Affairs, Industrial Development Branch, *Economic Survey of the Town of High River* (Edmonton: by author, 1952), 4.
17. HRT, 24 Sept. 1959.
18. HRT, 25 Mar. 1948, 18 Aug. 1955, 2 Apr. 1959, 6 Apr. 1961; High River, *Good Medicine*, 27; HRT, *This is High River*, 4.
19. HRT, 14 July 1960, 25 Oct. 1956; High River, *Good Medicine*, 74–75, 79.
20. HRT, 7 Jan. 1954, 18 Aug. 1955, 22 Feb. 1962, 3 Feb. 1966; Alberta Association of Municipal Districts and Counties, *Story of Rural Municipal Government in Alberta, 1909 to 1983* (Edmonton: by author, 1983), 400–404; Walchuk, *Local Governments*, 63–83.
21. Patrick G. Cadden, "The Economic Role of Public Employers in the Urban Communities," in Barr, *Environment and Economy*, 161; also Alberta, *Survey of High River* (1959), 6.
22. Carle C. Zimmerman and Garry W. Moneo, *The Prairie Community System* (Ottawa: Agricultural Economics Research Council of Canada, 1970), 13–14, 99.
23. Gerald Hodge, Small Town Canada Today and Tomorrow," in Frank Jankunis and Barry Sadler, eds., *The Viability and Livability of Small Urban Centres* (Edmonton: Environment Council of Alberta, 1979), 60; Edmund H. Dale, "The General Problems of Western Canada's Small Rural Towns," in J.E. Spencer, ed., *Saskatchewan Rural Themes* (Regina: University of Regina Geographical Studies No. 1, 1977), 87–100.
24. P.J. Smith, "The Changing Structure of the Settlement System," in Barr, *Environment and Economy*, 22.
25. "Legal Memorandum, 1942," CFP.

26. Munro interview; Herbert Laycraft, interviewed by Paul Voisey.
27. "High School and University Matriculation Examinations Board Departmental Examinations for Charles A. Clark," 1927, 1928, 1929, CFP; Pickersgill interview; Tanner interview.
28. Various manuscripts and correspondence, CFP; Knupp, taped interview; Pickersgill interview; Tanner interview.
29. Various publications and correspondence, AWN; framed certificates, CFP; D'Albertanson, Printed Word, 47; Johnston, The Weeklies, 339.
30. Bill Holmes, "Up a Windmill."
31. HRT, 6 June 1946.
32. Charles A. Clark, taped interview.
33. Charles A. Clark, "President's Address, 1950 Convention," box 2 file 12, AWN.
34. Joe Clark, taped interview; Progressive Conservative Party files, Short/Knupp Papers.
35. Charles A. Clark to Hugh Clark, 6 Mar. 1957, CFP.
36. Knupp, taped interview; David L. Humphreys, Joe Clark: A Portrait (no city: Deneau and Greenberg, 1978), 62.
37. Holmes interview; Tanner interview.
38. Calgary Herald, 25 June 1956.
39. Knupp, taped interview; HRT, 26 Oct. 1961.
40. Various letters, scrapbooks, and yearbooks, CFP.
41. "Time Book," 1945–49, Charles A. Clark Papers, GA; Knupp, taped interview; Tanner interview, Munro interview. Employees were usually identified by name and job in the Christmas issues of the HRT.
42. Pickersgill interview.
43. Kesterton, History of Journalism, 124; HRT, Special Edition: "The Times" (High River: by author 1979); Pickersgill interview; Munro interview.
44. Charles A. Clark to Joe Clark, 14 Mar. 1961, CFP; Holmes interview; Tanner interview; Charles A. Clark, taped interview. See also David R. Bowers, "Impact of Centralized Printing on the Community Press," Journalism Quarterly 46 no. 1 (1969): 43–46.
45. R.C.R. Munro, "History of the Vulcan Advocate," Vulcan Advocate, 29 July 1998; Munro interview; HRT, 9 Nov. 1944; Charles Clark to C.F. Heseltine, 19 Nov. 1947, CFP; Strathern, Alberta Newspapers, 235–36; D'Albertanson, Printed Word, 98–99.
46. Various rate and circulation cards, and Data publications, 1948–1966, AWN.

47. Ibid.
48. *Data* (Nov. 1966), 15–19, AWN.
49. Johnston, *The Weeklies*, 157, 160; Pickersgill interview; Munro interview.
50. Tanner interview. Some editors still complained that national advertisers ignored the weeklies; Chuck McLean, taped interview with Joe Clark, 1971?, CFP.
51. D'Albertanson, *Printed Word*, 52.
52. "Conditional Sale Agreement," n.d., CFP; Tanner interview; Charles A. Clark to Joe Clark, 26 June 1964, CFP.

9   FEARING FOR THE FUTURE

1. HRT, 20 Sept. 1951, 4 Dec. 1952, 23 Sept. 1954; Alberta, *Economic Survey*, 16.
2. HRT, 27 Mar. 1952.
3. Joe Clark to Charles and Grace Clark, 27 Oct. 1964, CFP.
4. HRT, 7 Feb. 1963.
5. HRT, 30 Sept. 1948.
6. HRT, 18 Aug. 1955, 17 Nov. 1960, 31 Aug. 1961, 22 Nov. 1962.
7. HRT, 21 Apr. 1955.
8. HRT, 9 and 23 June 1955, 1 and 8 Dec. 1955, 12 and 26 Jan. 1956, 13 Sept. 1956.
9. HRT, 28 Apr., 9 and 23 June, 18 Aug. 1955.
10. Alberta, *Economic Survey*, 17; Alberta, *Survey of High River* (1959), 18; Alberta, *Survey of High River* (1969), 19.
11. HRT, 16 Feb. 1961.
12. HRT, *This is High River*, 9.
13. HRT, 31 Aug. 1950, 24 Sept. 1953, 10 May 1956.
14. Pickersgill interview.
15. HRT, 15 May 1961, 4 June and 5 Nov. 1964.
16. HRT, 18 Nov. 1952, 24 Oct. 1957, 20 May 1963. See Thomas and Marilyn Wessel, *4-H: An American Idea, 1900–1980* (Chevy Chase, Md.: National 4-H Council, 1982).
17. A standard reference is Victor Peters, *All Things Common: The Hutterian Way of Life* (Minneapolis: University of Minnesota Press, 1965); see also Robert Macdonald, "The Hutterites in Alberta," in Howard and Tamara Palmer,

eds., *Peoples of Alberta: Portraits of Cultural Diversity* (Saskatoon: Western Producer Prairie Books, 1985), 348–64.
18. Simon M. Evans, "Spatial Bias in the Incidence of Nativism: Opposition to Hutterite Expansion in Alberta," *Canadian Ethnic Studies* 6 no. 1–2 (1974): 4.
19. HRT, 11 July 1940; see also D'Albertanson, *Printed Word*, 47.
20. HRT, 9 June 1960.
21. HRT, 1, 8, 22 Dec. 1960.
22. HRT, 7 and 21 Dec. 1961. The general hostility of the weekly press in Alberta towards Hutterite expansion is noted in Isaac Obeng-Quaidoo, "Hutterite Land Expansion and the Canadian Press" (Ph.D. Thesis, University of Minnesota, 1977), 189.
23. HRT, 26 Mar., 7 May 1964.
24. HRT, 24 Sept. 1964; Macdonald, "The Hutterites," 359; Obeng-Quaidoo, "Hutterite Land," 53–56.
25. Cited in Howard Palmer, "The Hutterite Land Expansion Controversy in Alberta," *Western Canadian Journal of Anthropology* 2 (July 1971): 32.
26. Evans, "Spatial Bias," 10.
27. Palmer, "Hutterite Land," 36–37. For impediments to continued Hutterite expansion see Karl Peter, "The Instability of the Community of Goods in the Social History of the Hutterites," in A.W. Rasporich, ed., *Western Canada Past and Present* (Calgary: University of Calgary and McClelland and Stewart West, 1975), 99–120.
28. Alberta, *Economic Survey*, 15–6; Alberta, *Survey of High River* (1959), 17; Alberta, *Survey of High River* (1969), 18.
29. HRT, 20 Jan. 1966; also High River Community Development Association, "A Statement on Urban Renewal in High River, Alberta," unpub. ms., 1968, CFP; Blake, taped interview.
30. HRT, 26 Sept., 19 Oct. 1961; 26 Aug. 1965.
31. W.O. Mitchell, "My Home Town. High River: A Place to Love at First Sight," [Toronto] *Star Weekly Magazine*, 22 Sept. 1962, 4; also Tanner interview.
32. D'Albertanson, *Printed Word*, 76; also Charles A. Clark, taped interview.
33. HRT, 10 June 1948, 8 Apr. 1954; Ormond and Barbara Mitchell, *W.O.: The Life of W.O. Mitchell: Beginnings to Who Has Seen the Wind, 1914–1947* (Toronto: McClelland and Stewart, 1999), 306, 327–28.
34. For Mitchell's appreciation of her work generally see Hughena McCorquodale files, Mitchell Papers, file 19.8.19.

35. Documents and manuscripts related to "The Alien" are located in the Mitchell Papers.

10 THE OLD, WILD WEST

1. W.O. Mitchell, *Roses Are Difficult Here* (Toronto: McClelland and Stewart, 1990), 50–58.
2. Evans, *Prince Charming*, 180–4; HRT, 13 Apr. 1950, 8 Mar. 1962.
3. Richard Aquila, ed., *Wanted Dead or Alive: The American West in Popular Culture* (Urbana and Chicago: University of Illinois Press, 1996); William W. Savage, *The Cowboy Hero: His Image in American History and Culture* (Norman: University of Oklahoma Press, 1979).
4. Tom Primrose, "Prospecting a Legend," in Dan Riley, Tom Primrose, and Hugh Dempsey, *The Lost Lemon Mine* (Surrey, B.C.: Frontier Publishing, 1968), 16, 36. The first published, but less fanciful account appeared in the *Helena Herald* in 1870; see Hugh Dempsey, "An Historian's View," in Riley, *Lost Lemon*, 30–33. Another claim for the High River origins of the tale is provided in a letter from Phil Weinard to Kenneth Coppock, 1 Sept. no year, Coppock Papers.
5. Versions of the legend include Dan Riley's 1946 account, which appears as, "The Original Legend," in Riley, *Lost Lemon*, 5–10; and as Dan Riley, *The Lost Lemon Mine: The Great Mystery of the Canadian Rockies* (Edmonton: Lone Pine, 1991); Garnet Basque, "The Lost Lemon Mine," *Canadian West* 13 (Fall 1988): 86–90; Ron Stewart, *Goldrush: The Search for the Lost Lemon Mine* (Edmonton: RLM Publications, 1989), republished as *The Mystery of the Lost Lemon Mine* (Langley, B.C.: Sunfire, 1993); Elma Schemenauer, *The Lost Lemon Mine* (Markham, Ont.: Globe/Modern Curriculum Press, 1979); and the play by Astrid Twardowski, *The Curse of the Lost Lemon Mine* (Ottawa: Ottawa Little Theatre, 196_?).
6. Dr. G.D. Stanley, *A Round-up of Fun in the Foothills* (Calgary: by author, 1951?), Foreword, n.p.
7. HRT, 24 Mar., 21 Apr., 19 May, 15 and 19 Sept. 1955; see also High River Pioneers and Old Timers Association Papers, GA. For the nature of community-written local histories generally, see Joanne A. Stiles, "Gilded Memories: Perceptions of the Frontier in Rural Alberta as Reflected in Popular History" (M.A. Thesis, University of Alberta, 1985).
8. HRT, 28 Jan., 4 Feb. 1960.

9. High River, *Leaves*, 29, 272, 450, 500.
10. High River, *Leaves*, 143, 206, 258–59. See also Donna B. Ernst, "The Sundance Kid in Alberta," *Alberta History* 42 no. 4 (Autumn, 1994): 10–15. Alternate spellings of "Longdebough" include "Longabough" and "Longbough."
11. High River, *Leaves*, 170.
12. Praise for these efforts appeared in HRT, 22 Aug. 1946, 24 Jan. 1952, 25 Sept. 1955, 16 May 1957, 24 Sept. 1959.
13. HRT, 21 Oct. 1954, 23 Feb. and 26 Apr. 1956, 12 Sept. 1963. See also Bert T. Smith, *Cowboy Coloring Book* (High River: by author, n.d.), MH.
14. Many issues, HRT, especially 5 and 12 Feb. 1959, 17 Mar. 1960. See also High River, *Leaves*, 16–17.
15. HRT, 30 June, 7 July 1960; *Unveiling Ceremony, High River's Medicine Tree Arch* (High River: 1960), Programs Files, MH.
16. HRT, 11 Dec. 1958, 17 May 1962, 29 Oct. 1964; HRT stationery, 1963, CFP.
17. HRT, 7 July 1949; advertisements in *Souvenir of High River Rodeo and Annual Fair* (High River: 1949), and other rodeo pamphlets in Programs Files, MH.
18. HRT, 5 Oct. 1961, 28 Mar. and 24 Oct. 1963.
19. HRT, 4 May 1950, 27 Nov. 1952, 3 May 1962; Lillian Knupp, *Harness, Boots and Saddles* (High River: Sandstone Publishing, 1987?), 4–15, 17–20; *Bradley's Men's Wear — Leather Goods. Saddles, Boots, Stetson Hats.* (High River: 195_?), MH; Lou Bradley, taped interview with CHRB Radio, 29 Apr. 1978, MH.
20. *Eamor's Leather Works* (High River: n.d.), 4, MH.
21. HRT, 2 Feb. 1950, 17 May 1951, 23 May 1957, 11 May and 30 Nov. 1961; Knupp, *Harness, Boots*, 22–24. HRT, 11 June 1964 claimed that fifteen employees turned out 100 saddles a month.
22. Kristine Fredriksson, *American Rodeo: From Buffalo Bill to Big Business* (College Station: Texas A&M University Press, 1985); Michael Allen, "Real Cowboys? The Origins and Evolution of North American Rodeo and Rodeo Cowboys," *Journal of the West* 37 no. 1 (Jan. 1998): 69–79.
23. HRT, 18 June 1908, 14 Aug. 1924, 9 Aug. 1928, 11 July 1929; see also Claire Eamer and Thirza Jones, *The Canadian Rodeo Book* (Saskatoon: Western Producer Prairie Books, 1982), 6–10; James Gray, *A Brand of Its Own: The 100 Year History of the Calgary Exhibition and Stampede* (Saskatoon: Western Producer Prairie Books, 1985); Dempsey, *Canadian Cowboy*, 119–22.
24. High River, *Leaves*, 271.

25. High River Rodeo Committee, *Rodeo, Fair, and Horse Show* (High River: by author, 1948), Program Files, MH. See also *Souvenir Programme, 1947 High River Rodeo and Annual Fair* (High River: 1947), BU.
26. HRT, *High River's Three-Star Events* (High River: by author, 1951), 1, MH.
27. L.V. Kelly, *The Range Men: The Story of Ranchers and Indians of Alberta* (Toronto: William Briggs, 1913), 3.
28. HRT, 28 June, 12 July 1962; see also Hugh H. Dempsey, "Calgary's First Stampede," *Alberta Historical Review* 3 no. 3 (Summer 1955): 5. On Canadian cowgirls generally see Candace Savage, *Cowgirls* (Vancouver: Greystone Books, 1996).
29. Mary Lou LeCompte, *Cowgirls of the Rodeo: Pioneer Professional Athletes* (Urbana: University of Illinois Press, 1993).
30. For the origins of Little Britches see HRT, 30 Apr. 1959; Agricultural Society Minutes, Annual Meeting, 20 Jan. 1960; Lou Bradley, taped interview with CHRB Radio, 20 May 1978, MH.
31. Favourable impressions of Indians in their role as historical figures appear in HRT, 27 May 1909, 12 Aug. 1920, 20 July 1961. See also Keith Regular, "On Public Display" *Alberta History* 34 no. 1 (Winter 1986): 1–9. The advent of Banff's Indian Days in the 1890s exploited the popularity of Indians as living artefacts; see Laurie Meijer Drees, "'Indians' Bygone Past:' The Banff Indian Days, 1902–1945," *Past Imperfect* 2 (1993): 7–28.
32. Reprinted as Fred A. Ackland, "Cattle on a Thousand Hills," *Alberta Historical Review* 19 no. 4 (Autumn, 1971): 25–29.
33. A description of a cowboy costume used by a professional photographer appears in a letter, Edward F.J. Hills to Mother, 22 Nov. 1884, Edward F.J. Hills Letters, GA.; Dempsey, *Canadian Cowboy*, 24–25; John Lenihan, "Westbound: Feature Films and the American West," in Aquila, *Wanted Dead or Alive*, 110–13; Kenneth J. Bindas, "Cool Water, Rye Whiskey, and Cowboys: Images of the West in Country Music," in Aquila, *Wanted Dead or Alive*, 220–22; Laurel E. Wilson, "The Cowboy: Real and Imagined," *Dress: Annual Journal of the Costume Society of America* 23 (1996): 3–15.
34. Bradley, taped interview, 29 Apr. 1978.
35. Bill Holmes, "Up a Windmill."
36. See also Collette Lassiter and Jill Oakes, "Ranchwomen, Rodeo Queens, and Nightclub Cowgirls: The Evolution of Cowgirl Dress," in Catherine A. Cavanaugh and Randi R. Warne, eds. *Standing on New Ground: Women in Alberta* (Edmonton: University of Alberta Press, 1993), 55–69.

37. High River, *Rodeo, Fair*; HRT, 1 Aug. 1957; District of High River Centennial Committee, "List of Projects and Events," CFP; W.O. Mitchell, "Billy Henry," unpub. ms., n.d., Mitchell Papers, file 19.18.9.
38. HRT, 30 Mar. 1961.
39. HRT, 28 June, 12 July 1962.
40. HRT, 22 Sept. 1949; Johnston, *The Weeklies*, 49.
41. HRT, 26 Sept., 3 Oct. 1957; 26 May 1960.
42. HRT, 11 Feb. 1954, 18 Jan. 1962, 4 June 1964.
43. Lillian Knupp, taped interview with Margaret Crosby, 3 Feb. 1987, MH.
44. Knupp, *Life and Legends*; *Harness, Boots; Twigs of the Medicine Tree Country* (High River: Highwood Heritage Books, 1998); *Heritage on the Highwood* (High River: Highwood Heritage Books, 1986); *History of a Pioneer Family: Joseph and Julia Anna Short* (High River: Highwood Heritage Books, 1987).
45. HRT, 3 Oct. 1957.
46. HRT, 13 Jan. 1955.
47. HRT, 22 May 1947, 28 July 1955, 24 Mar. 1960; HRT, *This is High River*, 23.

11 A PARADE OF INDIVIDUALS

1. Johnston, *The Weeklies*, 23–24, 81–88.
2. HRT, 19 July 1917, 2 July 1931.
3. Kesterton, *History of Journalism*, 147.
4. HRT, 1 Jan. 1914, 18 Oct. 1923, 13 Aug. 1931.
5. Canadian Weekly, "Readership Study," 25.
6. Quoted in Johnston, *The Weeklies*, 21–22.
7. HRT, 27 Jan. 1927, 23 Aug. 1928.
8. Holmes interview; see also Johnston, *The Weeklies*, 28.
9. See, for example, HRT, 7 Dec. 1933.
10. Charles A. Clark to Peter Clark, 7 May 1964; also Charles A. Clark to Joe Clark, 6 May 1964, CFP.
11. Perhaps the most damning critique of rural weeklies appears in Robert R. Dykstra, "Town-Country Conflict: a Hidden Dimension in American Social History," *Agricultural History* 38 no. 4 (Oct. 1964): 195–205.
12. An assessment of the major studies appears in Lingeman, *Small Town America*, 396–440.
13. HRT, 1 Feb. 1934; also 20 Mar. 1924, 19 Aug. 1926, 9 Dec. 1937.
14. Unsigned letter to Mrs. Clark, 19 Mar. 196–?, CFP.

15. Munro interview.
16. Mitchell, "My Home Town."
17. Grace Clark, taped interview.
18. Livingstone, "Joe Clark's West," 4–5.
19. Ellison Capers to Charles Clark, 17 July 1945, CFP.

12 POSTSCRIPT

1. Joe Clark, taped interview; Humphreys, *Joe Clark*, 18; Charles A. Clark to Joe Clark, 8 Mar. 1960, CFP.
2. Charles A. Clark to Jack Sanderson, 16 Jan. 1964, CFP.
3. Charles A. Clark to Joe and Peter Clark, 12 Nov. 1964, CFP.
4. HRT, 1 Dec. 1955, 15 Jan. and 15 Oct. 1959; Toronto *Globe and Mail*, 1 Sept. 1964.
5. HRT, 28 Sept. 1961.
6. HRT, 20 Jan., 21 Apr. 1966; 8 and 28 Mar. 1968; High River Community Development Association, various unpub. ms., 1968?, CFP.
7. Bob Snodgrass and R.D. "Don" Tanner, taped interview with Joe Clark, 4 Aug. 1973?, CFP. The town increased its own commitment rather than let the project fail; Don Blake, taped interview.
8. Michael Broadway, "Here's the Beef: The Social Costs of Beefpacking's Move to Rural Alberta," *Alberta Views Magazine* online (Jan.–Feb. 2001).
9. Ibid.
10. High River Tourism Action Committee, *Tourism Action Plan for the Town of High River* (High River: by author, 1988); John H. Stark, "Cultural Tourism Development Strategy to be Based on Ranching for High River" (M.A. Project, University of Calgary, 1991).
11. Some of these projects are profiled in the *Edmonton Journal*, 9 June 2001, section K, 1; see also the website "Big Things in Alberta."
12. Typical examples include Underwood, McLellan and Associates Ltd., *Engineering Appraisal of Designated Potential Development Areas: Town of High River* (Calgary: by author, 1973); Calgary Regional Planning Commission, *High River Downtown Parking Study* (Calgary: by author, 1977); Alberta Dept. of Municipal Affairs, *Impact Model for Planning Alberta Communities Over Time: Town of High River* (Edmonton: by author, 1987).
13. HRT, *The Times*; Tanner interview; Holmes interview; Munro, "Vulcan Advocate."

A NOTE ON SOURCES

1. Don Tanner, ed., *The Best of Times: Forging the Frontier, Volume I, 1905–1911* (High River: HRT, 1999); *The Best of Times, Volume II, 1912–1918: The War Years* (High River: George Meyer, Bill Holmes, Don Tanner, 2001); *The Best of Times, Volume III, 1919–1925: The Roaring Twenties* (High River: George Meyer, Bill Holmes, Don Tanner, 2002).

A NOTE ON SOURCES

IT SHOULD COME AS NO SURPRISE that the most important source for this study was the *High River Times* itself. Complete runs of the paper from 1905 to 1966 and beyond may be found on microfilm in several depositories, including the University of Alberta Library. Former *Times* owner Don Tanner has also reprinted much of the newspaper in book form.[1] I cannot claim to have read every word the *Times* printed over a 61-year period, but I scanned every page and read a great many of them.

Records retrieved from the Clark residence in High River and stored in Peter Clark's basement in Calgary provided valuable information on the family from the nineteenth century to the 1960s. Most of those papers were donated to the Glenbow Archives in Calgary after I viewed them, so my references do not correspond to the current Glenbow collection. There are references in my notes to a smaller Charles A. Clark collection that had previously been deposited at the Glenbow. Unfortunately, the Clark papers contained limited information about the operation of the *Times*. Apparently most of the business records generated before 1966 were destroyed, perhaps on those occasions when the newspaper moved to new premises. The credit ratings of the R.G. Dun agency partly compensated for the paucity of financial records by providing snapshot summaries of the state of the business in various years.

The Glenbow Archives and the Museum of the Highwood in High River contained many record collections that illuminated parts of this study. The

Bar U Ranch National Historic Site Project at the Parks Canada office in Calgary provided materials about ranching in the High River district, and the W.O. Mitchell papers at the University of Calgary Library yielded useful information on some points. Interviews and discussions with former owners, employees, and business associates of the *Times* provided information that was difficult or impossible to obtain otherwise.

SELECTED BIBLIOGRAPHY

PRIMARY SOURCES

Calgary. Privately held by Peter Clark.
Clark Family Papers. (Most now deposited in Glenbow Archives, Calgary.)

Calgary. Glenbow Archives.
Alberta Weekly Newspapers Association Papers.
Blake, Don. Taped interview with Tom Kirkham, 22 Oct. 1980.
Charles A. Clark Papers.
Clark, Charles A. Taped interview with T.W. Kirkham, 1981.
George and Norma Piper Pocaterra Papers, 1848–1978.
Guy Weadick Papers.
High River Agricultural Society Minutes, 1925–36.
High River Club Papers, 1906–10.
High River Fish and Game Association Papers.
Hunt and Watt Ltd. Papers.
Pocaterra, George. Taped address to Calgary Kiwanis Club, 16 Nov. 1965.
Short/Knupp Family Papers.

Calgary. Parks Canada.
Bar U Ranch Collection.

Calgary. University of Calgary Library.
W.O. Mitchell Papers.

Edmonton. University of Alberta Library.
Alberta Department of Business and Tourism, Regional Services Branch. *High River Community Survey*. Edmonton: by author, 1974.
Alberta Department of Economic Affairs, Industrial Development Branch. *Economic Survey of the Town of High River*. Edmonton: by author, 1952.
Alberta Department of Economic Affairs, Industrial Development Branch. *Survey of High River*. Edmonton: by author, 1959.
High River Times, 1905–1966.

High River, Alberta. Museum of the Highwood.
Clark, Grace. Taped interview with Margaret Crosby, 18 June 1987.
High River Times. *High River and District at a Glance*. High River: by author, 1927.
High River Times. *High River's Three-Star Events*. High River: by author, 1951.
High River Times. *This is High River, Alberta: The Cowtown Capital of the Foothills*. High River: by author, 1950.
Knupp, Lillian. Taped interview with Margaret Crosby, 3 Feb. 1987.
Lillian Knupp Papers.
Politics Files.
Programs Files.
Ranching Files.

Ottawa. National Library of Canada.
R.G. Dun and Co. *The Mercantile Agency Reference Book....* Selected years, 1908–1937.

Interviews by Kimberly Speers.
Clark, Joe. Taped interviews, 12 Jan., 3 Mar. 1998, privately held by Kimberly Speers.
Knupp, Lillian. Taped interview, 1 July 1998, privately held by Kimberly Speers.

Interviews by Paul Voisey.
Clark, Peter, various conversations, 1998–2003.
Holmes, William "Bill," 3 Oct. 1998.
Laycraft, Herbert, 8 Apr. 2003.
Munro, R.C.R. "Bob," 2 Aug. 1998.

Pickersgill, Peter, 2 Aug. 1998.

Tanner, R.D. "Don," 8 July 1999, and various conversations, 2000–2003.

SECONDARY SOURCES

Adam, G. Stuart. "The Sovereignty of the Publicity System: A Case Study of the Alberta Press Act." In *Journalism, Communication and the Law*, edited by Adam, 154–71. Scarborough: Prentice-Hall, 1976.

Allen, Michael. "Real Cowboys? The Origins and Evolution of North American Rodeo and Rodeo Cowboys." *Journal of the West* 37 no. 1 (Jan. 1998): 69–79.

Anderson, Clifford B. "The Metamorphosis of American Agrarian Idealism in the 1920s and 1930s." *Agricultural History* 35 no. 4 (Oct. 1961): 182–88.

Aquila, Richard, ed. *Wanted Dead or Alive: The American West in Popular Culture.* Urbana and Chicago: University of Illinois Press, 1996.

Artibise, Alan F.J. "Boosterism and the Development of Prairie Cities, 1871–1913." In *Town and City: Aspects of Western Canadian Urban Development*, edited by Artibise, 147–76. Regina: Canadian Plains Research Center and University of Regina, 1981.

Bantjes, Rod. "Improved Earth: Travel on the Canadian Prairies, 1920–50." *Journal of Transport History* 3rd series 13 no. 2 (Sept. 1992): 115–40.

Borne, Lawrence R. *Dude Ranching: a Complete History.* Albuquerque: University of New Mexico Press, 1983.

Bowers, William L. "Country Life Reform, 1900–20: A Neglected Aspect of Progressive Era History." *Agricultural History* 45 no. 3 (July 1971): 211–22.

Breen, David H. *The Canadian Prairie West and the Ranching Frontier, 1874–1924.* Toronto: University of Toronto Press, 1983.

Canadian Weekly Newspapers Association and the Alberta Division of the Canadian Weekly Newspapers Association. "A Readership Study of a Canadian Weekly Newspaper." In Alberta Weekly Newspapers Association Papers, box 15 file 145, Glenbow Archives, Calgary. Unpublished, 1960.

Clark, Wade D. "Big Business on the Big Ranch: The Making of the Modern Cattle Industry in Alberta in the Post-World War Two Era, 1950–1976." Honours thesis, University of Calgary, 1995.

Colpitts, George W. "Fish and Game Associations in Southern Alberta, 1907–1928." *Alberta History* 42 no. 4 (Autumn 1994): 16–26.

———. *History of the Highwood River.* High River, Alta.: Highwood River Restoration and Conservation Association, 1991.

D'Albertanson, Leonard, ed. *The Printed Word, 1904–1955: The Story of Alberta Division, Canadian Weekly Newspapers Association.* Wainwright, Alta.: Alberta Division, Canadian Weekly Newspapers Association, 1955.

Dale, Edmund H. "The General Problems of Western Canada's Small Rural Towns." In *Saskatchewan Rural Themes*, edited by J.E. Spencer, pp. 87–100. Regina: University of Regina Geographical Studies No. 1, 1977.

Davis, Angela E. "'Valiant Servants': Women and Technology on the Canadian Prairies, 1910–1940." *Manitoba History* 25 (Spring 1993): 33–42.

DeFleur, Melvin L., and Ball-Rokeach, Sandra J. *Theories of Mass Communication.* 5th ed. New York: Longman, 1989.

Dempsey, Hugh. *The Golden Age of the Canadian Cowboy: An Illustrated History.* Saskatoon and Calgary: Fifth House, 1995.

Dunae, Patrick A., ed. *Ranchers' Legacy: Alberta Essays by Lewis G. Thomas.* Edmonton: University of Alberta Press, 1986.

Dunlop, J.S. "Changes in the Canadian Wheat Belt, 1931–69." *Geography* 55 part 2 no. 247 (Spring 1970): 156–68.

Dykstra, Robert R. "Town-Country Conflict: a Hidden Dimension in American Social History." *Agricultural History* 38 no. 4 (Oct. 1964): 195–205.

Eamer, Claire, and Jones, Thirza. *The Canadian Rodeo Book.* Saskatoon: Western Producer Prairie Books, 1982.

Edelstein, Alex S., and Schulz, J. Blaine. "The Leadership Role of the Weekly Newspapers as Seen by Community Leaders: A Sociological Perspective." In *People, Society and Mass Communications*, edited by Lewis A. Dexter, 221–38. London: Free Press of Glencoe, 1964.

Elgaard, Knud. *Cattle Ranching in Southern Alberta.* Regina: Economics Branch, Canada Department of Agriculture, 1968.

Elliott, David R., and Miller, Iris. *Bible Bill: A Biography of William Aberhart.* Edmonton: Reidmore Books, 1987.

Elofson, Warren M. *Cowboys, Gentlemen and Cattle Thieves: Ranching on the Western Frontier.* Montreal and Kingston: McGill-Queen's University Press, 2000.

Evans, Simon M. "The Burns Era at the Bar U Ranch." In Bar U Ranch Collection, Parks Canada, Calgary. Unpublished, 1997.

———; Carter, Sarah; and Yeo, Bill, eds. *Cowboys, Ranchers and the Cattle Business: Cross-Border Perspectives on Ranching History.* Calgary and Boulder: University of Calgary Press and University Press of Colorado, 2000.

———. "George Lane: Purebred Horse Breeder." In Bar U Ranch Collection, Parks Canada, Calgary. Unpublished, 1994.

———. "Land Acquisition: The Bar U Ranch." In Bar U Ranch Collection, Parks Canada, Calgary. Unpublished, no date.

———. *Prince Charming Goes West: The Story of the E.P. Ranch*. Calgary: University of Calgary Press, 1993.

Fencelines and Furrows History Book Society, *Fencelines and Furrows*. 2d rev. ed. Calgary: by author, 1971.

Fredriksson, Kristine. *American Rodeo: From Buffalo Bill to Big Business*. College Station: Texas A&M University Press, 1985.

Fulford, Robert. "The Press in the Community." In *The Press and the Public*, edited by D.B.L. Hamlin, 23–34. Toronto: University of Toronto Press, 1962.

Hanson, Eric J. *Local Government in Alberta*. Toronto: McClelland and Stewart, 1956.

High River Hospital and Nursing Home. *"In the Spirit of Good Medicine:" A Story of Health Care in the High River Hospital District*. High River: Sandstone, 1990.

High River Pioneers and Old Timers Association. *Leaves From the Medicine Tree: A History of the Area Influenced by the Tree, and Biographies of Pioneers and Old Timers Who Came Under Its Spell Prior to 1900*. High River, Alta.: by author, 1960.

Hill, Robert C. "Social Credit and the Press: The Early Years." Master's thesis, University of Alberta, 1977.

Hudman, Lloyd E. "Tourism and the American West." *Journal of the West* 33 no. 3 (July 1994): 67–76.

Hudson, John C. *Plains Country Towns*. Minneapolis: University of Minnesota Press, 1985.

Ings, Frederick W. "Tales from the Midway Ranch." Glenbow Archives, Calgary. Unpublished, 1936.

Ironside, R.G. "Rural Alberta: Elements of Change." In *Environment and Economy: Essays on the Human Geography of Alberta*, edited by B.M. Barr and P.J. Smith, 95–110. Edmonton: Pica Pica Press, 1984.

Jellison, Katherine. "Women and Technology on the Great Plains, 1910–1940." *Great Plains Quarterly* 8 no. 3 (Summer 1988): 145–57.

Johnston, J. George. *The Weeklies: Biggest Circulation in Town*. Bolton, Ont.: Canadian Weekly Newspapers Association, 1972.

Jones, David C. "'There is Some Power About the Land'—The Western Agrarian Press and Country Life Ideology." *Journal of Canadian Studies* 17 no. 3 (Fall 1982): 96–108.

Keen, Elizabeth. "The Frontier Press." *Studies in Literature of the West* 20 (1956): 75–100.

Kennedy, Margaret A. *The Whiskey Trade of the Northwestern Plains*. New York: Peter Lang, 1997.

Kester, Randall B. "Recollections of a Printer's Devil." *Oregon Historical Quarterly* 99 no. 1 (Spring 1998): 62–78.

Kesterton, W.H. *A History of Journalism in Canada*. Toronto: McClelland and Stewart, 1967.

Knight, Oliver. "The *Owyhee Avalanche*: The Frontier Newspaper as a Catalyst in Social Change." *Pacific Northwest Quarterly* 58 no. 2 (April 1967): 74–81.

Knupp, Lillian. *Life and Legends: A History of the Town of High River*. Calgary: Sandstone Publishing, 1982.

Lapp, Diana M. *The Structure of Alberta Farms, 1941–1974*. Edmonton: Alberta Land Use Forum, Technical Report No. 11, 1974.

Lingeman, Richard R. *Small Town America: A Narrative History, 1620—The Present*. New York: G.P. Putnam's Sons, 1980.

Livingstone, Donna. "Joe Clark's West." *Glenbow Magazine* 13 no. 2 (Summer 1993): 3–6.

MacPherson, Ian, and Thompson, John Herd. "An Orderly Reconstruction: Prairie Agriculture in World War Two." *Canadian Papers in Rural History* 4 (1984): 11–32.

McCullough, A.B. "Frederick Stimson and the North West Cattle Company." In Bar U Ranch Collection, Parks Canada, Calgary. Unpublished, 1994.

McQuail, Denis. *Towards a Sociology of Mass Communications*. London: Collier-Macmillan, 1969.

Mitchell, W.O. *Roses Are Difficult Here*. Toronto: McClelland and Stewart, 1990.

Moline, Norman T. *Mobility and the Small Town, 1900–1930: Transportation Change in Oregon, Illinois*. Chicago: University of Chicago Department of Geography, Research Paper no. 132, 1971.

National Film Board of Canada with the Canadian Weekly Newspapers Association. *The Home Town Paper*. Ottawa, film by author, 1948.

Pike, Robert M. "A Chequered Progress: Farmers and the Telephone in Canada, 1905–1951." *Journal of Canadian Studies* 33 no. 3 (Fall 1998): 5–30.

Pocaterra, Norma Piper. "Son of the Mountains: The Story of George W. Pocaterra, Pioneer Alberta Rancher, Explorer, and Friend of the Stoney Indians." Glenbow Archives, Calgary. Unpublished, 1970.

Proudfoot, Bruce. "Agriculture." In *Studies in Canadian Geography: The Prairie Provinces*, edited by P.J. Smith, 51–64. Toronto: University of Toronto Press, 1972.

Riley, Dan; Primrose, Tom; and Dempsey, Hugh. *The Lost Lemon Mine*. Surrey, B.C.: Frontier Publishing, 1968.

Rothman, Hal K. *Devil's Bargains: Tourism in the Twentieth-Century American West*. Lawrence: University Press of Kansas, 1998.

Rutherford, Paul. *The Making of the Canadian Media*. Toronto: McGraw Hill-Ryerson, 1978.

———. *A Victorian Authority: The Daily Press in Late Nineteenth-century Canada*. Toronto: University of Toronto Press, 1982.

Savage, Candace. *Cowgirls*. Vancouver: Greystone Books, 1996.

Sharp, Paul F. *Whoop-Up Country: The Canadian-American West, 1865–1885*. 1955. Reprint. Norman: University of Oklahoma Press, 1973.

Sheppard, Bert. *Spitzee Days*. Calgary: by author, 1971?

Shideler, James H. "Flappers and Philosophers, and Farmers: Rural-Urban Tensions of the Twenties." *Agricultural History* 47 no. 4 (Oct. 1973): 283–99.

Short, Julia "Lula." "Grandma's Childhood: Pioneer Life in Southern Alberta." In Short/Knupp Family Papers, Glenbow Archives, Calgary. Unpublished, no date.

Siebert, F.S. "The Libertarian Theory of the Press." In *Four Theories of the Press*, edited by Siebert and others, 39–71. Urbana: University of Illinois Press, 1963.

Smith, Anthony. *The Newspaper: An International History*. London: Thames and Hudson, 1979.

Smith, P.J. "The Changing Structure of the Settlement System." In *Environment and Economy: Essays on the Human Geography of Alberta*, edited by B.M. Barr and P.J. Smith, 16–35. Edmonton: Pica Pica Press, 1984.

Sotiron, Minko. *From Politics to Profit: The Commercialization of Canadian Daily Newspapers, 1890–1920*. Montreal and Kingston: McGill-Queen's University Press, 1997.

Stanley, Dr. G.D. *A Round-up of Fun in the Foothills*. Calgary: by author, 1951?

Stephenson, H.E., and McNaught, Carlton. *The Story of Advertising in Canada: A Chronicle of Fifty Years*. Toronto: Ryerson, 1940.

Stiles, Joanne A. "Gilded Memories: Perceptions of the Frontier in Rural Alberta as Reflected in Popular History." Master's thesis, University of Alberta, 1985.

Strathern, Gloria. *Alberta Newspapers, 1880–1982: An Historical Directory*. Edmonton: University of Alberta Press, 1988.

Stutt, R.A. "Changes in Land Use and Farm Organization in the Prairie Area of Saskatchewan During the Period 1951 to 1966." *Canadian Farm Economics* 5 no. 6 (Feb. 1971): 11–19.

Sunshine Tales Book Committee. *Sunshine Tales: Over 100 Years of History From the Rural Area Surrounding the Sunshine Trail South and East of High River.* High River, Alta.: by author, 1998.

Szabo, Michael L. "Depopulation of Farms in Relation to the Economic Conditions of Agriculture on the Canadian Prairies." *Geographical Bulletin* 7 no. 3–4 (1965): 187–202.

Tales and Trails History Book Society. *Tales and Trails: A History of Longview and Surrounding Area.* Longview, Alta.: by author, 1973.

Vipond, Mary. *The Mass Media in Canada.* Toronto: James Lorimer, 1989.

Voisey, Paul. "Boosting the Small Prairie Town, 1904–1931: An Example from Southern Alberta." In *Town and City: Aspects of Western Canadian Urban Development*, edited by Alan F.J. Artibise, 210–35. Regina: Canadian Plains Research Center and University of Regina, 1981.

———. *Vulcan: The Making of a Prairie Community.* Toronto: University of Toronto Press, 1988.

Walchuk, Walter. *Alberta's Local Governments: People in Community Seeking Goodness.* Edmonton: Municipal Administrative Services Division, Alberta Municipal Affairs, 1987.

Weinard, Philip. "Early High River and the Whiskey Traders." *Alberta Historical Review* 4 no. 3 (Summer 1956): 12–16.

Wetherall, Donald G., and Kmet, Irene R.A. *Town Life: Main Street and the Evolution of Small Town Alberta, 1880–1947.* Edmonton: University of Alberta Press and Alberta Community Development, 1995.

Wilson, Laurel E. "The Cowboy: Real and Imagined." *Dress: Annual Journal of the Costume Society of America* 23 (1996): 3–15.

Zimmerman, Carle C., and Moneo, Garry W. *The Prairie Community System.* Ottawa: Agricultural Economics Research Council of Canada, 1970.

INDEX

Aberhart, William, 92, 108–17
absentee landowners, 53
Accurate News and Information Act, 110, 112, 114–15
advertising, 63–64, 100–101. *See also* High River Times
agrarian idealism, 119–20
agriculture, 17, 20–23, 44–45; after 1918, 81–82, 84–85, 123; after 1940, 143–44, 146–49
airport, 90, 144–45
Alberta and Eastern British Columbia Press Association, 37, 69
Alberta Social Credit Chronicle, 109, 111–12
Aldersyde, Alberta, 47, 72, 152
Americans, 11–14, 21, 39–40. *See also* Mormons
Audit Bureau of Circulation, 159
automobiles. *See* motor vehicles

Baker, William, 169
Banff, Alberta, 136–37
Bar U Ranch, 10, 12, 14–17, 19–20, 32–33, 220; sale of, 82–83, 149; visitors to, 129–31
Bateman, Lola, 158
Big Lake, Alberta. *See* Frank Lake, Alberta
Black Diamond, Alberta, 158
Blackfoot Indians, 3, 4, 6, 185, 193
Blackie, Alberta, 72, 92, 96, 152
boiler plate. *See* ready-made print
boosterism, 43, 70, 72–73, 81, 102–3, 217. *See also* High River Times
Boyd, Catherine, 76
Bradley, Bob, 104
Bradley's store, 186–87, 194, 197–98
Brant, Alberta, 48, 152, 173
British American Oil Company, 87
British Broadcasting Corporation, 115

British Canadian Pictures, 137–38
British Commonwealth Air Training Agreement, 144
Broomfield, John T., 113
brothels. *See* prostitution
Buffalo Head Ranch, 132, 134
Burnet, Jean, 177
Burns, Pat, 25, 82–83
Burns Ranches, 82, 149

Calgary, Alberta, 5, 7, 25–26, 32, 50, 71, 74; after 1918, 87, 91, 101; after 1940, 165, 168, 189, 216–18
Calgary Aero Club, 144
Calgary Albertan, 50, 109, 110
Calgary and Edmonton Railway, 18–19, 26, 33, 47, 72. *See also* Canadian Pacific Railway
Calgary Herald, xxvii, 33, 109–10, 157, 177
Calgary Power, 84, 123
Calgary Rebel, 110
Calgary Regional Planning Commission, 175, 217
Calgary Stampede, 188–92
Cameron, Stewart, 110
Canada Air Board, 90, 144
Canadian Broadcasting Corporation, 196–97
Canadian Northern Railway, 71, 83
Canadian Pacific Railway, 8, 18, 32, 40, 72, 85, 88, 217; Kipp-Aldersyde line, 72, 82; and tourism, 132, 136–37
Canadian Press Association, 69
Canadian Television Network, 197

Canadian Weekly Newspapers Association, xix–xx, xxiii, xxvi, 97, 103, 107, 154, 196, 206; Alberta Division, xxiii, xxvii, 101, 104, 110, 114, 154–55, 159, 161, 171–72
Canadian Western Natural Gas Company, 84
Capers, Ellison, 210
Cargill, 218–19
Casey, Ivan, 113–14, 116, 167–68
Casey, John, xix
Cayley, Alberta, 26, 92, 96, 152, 171
children and youths, 169–70
Chinese, 38–39, 172
Chinook Shopping Centre, 168
chuckwagon races, 190–91, 219
Circle Ranch, 9
Claresholm, Alberta, 49
Clark, Charles, 29–30, 57, 68, 87, 97, 152–53; newspaper activities, xix, xxvi, 59–60, 72, 96, 102, 152, 155, 158; newspaper associations, 57, 69, 87, 103, 104, 107; politics, xxv, 107
Clark, Charles A. (Archibald), 29, 104–5, 114, 154, 161, 176, 209, 218; newspaper activities, xix, xxvii, 152–53, 157–58, 207–8, 215–16, 220; politics, xxv, 114–16, 155–56
Clark, Charles Joseph (Joe), 105, 157, 161, 194, 209; newspaper activities, xx, xxvii–xxviii, 169, 215; politics, xxv, 116, 156, 164
Clark, Grace Roseline (*nee* Welch), 104–5, 154, 161, 169, 208–9, 216

Clark, Hugh, xxv, 29, 106, 156, 163
Clark, Mary Elizabeth (nee
    McDonell, sometimes
    McDonnell), 29, 56, 154
Clark, Mary Margaret (Marnie), 30,
    105, 155, 158, 169
Clark, Peter McDonell, 105, 156,
    169, 207–8, 215
clothing. See fashion
coal mining, 51–52, 83–85
Cochrane, Matthew, 9–10
Cochrane Ranch, 9, 18
Cody, (William) Buffalo Bill, 180
cold war, 163
Communal Property Act, 173–74
Communal Property Control Board,
    173
Conservative Party, 9, 16–17, 41,
    154–56, 167, 173
Coote, George, 108
cowboys, 13–14, 180, 191, 193, 197.
    See also ranching
crime, xxvii, 36–37, 155, 170
Crossing, The, (Alberta), 6–7
Cypress Hills Massacre, 4

de Foras, Barle, 129
de Foras, Odette, 204
Dick, Catherine Bond, 184–85
Diefenbaker, John, 156
Douglas, C.H., 111
drinking and disorderly conduct,
    14–16, 56–57
dude ranches, 131–34, 199

Eamor's Saddlery, 186–88, 196
Edmonton Journal, 109, 112
education. See schools

Edward, Prince of Wales, 129–31,
    179
Edwards, Bob, 28–29
Ellis, Ross, 167, 173
Emerson, George, 7
E.P. Ranch, 129–31, 179
Eye Opener, 28–29

farming. See agriculture
fashion, 193–95
fishing, 134–36
Foothills Circuit Rodeo Association,
    191
Foothills Health Unit, 92, 151
Foothills School Division, 93,
    150–51
Fort Benton, Montana, 4–5, 9
Fort Macleod, Alberta, 5, 47
Fort Spitzee, (Alberta), 4, 181
Fort Whoop-Up, (Alberta), 4
4-H clubs, 171
Fowler, Roy, 182
Frank Lake, Alberta, 23, 85, 135
Frankburg, Alberta, 39, 85
Fraser, Frances, 184
French, Lafayette, 180–81, 183
French settlers, 39
Frontier Days, 190–91, 198
fur trade, 3–4

Gibson, Hoot, 137–38
Glass, Ron, 191
Gleichen, Alberta, 49
Gleichen Call, 49
Gostick, Edith, 110–11
Grand Trunk Railway, 83
Great War. See World War I

Hanna, Alberta, 177
Harper, Lily, 184
Hart, Neil, 137
Henry, William S. (Billy), 195
Herron, John, 41
Herronton Social Credit Group, 115
High River, Alberta (district):
descriptions of, xxix–xxx, 45, 124, 128; environment, 7, 22–3; maps, 10, 73, 84, 166; population, 20, 147, 168, 217; rural municipal government, xxi, 70, 82, 85, 90, 93–95, 151; settlement, 7, 20–22, 23; urban sprawl, 216. *See also* agriculture; ranching
High River, Alberta (town):
beautification and urban renewal, 55–56, 125, 217; descriptions of, 124–25; economic development, 25–28, 48–49, 52, 69–72, 75–76; economic development after 1918, 81–82, 84, 88, 90–91; economic development after 1940, 144–45, 149–52, 164, 168, 173–76, 198–99, 217–19; municipal government, xxi, 27, 54, 85–86; origins, 3, 6–7; park, 125–26, 128, 185; population, 28, 47, 74, 76, 94, 163–64; services, xxvi, 27–28, 91–93, 126–27, 150–51, 154, 169; utilities, 27, 54–55, 84, 165
High River Agricultural Society, 45, 83, 86, 188

High River and Hudson Bay Rail Road, 52, 71–72, 83–84
High River Board of Trade, 53–54, 70, 86, 125
High River Businessmen's Association, 164
High River Chamber of Commerce, 86–87, 151, 198
High River Civic League, 56
High River Club, 33, 57
High River Community Development Association, 218
High River Fish and Game Association, 135
High River Oil and Gas Company, 52
High River Pioneer and Old-Timers Association, 182
High River Real Estate Association, 53
High River Rodeo Association, 187
High River Social Credit Group, 115
High River Times: advertising in, 30, 32, 62–66, 69; advertising after 1918; 99–101, 114, 159–160, 170, 186, 207; awards and prizes, xix, 103, 112; and boosterism, xxviii–xxix, 43–45, 49–55, 59, 67–69, 71, 74–75; boosterism after 1918, 86, 102, 128, 154–55, 175, 189, 195, 197; circulation, 53, 61–62, 95, 100, 158–59; collecting news, 60–61, 95–96, 158, 206; editorial policies, xxv–xxix, 34, 36–37, 40–41, 107–8, 122, 155, 207–8; employees, 59–61, 67–68, 104–6, 157; features of,

xix–xxii, xxiv–xxv, 30, 32–34, 145, 202–3; finances, 59, 68, 74, 97, 99–100, 161; format, 30–31, 98–100, 160, 214; founding, xix, 29; photography, 30, 157, 160, 202; printing jobs, 66–67, 101–2; printing technology, 61, 96–97, 99, 102, 160, 220; sale of, 215–16; subscription rates, 61, 95, 100
High River Trading Company, 26, 65
High River Turf Association, 11
Highway 2, 167
Highway 23, 165–66
Highwood Memorial Centre, 154–55
Highwood River, 3, 5, 25–26, 124; flooding, 3–4, 88–89, 126, 164; recreation, 135–37; resources, 51–52, 84
Highwood Western Railway, 84–85
Hoadley, George, 92
Holmes, Bill, 154, 220
Home Town Paper, 206–7
horses. *See* ranching
hospitals. *See* medical services
Howell, Harris, 181
Hunt, Frazier, 129
hunting, 134–36
Hutchison, Bruce, 121
Hutterites, 171–74

Indians, 3–5, 8, 193. *See also* Blackfoot; Stoney
Industrial Workers of the World, 42
Ings, Fred, 15–16
Intertype, 96–97, 100

John Lineham Company, 26–27, 83

Kananaskis Lakes, Alberta, 136
Kelly, H.V., 191
Kincardine Review, 29, 106
King, Don, 182, 184
Knupp, Lillian, 155–56, 197–98

labour, 41–42, 107
Lacombe Globe, xxiii, 206
LaDue, Flores, 131–32, 192
land speculation, 21–22, 28, 46, 73–74, 81
Lane, George, 12–13, 19, 82, 125, 129, 185, 188, 205
Leaves from the Medicine Tree, 182–83, 185
Lethbridge Herald, 54
Liberal Party, 18–19, 167
Lineham. *See* John Lineham Company
Linotype, 96
Little Bow River, Alberta, 3, 88–90
Little Britches, 193, 196–97, 212–13, 219
Little Chicago, Alberta, 87
Little New York, Alberta, 87
Logan, Tommy, 104, 203, 216
Longview, Alberta, 152
Lost Lemon Mine, 180–81
Lougheed, Peter, 156
lumbering, 26–27, 51, 83–84
Lynch, Tom, 7

Macleod Trail, 91, 166
mail order catalogues, 50–51, 66, 68, 72–73, 103
Main Street, 122

Manning, Ernest, 116
Mazeppa Ladies' Social Credit Group, 115
McCorquodale, Hughena, 105–6, 154, 156–57, 176–77, 210
medical services, 91–92, 151
medicine tree, 184–85
Medicine Tree Arch Committee, 185
Medicine Tree Manor, 185
Medicine Tree Pow Wow Committee, 185
Mencken, H.C., 122
Meyer, George, 220
Mill, John Stuart, xviii
Mills, Claude, 187
Mitchell, W.O., xix, 105, 175–77, 179, 195, 208–9
Mormons, 18, 21, 39, 85
Morrison, William, 109
Mosquito Creek, Alberta, 9
motion pictures, 137–38, 180, 196
motor vehicles, 90–91, 123–24, 146, 165, 167, 216–17
Mount Head Ranch, 10
Municipal District of Dinton, 95, 115, 158–59
Municipal District of Foothills, 94, 159, 175, 216
Municipal District of Highwood, 94, 151
Municipal District of Sheep Creek, xxi
Munro, Bob, 158
Museum of the Highwood, 219

Nanton, Alberta, 48, 91, 165
Nanton News, 95, 158

National Film Board of Canada, 196, 206
nativism, 37–39, 57, 172
newspapers, xvii–xviiv; dailies, xviii, xx, xxiii–xxv, 32–33, 122, 156, 204, 206, 210–11; weeklies, xix–xxv, xxvii–xxviii, 102–3, 122, 158, 202, 204, 206–11. *See also* specific newspapers
Next-Year Country, 177
Norma, Alberta, 47
North West Cattle Company. *See* Bar U Ranch
North West Mounted Police, 5–6, 8–9, 17
North-West Territories, 7
Number 5 Elementary Flying Training School, 144

offset printing, 157, 159, 220
oil and gas. *See* petroleum
Okotoks, Alberta, 26, 29, 48–49, 91, 165, 217
Okotoks Review, 29, 49–50, 95, 158
On Liberty, xviii
O'Neill, Moira, 15
Oxley Ranch, 9

Page, Percy, 185
Patterson, R.M., 132, 134
peddlers, 51, 67, 102–3
Pekisko, Alberta, 33
Pekisko Kids, 185
Penetang Herald, 102
petroleum, 52, 83, 86–88, 164
Pickersgill, Peter, 157
Pioneer Square, 218
Pocaterra, George, 129, 132

polo, 11, 15, 53, 131
pool halls, 57
postal service, 32–33, 68–69
Prairie Farm Rehabilitation Administration, 147–48, 164
Progressive Conservative Party. *See* Conservative Party
Progressive Party, 108
prohibition, 57, 86
prostitution, 16, 36, 56
Pulitzer Prize, 112, 115

Quebecor World, 220
Quorn Ranch, 9

racism. *See* nativism
radio, xxi, 100–101, 123, 196–97
railways, 46–47, 52, 71–72, 83–84; passenger service, 50, 91, 165. *See also* specific companies
ranching: depictions of, 45, 76, 128–29, 179; economic conditions, 81–83, 85, 143–44, 148–49; government policy towards, 9, 16–18; horse breeding, 19, 81–83, 197; national character of, 10–16; origins, 6–10; relations with farmers, 17, 34–35; techniques, 13, 20, 157. *See also* dude ranches
Range Men, 191
ready-made print, 30, 32, 160–61
reciprocity, 41
Riley, Dan, 19, 34, 108, 129, 144, 180–82, 205
roads, 47–48, 87, 90–91, 136–37, 165–67, 216–17

Robertson, Thomas, 11
Rocky View News, 158
rodeo, 188–93, 196–98, 219
Roses Are Difficult Here, xix, 176–79, 208
Round T Ranch, 132, 134
Round-up of Fun in the Foothills, 182
rural depopulation, 168–71, 216

saddle making, 186–88
Saddlemaker, 196
schools, 92–93, 150–51, 169
Scott, Bill, 156–57, 195
Sheep Creek, Alberta, 9, 26
Short, Lula (Julia), 16
Sinclair, Lewis, 122
Skrine, Agnes, 15
Smiley, Bill, 169
Smith, Bert, 184
Soby, Harold W., 105
Soby, Mrs. *See* Clark, Mary Margaret (Marnie)
Social Credit, xxvi, 108–117, 173–74, 177
Stampede Ranch, The, 132–34, 137
Stanley, George, 182
Stead, Robert J.C., 35–36, 73, 217
Stimpson, Fred, 10, 16, 19
Stoney Indians, 3, 16, 181, 185, 193
Strange, Kathleen R., 123
Sullivan, Mrs. J.J., 74
Sundance Kid, 183
Sunshine Trail, 90–91. *See also* Highway 23

Tanner, Don, 216, 220
Tanner, Glen, 220
Teen Town, 169

telephones, 55, 68, 123, 207
television, xxi, 180, 196–97
Temperance and Moral Reform League, 57
Thompson, E.E., 48
Toronto Type Foundry Company, 30, 59, 61, 97
tourism, 128–39, 189–93, 195–99, 219
Town Act, 70
towns, 46–48, 71–72, 75, 152. See also specific towns
trade-at-home campaigns, 50–51, 103
trucks. See motor vehicles
Turner Valley, Alberta, 52, 83, 86–87, 91–92, 96, 158, 164

United Farmers of Alberta, 41, 108, 113–14
United Trailer, 164

Vernon News, 206
Vulcan, Alberta, 72, 90, 92, 151, 173, 219
Vulcan Advocate, 72, 96, 157–58
Vulcan Review, 72

Walrond Ranch, 18
Ware, John, 14
Watt, Frank, 87
Weadick, Guy, 131–32, 134, 137–38, 182, 185, 196, 205
Weadick, Mrs., 131–32, 192
Weinard, Philip, 13
Westersund, Varno, 210
Westmount Publishing, 220
whiskey traders, 4–5
Wilson, T.R., 83–84
wolfers, 4
women, 15, 55–58, 101, 123, 192, 195; and the newspaper business, 60, 106; shortage of 15–16, 21, 56. See also prostitution
Women's Christian Temperance Union, 57
Wong, Marjorie, 172
Wood, Kerry, 184
World War I, 18, 33–35, 57–58, 81
World War II, 143–46
Wyatt, Jim, 197

TOWN LIFE
Main Street and the Evolution of Small Town Alberta, 1880–1947
Donald G. Wetherell and Irene R.A. Kmet

THE LITERARY HISTORY OF ALBERTA, VOLUME ONE
From Writing-on-Stone to World War Two
George Melynk

THE LITERARY HISTORY OF ALBERTA, VOLUME TWO
From the End of the War to the End of the Century
George Melynk

ALBERTA'S NORTH
A History, 1890–1950
Donald G. Wetherell and Irene R.A. Kmet

HIGH RIVER AND THE *TIMES*
An Alberta Community and Its Weekly Newspaper, 1905–1966
Paul Voisey